THE BEDSIDE 'GUARDIAN' 18

A selection from
The Guardian 1968-69

Edited by
W. L. Webb

With an introduction by
Harold Jackson

Collins
St James's Place, London, 1969

Printed in Great Britain
Collins Clear-Type Press
London and Glasgow

The Bedside 'Guardian' 18

Introduction

The reporter never knows for whom he is writing. His editor, obviously: but who are the shadowy individuals beyond his typewriter? What sort of lives do they lead? How do they relate them to the sometimes bizarre events presented by their morning paper? Around the office there is a vague notion of *The Guardian* Reader, but he turns out to be a figure of infinite variety. I suspect They are as unsure of us.

Through the pages of the paper, and of this selection, shine the joys, sorrows, interests, and boredoms of that zestful group who form the writing team. They have percussed and probed, tested and observed. And through their reports has emerged not only a picture of our often baffling world but a glimpse of themselves. The reader feels part of the group, learns to accept the quirks and eccentricities that inevitably emerge, and feels comfortably that he is certainly on personal terms with all those familiar names. He isn't.

The newspaperman's liaison with his keyboard is an affair of infinite subtlety—probably far more complex than his marriage. For those who burn it is a weapon, for those who yearn a sublimation. Some tell it all, some nothing. But they are not different people. They are all encompassed in the one familiar byline at the top of the copy. The great strength of the *Guardian*'s tradition is that it has been able to absorb these often unpredictable elements.

I was once stuck out in the Far East with a man from the *Express*. It was the sort of day one detests: barely anything happening and those few developments of such obscurity and tedium as to defy any reader's understanding. He sent nothing but found me bashing away. He looked over my shoulder. 'Good God!' he shrieked, 'they won't print that, will they?' It was a mild piece, tangential to the main events, and they did print it. I even got a cable of praise, which I showed him. 'They're all mad in your office,' he said.

They probably are. They accept the judgment of the man on

the spot. They are willing to abide by his assessment of the situation, to record his reactions, print his conclusions. They are not unique in this, but they are members of a shrinking band. We seem to be entering the age not only of electronic journalism —which sees all and gets it largely wrong—but of committee reporting, which does the same less efficiently. So, while the Probe Teams and Vision Squads thrash around, the *Guardian* still believes in the seeing eye. Partly, of course, this is of necessity but it springs from conviction too.

Nothing, however, is more daunting than total freedom. I find myself from time to time in situations which seem to me absolutely insupportable, not in personal terms but in those of human degradation and suffering. I get into the sort of blind rage which comes on the helpless bystander. I want to rush off a diatribe against the injustice or inhumanity I have witnessed. I want to burst out on the reader, to make him feel as sick as I do. Why should he be able to sit smugly over his breakfast while I have to gaze down on the shattered remnants of nineteen young men and heave at the putrefaction of their bodies?

But, as I turn away with these thoughts in my mind, I know I will not do it. The paper would print it but you would not read it. Your mind is not prepared to accept the full import of the horrors normally told you in metaphor. So I bite back the urge and compose a calmer, more objective-sounding account. And you swallow your cornflakes, and catch your train, and murmur to the chap next to you about 'that dreadful business in Ruritania.'

The truth is that, given all the freedom in the world, the reporter never tells all. Sometimes his restraint is deliberate, sometimes a reflection of his own inhibitions or sensitivities. There is really no such thing as impartiality or objectivity in journalism. The mere act of reporting is a distortion of an event by separating it from the rest of life. It is not normal to be the focus of wide public attention. And the occasion is then filtered through the observer and emerges duly shaped by his experience, convictions, and blindnesses.

In a perfect world it will always be so. It is ludicrous to imagine that human affairs will ever draw the same response from all. The fallacy underlying the idea of committee reporting is

6

that there is one authentic version of anything, that if ten men each talk to twenty others they will arrive at the absolute truth. Rubbish! What they arrive at is the version acceptable to the dominant member of the squad.

The special quality of the *Guardian* is to have appreciated throughout its existence that this is so. Its reporters, in turn, have accepted the responsibility of restraining themselves appropriately, most of the time anyway. They can occasionally appear rude, smug, flippant, uncaring, or supercilious because no one is going to save them from themselves. They can also turn in the finest reporting being published today—as you may find by turning the page.

HAROLD JACKSON

Trouble at t' airport

In the grim little airline towns within an hour or so's drive from Heathrow (Sunningdale, Ascot, Woking, Leatherhead, Kingston, Maidenhead)—places whose dour, closely-knit people have been identified with the flying industry since the bad old balloon-and-stringbag days—there is an eerie silence instead of the roar of jets. In happier days the fierce folk loyalty of these people would be expressed in the famous gatherings at White Waltham or Farnborough; no one who has heard the crowds of pilots and their wives and often quite tiny children, after the long open-air day of processions, carnival fun and ripcord dancing displays, as they bawl out the lusty old favourites like *Don't Go Up In the Plane Daddy*, can ever forget the extraordinary sense of unity forged in the sweat of a hard, traditional craft; a craft which, as is too often forgotten, was one of the foundations of Britain's modern greatness.

But today the outsider is aware of hostile glances, especially if he is from the press, which these sturdy pilot-folk all regard as being on the side of the boss class and the hated Guthrie. Sullen groups of pilots, the fag-ends of Corona Coronas or other duty-free cheap cigars dangling from their lower lips, stand aimlessly at street corners or dawdle endlessly, in Skindles' or the Castle Hotel, Windsor, over champagne cocktails and the ubiquitous home counties delicacy, 'smoked salmon.'

In the simple detached residences, often without colour television and standing in less than an acre of gardens, they are preparing for a long siege.

I spoke to Mrs Venetia Sopwith-Vere-Benson, a grim-faced pilot's wife whom I met outside one such typical home, as she struggled to unload a case of a dozen Beaujolais from her car, a Mini with well over 5,000 miles on the clock.

'This is all we can manage for a second car. If Barbara Castle and some of them at Whitehall were to come down here and see for themselves what it's like trying to live on a captain's wages of £5,800 a year they wouldn't talk so fancy about us holding the nation to ransom, and the balance of payments. What about *our* balance of payments? Let them try scrimping and scraping to pay for the filtration plant on a miserable thirty-foot swimming pool!'

This is a town with long, bitter memories going back to the George Strike, when the pilots came out against the controversial automatic pilot—one of the many issues still plaguing the industry after the inconclusive settlement of 1948. 'Aye,' said Mrs Sopwith-Vere-Benson, 'there's many here recall the George Strike. That's why I've got this stuff. Several wine merchants refuse credit altogether. We had a hell of a job to keep the Sunday morning patio parties going at all; but they're an institution in these parts and somehow we managed with beer and stuff. But this time B A L P A are going to help us with the banks, and we're getting this stuff from the Duty-free. Most of us wives are with the Drivers and the Men Up Front to hell or harry prangers. But why am I saying all this to the filthy, revisionist, Guthrie-toadying, B A L P A-hating press, where it's always harry clampers on the truth and justice of our claims?'

But the minds of these sorely-tried workers are not entirely closed, and after a few hundred-pound notes had changed hands her husband, Toby Sopwith-Vere-Benson, a sky-steward and district convener of B A L P A, agreed to smuggle me into their meeting to discuss the Guthrie offer of an extra £75 a week.

'It's derisory, old boy, they'll turn it down harry nem-conners. Guthrie really wants to break B A L P A this time. The so-called settlement of the George Strike broke the old unwieldy GAU (General Airline Union); harry shambles, old boy, and now the industry's full of breakaway unions like NUTS (Navigators Union and Trade Society) and RATS (Radio and Allied Types Staff), riddled with Trots and scabs and Guthrie spies. In the old days GAU spoke for the old unit of the trade, the Cot (crew of three, old boy). Captain, Engineer and Steward. Each could pretty well do the other's job in the old Imperial Airways days. There was comradeship, variety. Often I'd pour out the tea for the passenger bods in their wicker chairs, the steward would get out on the wing to tighten up some loose wire and the engineer would bring the old kite down harry plonkers on the grass at Hendon.

'It was a tough life, and many people scraped and saved to get their boys into nice comfortable jobs like stockbroking or property speculation—anything but up in the dreaded air like their fathers. But at least we were together. After the George Strike we were too disunited to cope with either nationalisation or the awful boredom of the pilot's job, all those little dials to watch, and not even a private toilet for him. But really B A L P A is fighting for everyone. You'll see, old boy.'

I sensed the passion and purpose of these men the moment my eyes became accustomed to the dim lighting of the austere, red-plush ballroom of the simple four-star hotel where their secret meetings are held. They began with a full-throated rendering of the B A L P A Revolutionary Hymn:

> *Onward, brothers of the skies*
> *Though management wildly rages*
> *Confound those dastards, shame their lies*
> *And fight for honest wages*
>
> *From old Heathrow to Idlewild*
> *Our glorious banner streaming*
> *Fly, comrades, honour undefiled*
> *To salaries past dreaming*
>
> *We who guide the mighty jets*
> *Through stormy skies and sunny*
> *As the planes grow mightier yet*
> *Want lots and lots more money*
>
> *Bold captains on our worldwide rounds*
> *Let no boss try to reason*
> *On! On! To thirteen thousand pounds!*
> *One penny less is treason.*

As my guide had predicted, the £75 offer was rejected with howls of execration, and as I slipped out unobtrusively they were excitedly discussing plans for a sleep-in at the BOAC terminal at Victoria and the burning of Sir Giles Guthrie in effigy. It will be a tough fight, and one can only hope that out of the despair of Sunningdale, Ascot, Woking, Leatherhead and the rest, out of the old tragedy and heartbreak of this violent and passionate industry, a new hope will eventually be born.

PAUL JENNINGS

The Moonwalkers

Men are on the moon. At 3 39 a.m. this morning—nearly four hours ahead of schedule—Armstrong, the lunar module commander, opened the hatch and clambered slowly down to the surface of the moon. Minutes later Aldrin followed him down the steps of the ladder—already renamed Tranquillity Base—to join in this moving, clumsy culmination of eight years of intense dedication. It was the fulfilment of a dream which men have shared since the beginning of recorded history.

The decision to walk early was made three hours after the lunar module Eagle had made a perfect landing at 9.17 p.m., four miles downrange from the chosen site. The spacecraft was steered manually to clear a boulder-strewn crater 'the size of a football pitch.' It was a moment of extraordinary tension and silence. The lunar module curved gently down over the Sea of Tranquillity, the drama heightened by the calm, almost casual voices of the astronauts and the mission controller at Houston.

The casualness was deceptive: from 500ft. above the surface and all too aware that an error could lead to irretrievable disaster, Aldrin brought the spacecraft down under Armstrong's direction. At the moment of approach Armstrong's heartbeat rose from its normal 70 to 156. Yet his voice was calm and flat: 'Contact light: engines stopped . . . the Eagle has landed.'

The landing was perfect. Spaceflight Centre and the world seemed momentarily stunned by emotion: only Armstrong, Aldrin—and above them, Collins—seemed unmoved at the end of the drama which began with a characteristically laconic acceptance of the 'go' for separation of the lunar module shortly before 7 p.m.

'You got a bunch of guys who're about to turn blue,' said the Houston space controller, when the module had landed. 'We're breathing again. Thanks a lot.'

Within a few minutes of landing Armstrong was saying they did not know exactly where they had landed. Houston replied 'We'll figure it out for you.'

Armstrong reported that the site was pitted with craters, 'in the five to fifty feet range' with rocks of five to 10 ft., and ridges of five to 30ft.

Ten minutes after landing Aldrin radioed: 'We'll get to the details of what's around here, but it looks like a collection of every variety of shape, angularity, granularity, a collection of just about every kind of rock. Colour depends on what angle you're looking at . . . rocks and boulders look as though they're going to have some interesting colours.'

The close look already began to belie the image gained from centuries of examining lunar reflectivity—for that is what we see by—and the more detailed examination from orbit by man and camera. And from there, in the Sea of Tranquillity, the colourful earth is simply bright. 'It's big, and bright and beautiful,' said Armstrong.

They said they had no difficulty in adapting to the moon's

13

gravity. The conversation from the moon's surface came through loud and clear.

Separation began on this side of the moon, but the descent itself—the journey to which President Kennedy committed his nation eight years ago—began with a firing of the lunar module's motor after a long separating half-orbit on the far side of the moon and out of touch with the control centre back at Houston.

The world waited for the static-filled radio silence to be broken by an astronaut's affirmative. After what seemed on earth to be an age, the disappointed millions who had hoped to watch the first steps of separation on television, at last heard a calm and distant Armstrong confirm that the landing trajectory was good. The first minor miracle had been performed.

From that moment, with the tension mounting second by second and with the minimum of interrogation from earth, or from the orbiting Collins, the lunar module bore Armstrong and Aldrin downward, using its motor as a brake and slowly tilting until it was upright and ready for landing.

On and down, past 'high-gate' at 7,000ft. with the braking phase complete and the spacecraft rotated so that its windows faced forward—the point at which the final approach began.

Still onward and down, but more slowly now, the spacecraft moved with the astronauts checking, checking and checking again that all systems were 'go.'

Visual approach, but still under automatic control, began at 500ft. up with the spacecraft still nosing slowly forward. At 250ft. with all forward motion stilled and the descent rate only $2\frac{1}{2}$ft. a second, the spacecraft seemed to pause and wait as Armstrong searched the ashen-grey landscape for the hidden flaws, sudden rock which would shatter the landing.

With a permitted tolerance of 12 degrees about the horizontal—a tilt of 6 degrees in any direction—if the spacecraft was ever to rise again, the search for a landing area had to be as knowledgeable and as perfect as man could make it. A few minutes later, although time seemed to have slowed down, we knew that it had been good. The tilt was $4\frac{1}{2}$ degrees. A second minor miracle had been worked.

Every step of the preparation for landing yesterday went

14

smoothly. Armstrong and Aldrin transferred from the command module—codenamed Columbia—to the lunar module 'Eagle' during the tenth orbit, and on the eleventh orbit Glynn Lunney, the flight controller at Houston, told the world that all spacecraft systems were 'operating just fine.'

With the deceptive casualness which is now a hallmark of space-craft control, he added that the astronauts were 'a jump ahead in their work.' They took only six hours' sleep instead of eight and were in their lunar module spacesuits ahead of schedule.

ANTHONY TUCKER

Someone had blundered . . .

The unhappiest coincidence of this jubilant weekend is surely the leak, from a broken container, of the deadly nerve gas VX at the American base on Okinawa. It is the first word to reach the public that the United States is apparently deploying chemical war weapons overseas.

There was no way of suppressing the news that 25 men had been sent to hospital after exposure to this hideous item in the US arsenal. On Thursday night there was an emergency meeting of White House and Defence Department officials, who for a time did little more than sit around and curse the fate that blew the seal off one of the Pentagon's secrets.

The military is in bad odour just now, not only with radicals and student demonstrators but with the Congress as well. The Safeguard ABM is going to have a rough time squeaking through the Senate without people being suddenly reminded of the 6,000 sheep that died at a bacteriological testing range in Utah last year, and of the hullabaloo that arose in the spring when it became known that the army was about to put 27,000 tons of chemical war products on a train and ship them East to be dropped into the ocean off the summer beaches of New Jersey.

Now it comes out that lethal gas is deployed on a Japanese island, off which, last summer, a hundred children collapsed from an undisclosed ailment after swimming near the American base.

Mr Nixon will have to call, this week, on his best repertory of capital beaming father faces. If he is seen to crouch slightly as he watches the heroes splash into the Pacific, it could be a reflex protective gesture against the tornadoes of criticism blowing in from Moscow and Japan and, at his back, from the Congress of the United States.

ALISTAIR COOKE

Other people's rubbish

What the London dustbin-men call totting, my father, who was a Lancashire dustman, called chatting. By either name it is the collection and sale of unconsidered trifles thrown in the dustbins by householders who don't know their value. Dustmen know the value of almost anything that finds its way into a dustbin. Which explains why the Lambeth dustmen came out on strike when their employers tried to stop the practice. They were out for five weeks and only went back the day before yesterday, having sold their right to tottage for a lump sum of £450 each—equal, so one dustman says, to about two years' totting revenue.

I don't know if my father ever worked out how much he made a year from his chatting. What I do know is that his children would have deeply resented any bargain on the Lambeth pattern which would have robbed them of one of the most fascinating half hours of the day. This was when at the end of his round my father slipped his chatting sack off his shoulder and spread out the day's booty on the back-yard flags. As we children gathered round him he would begin the nightly task of sorting it out.

Kettles, pans, and tins. As he took each one from the pile he would stamp on it with his clog to flatten it and then slip it into one of a row of sacks hanging from the wall; one for aluminium, one for lead, one for bottles, and so on. Once, I remember, he ran out of sacks and had to stack some of the chats in a corner of the yard. By chance that day's haul had consisted mostly of aluminium hot water bottles. A visiting neighbour seeing half a dozen of them squashed flat and apparently thrown away asked who was the heavyweight in the family who was overlaying all our hot water bottles.

The next act in the entertainment took place indoors. My father would spread a newspaper on the kitchen table and empty on to it the contents of a smaller sack he kept in his pocket. On a good day there would be a wide range of items but one thing they had in common—they might contain gold or silver.

Spectacle frames were the most common of these possible sources of bullion but there were also from time to time broken dental plates that might conceal bits of gold wire, metal bands from umbrellas and walking sticks, pieces of watch chains and empty watch cases and, very occasionally, broken items of jewellery. After weighing each separate item in his hands and rubbing it clean my father would then go to the kitchen cupboard where the accumulated hauls of previous days were kept knotted up in a large handkerchief. The day's takings were added, the handkerchief reknotted, and the cupboard doors closed as a signal that it was over for the day.

The purpose of the exercise, of course, was not to entertain us children but to get money to help out my father's wages. About once a week a man came to collect the sacks from the backyard wall. He weighed them with a spring balance and what he gave in return was no more than a few shillings. It took care of the small extra expenses of the family; new boots for me, new dresses for my sisters.

Mostly we didn't bother to attend these weekly dealings but we never missed being there when the hoard in the cupboard was sold. It couldn't have happened more than twice a year. An old man dressed all in black came to the house in the evening sometime in the summer and just before Christmas. My mother sat him down in the living room and gave him tea and a piece of cake while my father got the bundle from the cupboard and spread it in front of him. The old man took from his waistcoat pocket a magnifying glass which he screwed into his eye and from another hiding place a small bottle of acid which he placed on the table.

For my sisters and I it was better than the pictures; better than the pantomime. He dabbed the acid on every piece and we watched it bubble on the metal. Then with his magnifying glass he read out the hall marks and explained them to us. Finally he placed each item to his left or his right; the real gold spectacle frames and the real silver umbrella handle on one side, the rolled gold brooch, the EPNS vase on the other. When he had finished sorting he weighed the gold and silver out on a pocket balance. The payment was always big enough to be in notes. Out of them came our Christmas and birthday presents and our holidays. And we could measure the size of each treat in advance by the size of the piles of twisted metal at the old man's elbow.

'There was always a certain thrill about totting, this job will never be the same without it,' lamented one of the Lambeth dustmen this week. No doubt his children will share his feelings.

HARRY WHEWELL

The girls behind the goalposts

Beyond the barrier, a few yards away, is the sanded arena. We are waiting for the Lions—we and some thousands of other roaring Christians of both sexes.

A mistake, it turns out, to believe rumours that the traditional football supporters are staying away, leaving the field to dons, literary critics, politicians, resting actors, and women. But true, equally obviously, that yet another male sanctuary—once the most exclusive of all—has been massively breached. They may not have reached the moon, or made the front of the buses, but they've certainly established themselves at the back of the goalposts.

That's the place for the real heat of the battle, though heat is not the first word that springs to mind in the Den. Cold Blow Lane, this January night in dockland, is no place for miniskirts. Thick coloured scarves spiralling downwards, sheepskin jackets, woollen hats are more the mode. A girl wears a wild fun-fur coat that could have been pinched from her brother. A pretty West

Indian is never alone with her blue-and-white bobcap: these are her flag, the only loyalist colours she knows.

Other girls, ostentatiously self-sufficient, cluster in twos and threes. They couldn't care less how they look. It's how they sound that matters. The Den is no catwalk, anyway on the spectators' side. This pitch behind the sand-sprayed goal area is the spot for serious watchers, where we pay least and demand most: no place for the lily-livered, the thin-ribbed, or the delicately-nurtured. From behind us a male voice choir chants its rude songs, no worse than the one Aunt Edna smiles at every night, sung by young gentlemen, in the most approved show of the current London stage. But art is longer-winded than life. The favourite word, back of the goalposts, rhymes with luck.

The language mostly passes over the girls' heads though occasionally it slips into their mouths. There are no Mrs Capps in sight, anyway on this part of the ground, but any number of Rita Garnetts. Perhaps they go home and tell the old man all about it, filling in the bits he didn't see on the telly.

What the box misses is the spectator tension. This is compulsive, and so is the scene itself—the unreality of the pale-green moon-meadow, the four-eyed arclamps glaring down on it from the huge purple bruise of the night sky. All explodes into action as the red invaders (boo!) charge on to the field, followed by the whiter-than-white home team (hooray!). Yet it turns out a gentlemanly affair at first, and the full team of policemen gathered on the left of our goal look as though they'll be staying in the reserves.

The girls want more action. 'Why don't you kiss him?' one of them shouts derisively as a floored forward grasps the hand of the man who bowled him over. Our goalkeeper has little to do; but once when he makes a save, rolling over on his sand several times, the girls dance and hug each other with glee. They make their own ritual, take their own initiatives. They preserve a kind of sexual apartheid, failing to join in the rhythmical shouts and chants of the men. They look bored and tense at the same time.

'What does that bleeding winger think he's playing at?' a Madonna-faced girl asks quietly. She seems to know the answer, and it isn't football. Occasionally they exchange private jokes, but mostly they stay silent as coiled springs. Hold-ups are frequent but the fouls are on the dull side. The problem is keeping warm. How does our goalkeeper manage, a cliff of a man perched on icicle-legs? Remembering his lionhood, he paces between his bars. The girls rub each other's ears. The rest of us shiver and wait.

Then one of them, who has hitherto been sunk deep in her tweed collar like the broody heroine of some lost Strindberg play, shoots off a sudden yell of 'Up the Lions!' Whether or not this galvanises the players, everything happens. Rolls of toilet paper snake across the ground and festoon our net. 'Off—off—off!' a woman repeats in a series of staccato screams. 'The bastard!' shrieks the sweet-faced girl. Somebody gets taken away on a stretcher. The game is coming along nicely. And when the home team scores, three leather-clad Gorgons launch themselves into space like one girl, kissing each other violently in mid-air. One lands on my foot, but my howl of anguish is lost in the universal joy.

So the Lions, and the Christians, are fed. Certainly there's been as much London football in recent days as even we aficionados can take, including the ladies. Limping on to the local Derby at the Palace (Crystal, not Buckingham), one finds the birds looking a rather more mature flock; a local Darby and Joan, I suppose you could call it. There are so many of them that a special record is played to keep them sweet. 'My Sunshine Girl,' it is entitled. (Moonshine, they have to mean.) A policeman jogs blithely to the tune, keeping his feet warm.

But there is never a dull moment at the Palace. Toilet rolls streak against the night sky like meteors. And here the women show that they know all the finer points of the game—beating the referee to an offside verdict, spotting fouls before they happen. 'Don't you do that to our Alec, you *****!' The most charming sight is a boy and girl linked together with a kind of love-knot scarf, Charlton colours. When Charlton score they nearly strangle each other. A blissful death that would be.

NORMAN SHRAPNEL

The prophet Paisley

The temptation is to find the face of bigotry brutish and dull. The reality is ordinary, frighteningly ordinary. Wallace Park Gates were white and the air damply glistening with sleet as we waited for Mr Ian Paisley to reach Lisburn. No one knew why he was so late, but the pinched boyish lips and fingers of the Shankill Road Young Conquerors tootled and banged out the rhythms of Protestant fervour. We banged our feet, blew our fingers, and wondered about the Catholic chapel (the Pope has the chapels here) that lay on the route of the march.

Suddenly the crowd was sucked away from the blood-stirring fifes and drums. 'There he is,' shrilled a middle-aged woman, and they clustered round the huge figure, goloshed and fur-hatted. Everything about him is larger than life: nature seems to have added 50 per cent to all his features. The nose, teeth, hands, and feet dwarf the ordinary mortals around him.

The delay, he explained, was because 'they' had been smashing the windows of his new church in Belfast. A thrill of outrage at the blasphemy coursed round. Only later did we discover from the police that the official complaint had been of snowballs being thrown.

So the march set off, four large policemen first, union flags and Orange Order banners next, Mr Paisley and officials behind that, and then the band and the faithful. Many wore sashes—orange, red, white, and blue; and purple, with their lodge number or 'Ulster Volunteers' blazoned across them. External display seems to be crucial to both sides here. The lapel, where he pins his heart, proclaims the man.

As we progressed, the Moderator of the Free Presbyterian Church, plonking his feet down into the slush with a curious deliberation, tied on a ritual smile and waved in a blessing kind of way at the groups lining the pavements and hanging from the houses. But his eyes, screwed up by the smile, darted around uncommitted by the benevolence beneath them.

'He's there, he's there,' nudged the crowd to one another, but the harsh brogue made the sound emerge as 'Thurr.' So the thundering side-drums and the fifes, shrilling through the narrow streets, had the added accompaniment of this deep 'Thurr Thurr Thurr' heightening the ritualistic effect.

In some onlookers the commitment was total. Mostly it seemed to be the women, shopping baskets and kids hung around them, who gazed at the approach and then broke into fervent cheering. 'God keep you, Mr Paisley,' shouted one, tears rolling down. The men clapped, occasionally cheered, turned to their families with the proud smiles of those who commune with the great. Some made no overt show: but there was complete acquiescence in the necessity and propriety of the display; a quiet satisfaction that it should be their men holding the streets.

In the town centre, the band was drowned by the sinister bass voice of the Lambeg drums—the Protestant war drums banged for hours on end by the faithful. Their sound is a physical pain, deadening the senses which can only scream for escape. To the booming of the Lambegs, we plunged up the hill towards the Catholic quarter. Six busloads of police stood by around the chapel but the march surged on ignoring them and it. No people on the streets here, no faces at the windows. Just the banners, the sashes, and the Lambegs, daring any to defy them.

The ensuing election meeting, with the 1,000 marchers looking rather fewer in the Tonagh Estate, must be one of the weirdest to have been seen in the UK. They called on Brother Beattie to start the service—for that was how it was termed—with a prayer. Mr Beattie, young, sharp-featured and dog-collared, launched into a long hellfire incantation, punctuated with the sort of drawn out nasal cadences favoured by the Southern Baptists.

'Lo-o-ord, look down with favour on your servants. Lo-o-ord, give them strength to sustain them. Lo-o-ord, remember the faithful in this Province. Lo-o-ord, we know that evil is among us. Lo-o-ord, give us strength to smite our enemies . . .'

As the pleas grew more specific his voice rose and the delivery became a chant. His accent became overladen with distinctly American tones. Finally to 'Oh God our Help' and to Mr Paisley, by this stage mounted on the back of a lorry.

Cold print can never capture the demagogue. The timing, the

22

pauses, the cadences need to be fully scored. The words barely matter—the attack on the traitor O'Neill, on the lying reporters, on the corrupt magistrates, on the hated Papacy—they are just the stands on which the sheet music rests. What counts is the personality of the man, his uncanny ability to handle the crowd which is his instrument, to coax it through all the movements of the work to its triumphant crescendo. Just as his acolyte relied on the 'Lo-o-ords' of his prayer, Mr Paisley leaned heavily on the convenient punctuation of 'Pro-o-otestant.'

'I want to tell Terence O'Neill today that he is going to face the Pro-o-o-otestant electorate of Ulster. He may try to use the landed gentry to attack the Pro-o-o-otestant working class, but he will not succeed; They can send me to prison, for three months or three years, but I will be a Pro-o-o-otestant until the breath leaves this body.'

As the speech reaches its climax, repetition of the word increases in frequency and intensity. 'He's right, he's right,' said a woman behind me. 'So he is,' said the young man beside her. 'So he is, God save him.'

After 40 minutes it was ended and we drifted away to brood. The only dissentient voice all day had been the man who whispered to me during Paisley's speech: 'He doesn't speak for me.' Otherwise there had been a frightening acceptance.

I said as much to an Irish reporter, who looked as though I was daft. 'Sure, it's always like that,' he said. In the centre of the town a lone figure stood in the middle of the shopping crowd, apparently in a trance, banging away on his Lambeg drum. No one took any notice.

HAROLD JACKSON

Adult extremism

Sir,—As grant earning students we were deeply disturbed to read of the riots caused by bald-headed adults in Armagh. While all serious-minded students were in their libraries working, or representing their universities in sport, these militant extremists were allowed to run amuck in the innocent streets of the peaceful city.

We realise that these hooligans are a minority of their generation, but feel that the moderate majority should assert themselves to keep such unruly elements under control. Surely these reputably responsible adults should have been working to close the trade gap. That is, after all, what they are paid for. They should leave politics to students who understand these matters.—Yours faithfully,

Elizabeth Sage, Ruth Pickard, Robert
Pritchard, J. L. Williams.
The University of York

MPs hear a voice from the barricades

It may be too late to cure the deeply festering ills of Northern Ireland. Several authoritative speeches in the Commons last night took this pessimistic view. But the emergency debate was a great occasion, at least, for youth, for women, and for maiden speakers—all embodied in the small but modestly triumphant person of Bernadette Devlin, the new Member for Mid-Ulster.

The baby of the House sounded alarmingly wise, and her own words were far from hopeful. So perhaps the joy of her parliamentary christening was less hers than Westminster's.

For joy and admiration were undoubtedly there. Miss Devlin spoke within minutes of making her ritual entry into the Chamber, usually in itself a sufficient ordeal for newcomers twice her age. The tiny figure moved steadfastly between Mr Paul Rose and Mr Gerry Fitt, both looking like political giants, and was given a roof-raising cheer. Order papers were ecstatically waved by Liberals, Nationalists, and a good many Labour back-benchers. Tories, including Ulster Unionists, were more restrained. Dr King, the Speaker, shook hands as warmly as the occasion merited and instructed the House not to be jealous.

However, many a promising entrée has been let down by the

main dish. Miss Devlin turned out better than her most ardent backers could have anticipated. There was more here than curiosity value, and the MPs who crowded at the bar and round the Speaker's chair got more for their discomfort than most standing-room-only occasions provide.

It would have been a good speech from a veteran. For a 21-year-old newcomer it was superb. Without obvious rhetoric, Miss Devlin managed to combine the orator's most conflicting arts. She was straightforward yet witty, quietly charming without the least hint of self-admiration, unassuming, and utterly assured. Most of the time she ignored her copious notes. And the way she took Mr. Chichester-Clark apart aroused, at one point, what must have been a pale smile of admiration even from him.

Mr Chichester-Clark's speech was reasonable for an Ulster Unionist—which would not be saying much in Miss Devlin's opinion—and he had made the tolerably unprovocative remark that 'the Englishman has yet to be born who understands Ireland or the Northern Irish.' She seized avidly on this text. In Miss Devlin's view no Ulster Unionist, even the Member for Londonderry, could have the least understanding of the oppressed people she represented.

Next she echoed his phrase about the 'stark human misery' caused, as Mr Chichester-Clark had told us, by the window-breakers on Saturday. She was with him there, but her own view was from the other side of the barricades—'not one night of broken glass, but 50 years of stark human misery.'

She resented the false images he imposed, as she saw it, on the civil rights movement. First it was said to be purely a Catholic uprising. It was in the interests of the Unionists to say so, just as it was in the interests of the Member for Londonderry to come over 'with all his tripe about the IRA.' This was her final left hook for Mr Chichester-Clark and his suspicions that 'IRA and Communist elements' were now infiltrating into the movement.

She proceeded to question whether Mr O'Neill had the courage of his convictions, and even whether he had any convictions. By this time Miss Devlin could do or say no wrong in the eyes of the delighted Labour benches, and they even cheered adoringly when she started clobbering them.

'No, no!' they shouted when she feared, without obvious bash-fulness, that she was going to make herself unpopular with every-body. No? Then surely any decent Labour Government would have got rid of all those old Unionists by now. 'Hear, hear!' they roared.

Her final fierce joke about the irrelevance of any possible agree-ment between 'the two arch-Tories of Ireland' was rewarded with a grin from Sir Alec Douglas-Home; but both Mr Callaghan and Mr Heath looked as severe as Sir Knox Cunningham. Even smiles, in these explosive times, can have a back-lash. Mr Callaghan found Miss Devlin's speech over-negative. Apart from that he was as fervent in his praise as everybody else, and even looked to the day 'when she may be standing here.'

The prospect, however distant, of the Rt. Hon. Bernadette Devlin as British Home Secretary made Sir Knox and some others visibly blanch. As for the heroine herself, she looked safe from the reformer's deadliest enemy of all. The intelligent girl knew, no doubt, that the days when Westminster could disarm its plain speakers with flattery are fast drawing to a close.

NORMAN SHRAPNEL

The technique of repetition

No two political speeches have been as widely reported this year as Mr Enoch Powell's two offerings on immigration. Yet he poses as a voice in the wilderness, the champion of unheard millions. 'The overwhelming majority of people on the one side, a tiny minority with almost a monopoly hold upon the channels of com-munication on the other.' That is the line-up which Mr Powell claims to see. The acreage of space devoted to him this weekend gives the lie to that. It must cause justifiable despair to all those who work slowly and steadily for better race relations and whose speeches are given an inch of space on an inside page if they are lucky. As a senior politician, Mr Powell knows how to exploit his position to get maximum publicity. Let no one feel sorry for him because he imagines himself to be underexposed.

His first speech was distasteful because of its racialist tone and its use of phrases like 'grinning piccaninnies'; his second one is as distasteful for its tone of self-pity, and the self-pity he attempts to arouse in his audience. In his first speech, we were told (by him) of his courage in speaking out. Now we are told of his courage in keeping silent (in the face of 'endless abuse and vilification'). The truth is that Mr Powell's silence since April is one of calculation and self-interest, not one of courage. He could have spoken in the House of Commons on many occasions. That, after all, is his job. But of course the House of Commons does not sit on a Saturday. It does not get such good coverage in the Sunday press.

A tone of self-pity is the oldest stock-in-trade of demagogues. The little man who speaks up for the masses against their un-representative rulers. The discovery of a scapegoat is the second oldest. Mr Powell's invective against his scapegoat, coloured immigrants, contains at least two distortions. It overlooks the whole context of migration into and out of Britain. Mr Powell forgets the almost 20,000 aliens who settle here permanently every year. (And that is not Mr Powell's au pair girl: it is per-manent settlement, as estimated by the Home Office.) He forgets the thousands of Irish citizens who settle here annually. He for-gets the thousands of people who migrate within the United Kingdom from England's green and pleasant land into the cities, and into Wolverhampton and the Midlands from the depressed areas. (As Chancellor of the Exchequer, Mr Powell would acceler-ate this, since he wants to abolish grants to the depressed areas.)

But then he is not interested in migration and urban over-crowding. He is worried by colour. And here he makes his second major distortion. British children who happen to be coloured are not British; they are 'immigrant-descended.' West Indians who speak English and number half the coloured immigrants here are conveniently lumped in with 'the great mass of immigrants speak-ing their own languages.' Anything that tends to show that immigrants can, will, and want to mingle peacefully here is ig-nored by Mr Powell. Anything that tends to divide people, he exacerbates. Anything that reflects discredit on one or two coloured individuals is highlighted out of all proportion. Anything that reflects credit is overlooked. In his reference to the article on Wolverhampton's maternity statistics in the 'Lancet,' why did he omit the sentence 'They (immigrants) also provide 10 per cent of the general practitioners, 10 per cent of the hospital nurses, 20 per cent of the domiciliary midwives, and 60 per cent of the junior hospital medical staff'?

Division is what Mr Powell emphasises. And division is the key to perhaps the most dangerous proposal which Mr Powell makes. It is not the policy of repatriation, because that is so widely condemned that it must hopefully be a non-starter. It is the proposal to stop immediately the immigration of virtually all descendants of those immigrants already here. Wives and children of men here would be banned at once. Mr. Powell concedes that this would be an 'evil,' but after a pause he adds, predictably, that it would be the lesser evil.

The political history of the immigration debate in Britain has shown a consistent pattern. First there is a 'Right-wing extremist' speech, followed by general condemnation, then little by little pressure mounts, the 'extremists'' proposal is adopted by one party, then by both parties, and it finally becomes law. 'Suppose,' to paraphrase Mr Powell, 'that any Government fifteen years ago had declared: it is our intention that by 1968 we shall have legislation to deprive hundreds of thousands of UK citizens of their passports; people would not have believed their ears.' Let this Government stand by its pledge repeated by Mr Callaghan only on Wednesday, that there will be no tampering with the rights of women and children to join their menfolk here.

LEADER

The wrath of Calcutta

As these things go hereabouts, we are having a quiet time in Calcutta at the moment. We have not had a decent riot for over a fortnight, since a student was killed in a bomb-slinging barney up

at the university. The late and unlamented Governor of Bengal has been allowed to evaporate quietly to Delhi, instead of fetching up at the bottom of the Hooghly, which seemed a more likely destination at the beginning of March. True, the secretary of the local Communist Party (Marxist) which now dominates politics here, has virtually promised us a bloody revolution, but it has not happened yet. Unless Jyoti Basu and his bully boys manage to start hauling Calcutta out of the nineteenth century fairly soon, though, it might.

The onus actually falls on the Central Congress Government in Delhi and on West Bengal's United Front Government, which is now two months old. But as the first has mis-spent twenty years helping to get Calcutta into its present frightening mess, only a ridiculous optimist can expect salvation from that direction. And as the second has started work by reducing bus fares and promising the teachers more pay out of a bankrupt exchequer, God alone knows where it will go from here. If it were not for the cold and very hard fact that Jyoti Basu has become the bossman in these parts I should not be at all surprised to see Mr Secretary Dasgupta's revolution break out any minute now. But Basu is there, tough enough to twist Delhi's arm behind its back for aid it ought to have sent a decade ago, shrewd enough to know just how much more these people can take before they go berserk and wipe this marvellous but very dreadful place out.

Nominally, Basu is Number Two in the United Front Government. The Chief Minister is a decent old Gandhian soul called Ajoy Mukherjee, who got sick of Congress corruption some years ago and now heads the Bengal Bangla Congress. This is only one of 14 different parties in the U F and Mukherjee wears the captain's braid to avoid frightening too many influential people, including a great squadron of British businessmen who, among other things, still own and run the city's electricity undertaking. The real power resides with the Communist Party of India (which follows Moscow) and even more with the C P M (which shadows Peking). It is quite a sign of the times in Calcutta that the C P M device—hammer, sickle and star—has been daubed on almost every wall in the city. And that means that Jyoti Basu is the real hero of the hour.

He comes from an old Calcutta land-owning family, one of the zamindaris whose once-gorgeous mini-palaces are dotted sadly, stucco peeling and Corinthian columns flaking, among the hopeless slums and pullulating bazaars north of Chowranghee. Just before the war he went to London to read law and learned communism as well at the feet of Palme Dutt. He did gaol time for his politics and he had it at the hands of Indian Congressmen, not British native-bashers. He tasted power for nine months a couple of years ago, before the U F Government of 1967 collapsed over a slender majority and Bengal was put under Governor's Rule by Delhi.

But now he has all the seats he needs to see him through as long as he wants. And before the shareholders of National and Grindlay's Bank, the Imperial Tobacco Company, or any other outfit still making money from Calcutta start to reach for their stock lists, it had better be recorded that relations between Jyoti Basu and Peking are a shade on the cool side at present. Chairman Mao doesn't like his lads forming coalitions with bourgeois politicians like Ajoy Mukherjee; and Basu, who is a Bengali even before he is a Communist, has told the Chairman to drop dead.

I should hate to face Jyoti Basu across the barricades because I do not think he would give a moment's thought to swatting me out like a mosquito. For once a cliché fits; he is utterly impersonal. His best friends try to recall when he last smiled and then remember that even that was only an unwonted movement of the lips. The pictures that catch his eyelids half shuttering his eyeballs are not the result of a blinding flashbulb; the man is permanently built like that. He is (of course) an ascetic, non-smoking, teetotaller who is not known to do anything but work. He believes in direct rule, in fixing things himself. When the unhappy management of Remington Rand the other day was subjected to the gherao—a local form of industrial torture in which the workers simply surround your building, your room or your car, and prevent you from even using the lavatory until you have given in to their demands—the blockade was lifted after eight hours only when the workers had been re-briefed personally by Mr Basu.

He is said to be a lousy speech-maker in Bengali, but in English he is lucid and chillingly pointed. He had not held office a week before issuing a statement which went like this: 'Some queries have been made to the Government regarding the course of action contemplated concerning the repressive measures initiated by the minority Government after the dismissal of the United Front in 1967, as also with regard to the events in connection with the agitation on an article in the *Statesman* (a local newspaper) by Professor Toynbee. At the very first meeting of the Cabinet it was decided to institute inquiries on both. The procedure and methods will be decided in a short time. The inquiries will be impartial and these will be carried out with speed.' They talked that way just after the October Revolution, and after Chiang Kai Shek was sent packing, and in Prague in 1948.

Yet he may be the best thing that has happened to Calcutta for at least as long as that. He is certainly a necessity at this desperate moment in its fortunes, if only because he is not known to be corrupt—as even British business people will concede—after years of corrupt and incompetent administration, It is fairly typical of this city's recent history that when, in the early fifties, a Bengal Government Commission produced hair-raising evidence of bribery in and around the Council chamber, misappropriation of funds and shifty aldermanic deals in the property market, its Biswas Report was printed but never published.

You will not find anyone in Calcutta today who believes that things have improved since then. And Calcutta looks, feels and smells like it. It badly requires a people's hero.

This is the fourth largest city in the world and (for what the computation is still worth) the second city of the Commonwealth. There are something like seven million living here, who will be 12 million by 1976 at the present rate of increase, and 79 per cent of all the families have fewer than 40 sq. ft. of living space between them. There are 400,000 men with no work at all, on top of the millions who work for a pittance. There are a million refugees from East (Pakistan) Bengal, who have been squatting in bamboo shanty towns since partition and after. There is a water problem, a drainage problem, a slum problem, a transport problem, and if it were not completely lost in far larger issues there would be the problem of suicides who jump off the Howrah Bridge in despair.

Anyone from the West who does not perpetually trail a guilty conscience around Calcutta should be a very hard case indeed. The truth is, of course, that even after three weeks you begin not to notice some of the things that shocked you at first. The stench from the open midden on a corner of Bentinck Street, which is as central and commercial as London's Holborn. The family of five who have decided to make their home in mid-pavement on smart Park Street, beneath a concrete stand which advertises the world's biggest-selling air-conditioner (mother washes the smalls at a broken stand-pipe in the gutter). The dwarf woman of 50 who, like every beggar child in town, chants 'No Mamma, No Pappa' as she craves your spare paise.

After three weeks you become so accustomed to these things that you turn your attention to the astonishing delights of Calcutta. To the Victoria Memorial, which would be as depressing as St Pancras Station if it were not also as gloriously daft (what on earth *do* the Indian schoolchildren make of Mr Finden's Portraits of The Female Aristocracy of the Court of Queen Victoria—all 56 of them?). To the Marble Palace off Chitpur Road, a wild extravaganza of Bohemian glassware, Italian paintings (and two by Rubens, they say), Sèvres vases and Australasian parakeets, collected by the zamindari Mullick family, who show visitors round their home and dispense charity to a couple of thousand needy at their gate every noon.

To the Khaligat, where the most unpleasant Hindu deity of all is worshipped with rapture and marigolds and the daily sacrifice of goats. To the Hooghly, which was the sea-green Ganges at Benares but which is now a kahki-coloured torrent carrying hay-boats and tramp steamers past docks and brick works and jute mills and eventually through proper Lord Jim jungle to the Bay of Bengal. In any of these things you can take refuge from the throbbing, superheated nastiness of Calcutta.

Twenty-odd years ago a Governor of Bengal took his first close look at the worst of this city and said that human beings must stop doing this to other human beings. He was right. Four or five years ago a badly shaken Professor Colin Buchanan decided that he had witnessed the depths of human degradation here. He was wrong.

For all its uncontrolled horrors Calcutta has not yet broken these people. They are aggressively bent on something better because they are Bengalis, who are as stroppy as the Irish when they see their moment coming. They can see it now and their rising belligerence is taking some fairly useless directions at the moment. The students have not only been bombing and belting each other (C P M boys versus Naxalites, who are somewhat to the Left of Mr Basu); they have also been wrecking the university and gheraoing the Vice-Chancellor because, they complain, the examination papers are too hard.

The poverty-stricken have not only started to resent their poverty, but to resent anyone richer peering at it too closely. In a refugee camp the other night my taxi was stopped by a bellicose young man and a hundred camp followers. They demanded that my guide (a first-rate Marxist, as it happened) should explain himself and they had us out on the road. They clearly thought I was from the C I A. I had an uncomfortable feeling for ten minutes that the pair of us were close to a beating-up, and when we came home to roost my Marxist confessed that had we not done precisely as ordered, and had he not eaten humble pie, we might indeed have had a sticky time.

I do not think Calcutta can wait very much longer before its aggressive instincts are channelled to better purpose than that. Its people have been plundered for too long, first by the foreigners and then by other Indians. Its poor and its disposed may be tired and hungry, but they still have enough energy left and will take what they want if someone will show them how.

I cannot for the life of me think why no one has shown them before. Nor can I get out of my head that old crack of Lenin's: the road to world revolution leads through Peking, Shanghai and—Calcutta. I do not suppose Jyoti Basu has forgotten it, either.

GEOFFREY MOORHOUSE

The brutal battle of Chicago

Vice-President Hubert Humphrey overwhelmingly won the Democrats' Presidential nomination last night but he, the Convention, and most likely the Democratic Party itself, were wounded beyond recognition by the spectacle, seen by stupefied millions, of a Chicago police force gone berserk in front of the biggest hotel in the world. In 30 years of attending Presidential conventions, I have seen nothing to match the fury and despair of the delegations inside this Chicago amphitheatre, or on the outside, anything like the jumping-jack ferocity of the police corps around the Hilton Hotel.

They began by clubbing and taming peace demonstrators and jeering hippies and ended by roaming the hotel lobby like SS men and roughing up astonished guests, marooned families, and other innocents sitting or walking through the hotel lounges.

By mid-evening, while nominating orators were extolling the

34

saintliness of five candidates (Humphrey, McCarthy, McGovern, a Southern Governor, and a Negro parson), the night air along Michigan Avenue was dense with tear gas, roaring multitudes of youngsters, the smart crack of billy clubs, and the clatter of running feet.

Senator Eugene McCarthy opened up his headquarters in the hotel as an emergency hospital, and he and his daughter moved among the injured comforting them and bathing their wounds. Senator McGovern, the other dove candidate, stood at the window of his fourth floor suite reeling with disbelief and nausea. He turned back from the thing itself to the wider view of it being shown on television.

He telephoned his floor manager, Senator Abe Ribbicoff of Connecticut, on the Convention floor. When Ribbicoff came to the rostrum to put McGovern's name in nomination, he abandoned his smooth text, stared coolly at Mayor Daley and the entire Illinois delegation no more than 50 feet away and cried, 'With George McGovern as President we would not have Gestapo tactics in the streets of Chicago.'

Through a tidal wave of boos and derisive cheers, the Illinois delegation stood and lunged their fists at him. Ribbicoff, an elegant and handsome man, slowly said: 'How hard it is to accept the truth.' This was too much for the Mayor of Chicago. Dropping his calculated Edward G. Robinson smile, he rose and shouted inaudible horrors at the first man to confess to this Convention that the Democratic Party had been mocked, in the name of security, to make a gangsters' holiday.

Thereafter, scores of young men employed by a private detective agency locked arms around the Illinois delegation and denied any access to them by other delegates, the press, the television floor reporters, or Convention officials.

These same 'security' boys, wearing nondescript armbands or flagrant Humphrey buttons or even no badges at all, have enraged the press and the television reporters all week by their dogging presence, their systematic jamming of the aisles, their blocking of the necessary contact between heads of delegations.

Last night, they outdid themselves, in their mulish way, and this morning the three television networks and a host of newspapers filed protests with the City of Chicago, the Governor of Illinois, and the National Committee of the Democratic Party.

Even in the clearing haze of the morning after, another crystalline day of late summer, it is almost impossible to describe the progress of the Convention plot; for every parliamentary move on the floor was baffled by the street battles thundering from the television screens in the corridors and soon after by the rage of the delegates who had watched them.

Let it be said, then, for the sober record, that the Convention was gavelled into a rough approximation of order at 7.15 by the midget chairman from Oklahoma, Congressman Carl Albert, the House majority leader. The actor Ralph Bellamy and Paul Newman, the national heart-throb, recited a memorial tribute to Adlai Stevenson of Illinois which very few people bothered to hear. But, for 30 seconds or so, the Convention rose and bowed its head. It was the first and last moment of silence or serenity in the whirlwind of the night.

The nominators came in turn and praised their man, but as the word of the battle of Chicago came in even the orators began to salt their bland stuff with acid asides. The television reporters were complaining, in full view of the nation, about these 'thugs' and 'faceless men' at their elbows.

Paul O'Dwyer, the Democratic choice for Senator in New York, walked out and held a caucus of New York, California, and Wisconsin delegates and urged them 'to decline to participate in this mockery.' The purpose of this rebel caucus was declared to be 'to bring to a grinding halt this Convention unless these atrocities are stopped.'

Don Peterson, a liberal of Wisconsin, was the man chosen to attempt this enormity, which has happened only once, 108 years ago. His first chance to be heard by the Convention came when Wisconsin was called, in the roll of the States, to put a name in nomination or to pass. Peterson, ignoring the niceties of protocol, shouted in a measured way, 'Mr Chairman, is there no rule that will compel Mayor Daley to suspend these police state tactics on the streets of Chicago?' In the following bedlam, little Carl Albert gavelled him down and went on with the roll.

The next and last challenge came when Peterson, in the middle of the actual balloting roll call, shouted into an ocean of sound a motion to 'adjourn this Convention forthwith for two weeks, three weeks, until we can meet in another city.' Justifiable or not, this was an irrelevance.

When Wisconsin was called to register its Presidential vote, Peterson asked 'in all courtesy' what had happened to his motion. The chairman, hoarse as a frog by now, shouted that the rules permitted no motion or other business to interfere with a roll call. 'Reluctantly,' Wisconsin cast its vote.

At the end Hubert Humphrey had run up the commanding total of 1,761 against McCarthy's 601, McGovern's 146, with 67 votes for the Negro parson, 12 for Senator Kennedy and a sprinkling of oddities, including three votes for the football coach of Alabama State University.

The band blared in with Roosevelt's victory song, 'Happy Days Are Here Again.' But it was a funeral march. There were almost as many boos as cheers.

The euphoria of the winners was, I suppose, genuine enough at the moment. But the sight of it on television revealed a gruesome irony. The only unreal place to be last night was in the Convention itself. Fenced in with barbed wire, ringed around with Mayor Daley's tough guys, cut off from the living world of television, the Amphitheatre was a circus in the middle of a plague.

Most of the delegates, it was obvious, had no idea what the grim Ribbicoffs and Petersons were talking about. Some personal grudge, no doubt, against Mayor Daley. It was a terrifying demonstration of McLuhanism: the only people who got the whole message were the millions frozen with terror in front of their television screens.

Today, delegates from New York and California and several other states lodged formal complaints with the Justice Department; and Attorney-General Ramsay Clark has promised a full investigation of the Chicago disorders and the behaviour of the police.

If there is any consolation in all this for the ordinary, agonised citizen it is that Mayor Daley was revealed as an arch bully-boy, the manager and dictator of this Convention inside and out, the last of the city bosses in his dreadful and final hour of glory.

The Chicago newspapers are the first to say so. From pundits to gossip columnists this morning, the local press is seething at the dictatorship of the man who only a few months ago roared into power for the fourth time with a 75 per cent majority of the votes. 'Hubert in a Shambles' was the 'Chicago Daily News' headline over a piece that began: 'Hubert H. Humphrey could have gotten a better deal in bankruptcy court.' And its national correspondent wrote: 'The biggest name on the casualty list from the battle of Michigan Avenue last night was Richard J. Daley.'

'How long will it be,' moaned a lady social columnist, 'before Chicago's name stands for anything but horror in the minds of the world?'

'At least,' said a Chicago police official this morning, 'no one was killed.' No one, that is, except the Democratic Party. Now that the smoke and clatter and weeping have died down, there is only a faint rhythmical sound ruffling the horizon on this beautiful day. It is the sound, North, South, East, and West, of the Republicans counting votes.

ALISTAIR COOKE

Saigon keeps up with the American Joneses

Like the war, the middle classes, and the Constitution, Christmas in Vietnam has become Americanised.

It is a consumer festival with all the trappings of tinsel, cards, plastic snow, and Father Christmases in every other shop window. In the centre of Saigon, the folksy totems of the free world serve as the lightest cover for a thousand eager entrepreneurs to make a thumping Christmas profit.

As the Americans say, the Vietnamese are an industrious people. For the past few days the whole of the top of what used to be called Boulevard Charner in another era has been smothered in a forest of greenery. By the hour, trucks arrive from the Central Highlands—Vietcong seem to be permitting—bearing tightly packed bundles of fir trees which in effect are huge lopped-off branches, soon united and displayed on cunningly constructed wooden stands; and costing anything from £5 to £30.

During the past week the shops have splurged out on to the pavements. Protection money rather than licences is sufficient to allow anyone to set up a stall. Those which are not overflowing with American duty-free stocks (still with the dollar price tags but now costing much in excess) are loaded with Japanese goods—most of which carry heavy import tax.

Scotch stands next to hair spray, soft American lavatory paper and camouflaged sleeping bags. You can buy a whole range of sophisticated weaponry modelled in plastic, and the war-plane of your choice with flashing engines and firing guns.

There is not a single luxury item that cannot be had for a price. The Government's attitude is that the goods soak up spare currency and help to prevent inflation. French scent is for sale at £10 a quarter ounce, handcream at 25s, a box of paper handkerchiefs for 8s. Buying presents for most people must be frustrated by the sheer expense—and the seeming absence of locally made objects of any charm. It is as if the commercial possibilities of the souvenir market have destroyed taste and sometimes skill in the makers.

Among the transformed arcades occasionally you can glimpse the Christmas wife. You can tell her by her pale face and apprehensive look. Even the small number who have come this year have put hotel rooms at a premium. For most Americans it will be a boozy bachelor Christmas and, in spite of cards, the shiploads of parcels from home, the plastic Christmas trees that don't wilt in the heat, and carol services on tape, they would rather be getting on with the job or getting out.

This seems to have been in the mind of Mr Bunker, the US Ambassador here, when he composed his Christmas message to Americans in Vietnam. He quoted Saint Paul to Timothy and Dietrich Bonhoeffer from prison, and encouraged his fellow countrymen to 'stand their ground.' President Thieu, on the other hand, in his Christmas greeting said that the Allies were fighting 'for Jesus Christ, for the establishment of justice and love of mankind which Jesus Christ came to earth to teach us all.'

Not to be outdone, we have the professionals well represented here, too. Yesterday the papal delegate visited North Vietnamese prisoners, today we had an archbishop from New York, and Billy Graham is already in the country. So are Miss World, Roosevelt Grier, and Bob Hope. The latter is somewhat ambivalent about the war: keen to have the best of both worlds, he calls himself a 'rough dove' and says with that famous twinkle: 'I planned to spend Christmas in the States, but I can't stand violence.' Is Hope getting sick in his old age?

There is still no sign of any extension of the 24-hour truce announced last week by the South Vietnamese, nor any mention of a truce at the New Year and Tet festivals. Evidently, after the last Tet, they are waiting to see how the other side behaves.

On Christmas Day itself five American officers will meet representatives of the NLF 50 miles from Saigon to talk about the handing over of prisoners. There seems to be some doubt that any men will actually be released at that time. The US mission here is taking great care to see that no one upsets the meeting. The area will be out of bounds to correspondents, road blocks have already gone up, and no aircraft will be allowed within three miles of the spot. For the news ban all but the keenest correspondents are thankful—they will be able to eat their Christmas dinner with a clear conscience.

IAN WRIGHT

A mission to shoot at what moves

'Have you guys got weapons?' The American major put the question with somewhat dramatic solicitude as we climbed aboard the tiny helicopter that was to take us into the rubber plantation. 'In there,' he said darkly, 'sure as hell you're going to need them.' We looked at each other apprehensively: we had only come to write about the war. 'Well, never mind,' said the major giving us a cheery wave, 'when you get in there they've got plenty of guns and I guess they'll fix you up.'

It was the third day of the American military operation code named 'Atlas Wedge,'and this part of it was aimed, we had been told, at clearing two North Vietnamese regiments (perhaps 4,000 men) from their hiding place in the huge Michelin rubber plantation some 40 miles north-west of Saigon. 'Rubber is perfect for tanks,' said a general, 'the VC have been shooting at us from the Michelin for too goddamn long.'

Seven days before the Americans had moved part of their highly mobile 1st Cavalry Division into what they called 'blocking positions' north of the plantation. The idea was that tanks and armoured personnel carriers should come through the plantation from the south-east and south-west and push the enemy into the arms of the blocking force in the north.

The little observation helicopter, an elegant Dragonfly that weighs less than a Volkswagen, was already hovering high over the distinctive privet green of the bushy rubber trees, set out square upon square of neat sections like a vast verdant Manhattan. There were hills to the north-west and, framing the plantation on the easterly side, you could see dense clouds of smoke where B-52 Stratofortresses had delivered some 400,000 lb. worth of bombs only 15 minutes earlier. 'That's to cut off their escape,' said the chopper pilot.

Ever since Vietminh days the Michelin has had a bad reputation. Its geographical position, half way between Saigon and the Cambodian border, surrounded by thick forest, made it a natural catchment for guerrilla bands and a good place for North Vietnamese soldiers to gather, rest, and collect supplies.

But the plantation has continued in partial production—one of the largest and potentially most profitable in Vietnam. In 1967, for instance, under the most difficult security conditions, it managed to produce almost a million dollars' worth of rubber. Rubber is the only export of any value left in South Vietnam and the Saigon Government must regard the plantation as most valuable.

As things have stood, the North Vietnamese and Vietcong have been relatively unmolested, and in turn have never damaged the trees. The company has managed to hold on to its precious asset in the hope that when peace comes it can open up full production. Thus everyone was tolerably happy.

Everyone except the Americans. Our helicopter set us down in a clearing and in two minutes we were perched precariously on top of tanks or personnel carriers, lumbering up the road and into the rubber. Up to the end of February the company claims that more than $3 millions' worth of damage had been done to the plantation by military operations—but not a cent of compensation has been forthcoming from the Saigon Government, which paradoxically perhaps is responsible for the doings of the Americans.

Rubber trees in the Michelin are planted a convenient 12ft. apart. The 30 tracked vehicles moved abreast very slowly. Some took much care to avoid the trees, a few pushed down anything in their way. Men in steel helmets and flak jackets watched with much concentration and every now and then some itchy-fingered trooper would let off a burst of tracer which sometimes ignited the undergrowth which in turn set fire to the rubber trees. 'Our mission is to shoot at everything that moves: it's open house in here,' said an officer.

As the day wore on the only sign of the enemy was of his speedy departure: bits of clothing, long sausage-shaped bags of rice, two rifles, some mortar rounds, and a couple of Chinese manufactured mines. The initial vigilance began to relax. Some men took off their flak jackets and opened tins of Coca-Cola as we jogged along.

There was no need to worry that day. 'Atlas Wedge' is the biggest sweep ever to be made through the Michelin Plantation and yet so far it has not discovered a tenth of the enemy troops supposed to be hiding there. Perhaps the rest have moved out: perhaps they are still in bunkers 30ft. beneath the ground. How do you tell without tearing the plantation apart? As it is soldiers, tanks and airstrikes have disrupted the place and it is possible that the company will have to close it down.

If it does, the Michelin Plantation will have become yet another casualty of the way the war is being fought. It has been proved time and time again that hitting the enemy in his sanctuaries does more damage to the sanctuaries than to the enemy. The alternative is very frustrating, and it means that the enemy can choose where he wants to fight. But as the Americans readily admit, once they have managed to 'clean out' a place the size of the Michelin, they cannot afford to leave sufficient troops to guard it. So is it worth the effort?

IAN WRIGHT

Verdict on LBJ

For the first time since John Adams in 1801, a retiring President of the United States went down to Congress to deliver his last State of the Union message. It is usually sent by courier and read by droning clerks to half-empty sessions in both Houses, which raise no objections and no applause. For the least Congress can do is to acknowledge the greater embarrassment of a Chief Executive who is suddenly about to lose all power. There is very little point in worrying over the legislative 'recommendations' of a President whose convictions about the country's needs are so shortly to be embalmed in his memoirs. In a Parliament, the defeated man would in all likelihood cross over and put his boots up for several years on the front bench of the Opposition.

The American system, at once more sentimental and more ruthless, insists that a man live and breathe and have his being in the constituency he speaks for; but, like a football coach or base-ball manager, when he loses the decisive game he is benched. And all his team go with him into obscurity of, to be sure, a rather cushy kind. Dean Rusk is going back to his old Foundation life. Clark Clifford, privy to the deepest secrets of defence, will presumably resume his profitable law practice. Walt Rostow, the Colonel House (or, in the New Left version, the Doctor Strangelove) of national security, will be securely exiled in Austin, Texas, teaching at the university. Brother Eugene V. Rostow, the Under-Secretary of State, will resume his law professorship at Yale.

43

Larry O'Brien, the big brother of Kennedy's Irish Mafia, lately the Postmaster-General and the manager of Hubert Humphrey's campaign, is suddenly the president of one of Wall Street's most impressive investment banking firms. And the Vice-President himself, from next Wednesday on, will be mushing through the sub-zero cold of Minneapolis to teach the mysterious science of politics to sceptical 20-year-olds.

And the captain himself, after 38 years in Washington, will retire to the peach and armadillo country by the Pedernales River and confide his most burning 'recommendations' to nobody but his wife as they 'take a little walk at sundown over the hills and commune with ourselves.'

It is almost too touching to resist. But whereas most departing Presidents receive the usual condolences in private phone calls and tear-stained letters, it was typical of LBJ that he invited the whole Congress to the wailing wall and led his own chorus of Auld Lang Syne. No doubt about it, last Tuesday evening's was a poignant performance. He did not recriminate or defy or look for any last ditches to defend. Stronger men have spoken ruefully of their vanishing power, and most get in a few wincing digs at the mulishness of their opponents. He was neither a Hector nor a martyr. He was the old, early Johnson at his meditative best.

'Every President lives,' he mused, 'not only with what is but what has been and what could be.' He looked back, with more wistfulness than passion, over the immense turbulence of the Johnson years and thanked two ex-Presidents, two Speakers of the House and several Whips and Opposition leaders for their counsel. He said an indulgence for the incoming President and he ended: 'I hope it may be said, a hundred years from now, that together we helped to make our country more just for all its people—as well as to ensure the blessings of liberty for our prosperity. I believe it will be said that we tried.'

Americans do not always love a winner. But they invariably love a man who's down, especially when it's certain that he's down and out. LBJ's most dedicated enemies were prepared to forgive if not forget in the throbbing tide of cheers that overwhelmed him at the last. A few weeks or months from now they will more briskly compare his style with that of the coming man.

What have we left, after five rocking years with the outsize Texan? What he has done, without question, is to enlarge the Roosevelt revolution, the original grand promise of the New Deal, far beyond the scope of its creator. He inherited, it is now possible to see, a critical stalemate in the American Presidency. Kennedy, before his tragic translation into martyr, was stalled to the point of despair by his own inability to move a stubborn Congress through the essential gift of persuading and wooing the chairmen of its crucial committees.

This, on the contrary, had been Johnson's formidable talent both as the Senate's minority and majority leader. Between January and October of 1964 the eighty-ninth Congress enacted a volume of domestic reforms which, in a period of complacent affluence and Congressional torpor, far surpassed that given to Franklin Roosevelt in the pit of the Depression by a Congress frightened into submission. And it was done in spite of a defence appropriation which gobbled up just less than half the total budget.

All his legislative programmes of any seriousness were passed. Medicare. The suspension of literacy and character tests in every State where 50 per cent of the eligible voters registered. The principle of Federal aid to schools and higher education was established on a universal scale. The traditional rule of admitting immigrants by nation of origin was abolished. Three billion dollars, an unimaginable figure, primed the pump for the general relief of poverty and committed the Federal Government for ever to a subsidised poverty programme, to job retraining and a permanent Youth Corps. The first Act to relieve the pollution of rivers and waterways. The creation of a Cabinet department of housing and urban development. An Act, at last, to redeem the national highways from disfiguring billboards and abandoned automobiles.

This was all done, admittedly, in the glow of discovering LBJ's immense powers of persuasion, manipulation, and exhortation, and before the stealthy shadow of Vietnam grew into a stalking monster that dogged and in the end downed the President.

45

The worst ordeal for Johnson, and in retrospect it may come to look like his best time, was the terrible $2\frac{1}{2}$ years (from the Gulf of Tonkin resolution in 1965 to his decision to quit in March, 1968) in which the dreaded land war in Asia was a fact, in which Johnson's country manners and his frustrated rage made him a ridiculous and impotent figure.

For it was then, of a Congress rising against the betrayal in Africa and Asia and against the violence of the cities and the black revolution, that LBJ went on demanding more foreign aid and asking for a more radical re-ordering of American society. Unheard-of commitments to public housing and welfare, the cure of air pollution, increased social security for millions, the setting apart of great forests and sea shores as public lands, above all a series of civil rights Acts that extended equal rights from transportation and schools to the heart of the matter, which is private housing.

It is true to say, I think, that Johnson provoked much of the racial turmoil by showing the black poor a strong ray of hope. Where there is a cowed and hopeless peasantry, there can be a quiet, if unjust, society. Where there is genuine hope of deliverance, the people stampede to achieve it.

But when he was most alive to his ambitions for the poor, whose plight was always strongly felt in the memories of his own childhood, the Congress and the people, and indeed the world, pointed without mercy to the cross of Vietnam on which he was eventually crucified.

Without this tragic commitment, it is entirely possible that he would have been seen in his own time to be the last of the great Presidents who held the middle ground, that vast body of restless middle-class opinion across a continent of sectional interests, that is or was, the only true American 'consensus.'

ALISTAIR COOKE

Nixon's first six months

Today Richard Milhaus Nixon has been in the White House for six months. And tomorrow he leaves for a trip to the Far East and Rumania. How has he fared in his first half year as President? What problems is he leaving behind him and what image is he taking with him?

Foreign affairs have probably been preoccupying him to a greater extent than domestic affairs. He fancies himself as a foreign affairs specialist. And in this field lies his biggest single problem—Vietnam. He knows that unless he can get a negotiated settlement before the end of the year or can clearly demonstrate that the United States is on the way out, it will become Nixon's war as much as it had become Johnson's war and it will engulf him as surely as it did his predecessor.

The way towards a negotiated settlement, however, has been blocked so far by Hanoi. And few people here have much confidence that the Paris talks will move forward in the next few months. No one has yet adduced any very convincing reason why the other side should want to negotiate—which involves mutual compromise—when they have reason to believe that patience and time will bring them all they want.

So Mr Nixon is thrown back on his only alternative, which is gradual withdrawal—what the Administration here calls 'Vietnamising the war' and what Saigon calls 'replacement.' Whatever the name, the game is to withdraw US combat forces as rapidly as their places can reasonably be filled by South Vietnamese units; to place major emphasis on the training and equipping of these forces; and to keep American casualties at the lowest possible level.

Another major problem which involves both foreign and domestic policy that has been preoccupying Mr Nixon is the deployment of the Safeguard antiballistic missile system. He has not handled it astutely. Until a week or so ago, opponents of Safeguard appeared to have gained a one vote majority in the Senate. Mr. Nixon has had to dig deep into his Presidential reserves of

47

political influence—a mixture of threats and promises—to buy off some of the opposition or the vacillating.

Mr Nixon believes that the European trip he made shortly after becoming President did something for his image both at home and abroad. Presumably he hopes the same from his current trip. Perhaps he also expects to cash in on the prestige of a successful American moon landing. Though nine tenths of the achievement for this is due to earlier Administrations, it will no doubt also resound to his own. It is about the only thing that is going for him just now. The achievement and the immediate prospects are otherwise a trifle bleak.

Since Mr Nixon had more or less been actively seeking the Presidency for the past decade, he presumably brought to it a clearer notion of what he wanted to do than most of his predecessors. It is ironic, therefore, that the most general criticism of his young Administration in the domestic field is that it has so far failed to throw up any guidelines or signposts pointing to the directions in which it is trying to move the country forward.

The most common theme of the political cartoonist these days is the President, legs and torso running in one direction, head and upper body running in the opposite direction. They indicate the veering attitude of his Administration towards the nation's major domestic problems, particularly in the fields of civil rights and welfare.

All this shilly-shallying on the domestic front, which is presumably intended to provide something for every taste, is in fact irritating and frustrating nearly everyone. It is giving the impression of an erratic Administration and one which does not know which way to move. And Mr Nixon is conscious that Congress is controlled by the Democrats who are now behaving like an opposition on many issues. The Congressional honeymoon has long passed.

And what of the President himself? He is said to be more calm, under firmer control, more self-assured than in the past. One can only judge from his rare public appearances (he has given six full press conferences compared with 13 by Kennedy and 18 by Johnson in their first six months in the Presidencies). Neither he not his senior advisers see the press if they can help it.

But in the view of a majority of the American public (according to the latest Gallup poll), President Nixon has been performing well during his six months in the White House. He enjoys a favourable rating of 63 per cent, but then at the same period in their Presidencies Mr Johnson won a 75 per cent rating and both Mr Kennedy and General Eisenhower 71 per cent. So Mr Nixon has nothing to shout about. And he is not shouting.

RICHARD SCOTT

" SOMEDAY SON ALL THIS WILL BE YOURS "

How we helped Hitler

'I wonder sometimes whether we are backing Henlein enough in London.'
—*Most Secret Despatch from Sir Neville Henderson, August 22, 1938.*

Henlein was Hitler's man in Czechoslovakia, the Sudeten German Führer. Henderson was British Ambassador in Berlin. And Henderson need not have worried.

The Cabinet papers for 1938, published today, confirm finally and in detail that throughout the Czechoslovak crisis—the violent prelude to the Second World War—the British Government's first purpose was to help Hitler dismember Czechoslovakia. The papers show:

That the British Government exerted continuous and heavy pressure on the Czechs to make them give in to Hitler. The Prime Minister, Neville Chamberlain, personally took steps to conceal this fact from Parliament:

That Chamberlain after his second meeting with Hitler, was convinced he had 'established an influence over Herr Hitler' and Hitler's word was trustworthy.

That the plans for Chamberlain's three visits to Hitler—at Berchtesgaden (Hitler's country house in Bavaria) on September 15, at Bad Godesberg on September 22, and at Munich on September 29—were prepared (as 'Plan Z') by Chamberlain and his three intimates, Sir John Simon, Sir Samuel Hoare, and Lord Halifax. These plans were revealed to the full Cabinet only on the eve of the first visit;

That the only Ministers who objected were Duff Cooper, (who resigned) and Oliver Stanley.

Chamberlain's main preoccupation at home was to prevent anyone from knowing how much pressure Britain was putting on the Czechoslovaks to persuade them to give in. The Leader of the Opposition, Clement Attlee, had been pressing for a White

Paper, and got one. But it did not tell the whole truth. On the 27th Chamberlain decided:

'. . . to print the White Paper as in proof subject to the excision of the message sent by the Czech Government accepting the Franco-British proposals. This document would have to be omitted since it referred to the strong and continuous pressure put upon the Czech Government by French and British representatives. If this was printed it would lead to a demand for the telegrams to the French and British Ministers in Prague urging them to apply pressure.'

Others applied pressure too. On the 16th Lord Runciman reported to a meeting of the 'Czechoslovakia Committee' (this consisted of Chamberlain, Simon, Hoare, Halifax, and three civil servants—Vansittart, the Government's diplomatic adviser, Cadogan, Permanent Under-Secretary at the Foreign Office, and Sir Horace Wilson, the Government's industrial adviser); Runciman said 'he had told Dr Beneš that he thought the latter had done more than anybody else to sacrifice his country.'

Dr Beneš was the Prime Minister of Czechoslovakia. Lord Runciman was, ostensibly, a neutral arbitrator sent by the British Government to mediate between the Czechs and the Sudeten Germans. Runciman appears to have been equally frank with Beneš's deputy, Hodza.

Others were being frank in London. On the 12th Lord Halifax (Foreign Secretary) reported to the Cabinet that Mr Churchill had proposed to him 'that we should tell Germany that if she set foot in Czechosolvakia we should at once be at war with her' and that Mr Eden agreed with Mr Churchill. The same day the United States ambassador offered to send two American cruisers to Portland.

At this stage 'Plan Z' was still being prepared in committee. The Cabinet's first real discussion of the Czechoslovak crisis took place on the fourteenth, the day before Chamberlain went to Berchtesgaden.

The Cabinet did not know what 'Plan Z' was and Chamberlain had to explain it. The thought behind it, he said, was that it might be agreeable to Hitler's vanity if a British Prime Minister were to take the unprecedented step of visiting him in person.

Chamberlain said that he would have to make it clear that he could not speak for Mr Beneš but at the same time he would undertake to put all the pressure he could on Mr Beneš and the French would do likewise.

The rest of the Cabinet were, by and large, delighted with this. The Lord Chancellor (Lord Maugham) said he thought very well of 'this magnificent proposal.' The Chancellor of the Exchequer (Simon) said 'he felt sure the Prime Minister must feel deeply moved by the way in which his colleagues had received this brilliant proposal.' The Minister of Defence (Inskip) said that we could not protect Czechoslovakia, nor was it likely that, once over-run, Czechoslovakia would 'ever be reconstituted in its present form.' Only the First Lord of the Admiralty (Duff Cooper) was unimpressed. The choice, he told the Cabinet, was not between war and a Czechoslovak plebiscite but between war now and war later. Nevertheless Chamberlain went to Berchtesgaden.

After he got back (on the 17th) Chamberlain said that he had detected in Hitler no signs of insanity but many of excitement. He had formed the opinion that Hitler's objectives were strictly limited. Hitler had, however, told him that any serious incident that occurred would release the spring (of the German military machine) and the pincers would close. Once the machine was put in motion nothing could stop it.

Chamberlain said that his impression was that Hitler would prove to be better than his word about the military machine and would in fact stop it. Chamberlain said that he attached great importance to 'the dramatic side' of his visit to Berchtesgaden. (The practical side was an offer by Britain to try to separate the Sudetenland from the rest of Czechoslovakia.)

Chamberlain said that a discussion of all this in Parliament would wreck very delicate negotiations. Parliament would hear about the Government's decisions after they had been taken.

Lord Maugham (once more) was the first to applaud and Duff Cooper the first to object. The difficulty, Duff Cooper said, was that in reaching a decision 'we might be led into a complete sur-render.' He said that he did not believe Hitler's 'last aim' was the Sudetenland; Hitler had, after all, also promised not to attack Austria and had gone ahead and done so. 'There was no chance of peace in Europe as long as there was a Nazi regime in Germany,' Duff Cooper is quoted as having said. But he thought there might be a chance that Hitler would be overthrown and this chance might be worth taking.

Once more Duff Cooper was almost the only real objector. Inskip said that a war to check Hitler might result in changes which would be satisfactory to no one except the Bolsheviks. Hoare said Czechoslovakia had lost the Sudetenland already and Europe would have no peace until this was recognised. The Marquis of Zetland (Secretary of State for India) added a plea that Britain would not support a plebiscite; if this were done, he said, Congress would ask for one in India. Only Oliver Stanley (President of the Board of Trade) supported Duff Cooper. He said that this was not the last of Hitler's coups. The Nazi regime could not survive without coups.

The Cabinet had also heard a brief report from Lord Runciman on his Czechoslovak mission. Lord Runciman said that Beneš was a man of great ability, so agile that he made those about him distrust him. Hodza was a man of limited experience and the rest of the Czech Cabinet were 'of poor quality.' On the other hand Lord Runciman described the Sudeten German separatist leader, Konrad Henlein, as genial and good-tempered. Lord Runciman had concluded that Czechoslovakia could not continue to exist as she was and something would have to be done 'even if it amounted to no more than cutting off certain fingers.'

Six days later (on the 22nd) Chamberlain flew off to see Hitler again, this time at Bad Godesberg on the Rhine. When he got back he told the Czechoslovakia Committee that he thought 'he had established some degree of personal influence over Herr Hitler.' Chamberlain said he was satisfied that Hitler would not now go back on his word. The most difficult part of the negotiations (Chamberlain told the committee) had been Hitler's insistence on an immediate occupation of the Sudetenland by German troops. This would be something which would be very difficult to deal with politically, Chamberlain said. But having once agreed to cession the sooner the transfer began the better.

When the full Cabinet met later in the day Chamberlain again spoke of the personal influence he believed he had gained. 'He was sure (the minutes say) that Herr Hitler now felt some respect for him. The Prime Minister was sure that Herr Hitler was extremely anxious to secure the friendship of Great Britain. The Prime Minister said he thought it would be a great tragedy if we lost the opportunity of reaching an understanding with Germany. He thought he had now established an influence over Herr Hitler and that the latter trusted him and was willing to work with him.'

Duff Cooper said he did not believe Hitler's promises. He said he was afraid that after the second rebuff that Hitler had delivered to Chamberlain the House of Commons and the country would not accept the proposed settlement. In that case, Duff Cooper asked, what would become of Chamberlain's newly established influence over Hitler. Hitler would not stop at any frontier which might result from any Czechoslovak settlement. Lord Halifax (Foreign Secretary) reported that the Czech Ambassador in London, Mr Jan Masaryk, had raised strong objections to what he knew of the proposals.

This was the interval between Chamberlain's Bad Godesberg visit, where the deal was done, and his visit to Munich where it was sealed. Masaryk wrote to Halifax on the 26th. He said in part: 'Having accepted the Anglo-French Note under the most severe pressure and extreme duress I have had no time to make any representations about its many unworkable features.'

That day Sir Horace Wilson flew to Berlin for what seems to have been the most businesslike of all the Munich crisis meetings. Its outcome was certainly clearer than the rest. Sir Horace reported to the Czechoslovakia Committee that 'Herr Hitler had said that he had given sufficient assurances that this was the last of his territorial aims in Europe. He had pledged his word to the Prime Minister and he had made the statement publicly. In Herr Hitler's view there were two alternatives; either we persuaded Dr Beneš to accept Herr Hitler's memorandum (demanding the occupation of the Sudetenland) or there would be smash.'

The minutes go on to say that Sir Horace suggested that a telegram should be sent to Prague urging the Czechoslovak Government tacitly to accept occupation by the German troops . . . 'This he felt was very likely the last opportunity of avoiding war.' The telegram was sent. The next day (the 28th) Chamberlain told the Commons that he hoped to meet Hitler and Mussolini in Munich to settle the Czechoslovak crisis. There was what the editor of *The Times*, Mr Geoffrey Dawson, called 'a wonderful demonstration' at this, and on the 29th Chamberlain set off on his last visit to Hitler.

On the 30th he was welcomed back by Mr Dawson at the airport, by the King at Buckingham Palace and by admiring colleagues in the Cabinet. Simon was filled 'with profound admiration for the Prime Minister's unparalleled efforts.' There was much enthusiasm. Chamberlain said that he had done his best for Czechoslovakia, even though the Czechoslovaks themselves had not been there (Hitler would not have them). Chamberlain said he thought the Munich meeting had been a triumph for diplomacy.

At this point the First Lord of the Admiralty (Duff Cooper) said he was resigning.

(This was not quite the end of the Duff Cooper resignation affair. The Lobby Correspondent reported Duff Cooper's apparently rather impressive resignation speech in terms which did not please Dawson. Back at Printing House Square Dawson wrote another version describing the speech as 'a damp squib' and attributing it to the Lobby Correspondent. The correspondent protested. Dawson would not budge. The correspondent, Anthony Winn, resigned. Dawson's biographer, Evelyn Wrench, says that 'Geoffrey constantly added a few lines or a sentence to emphasise some special point. His colleagues accepted these corrections readily as they recognised how to the point they usually were. This common practice at Printing House Square was apparently resented by Winn.')

MARK ARNOLD-FORSTER

The road to intervention

In common with other analysts I have believed for some time that the likelihood of Soviet military intervention in Czechoslovakia was minimal, and I have said so. I no longer believe this analysis to be correct.

The evidence now suggests that the Russians have already made one attempt to intervene—that is, to introduce their troops into the country and to keep them there. Although this attempt has partly failed, in that they have begun to withdraw their troops, the danger of intervention remains so long as any Soviet troops, however few in number, remain in Czechoslovakia.

And when they have all left, as they are supposed to have left by Sunday, the danger will be only slightly less real—because those leaders in the Kremlin who have tried it on once, and were thwarted, will be looking for other ways to achieve their objective. And their objective is to station Soviet troops in Czechoslovakia as the only insurance against the possibility that Czechoslovakia might drop out of what they call 'the Socialist community.'

The evidence clearly points to the conclusion that the Kremlin asked Prague to allow the stationing of its troops in Czechoslovakia and that, when Prague refused, it insisted that it was entitled to leave them there under the terms of the Warsaw treaty. This emerges from the statement made by General Vaclav Prchlik, the head of the Czechoslovak Communist Party's department which is in charge of military and security affairs.

General Prchlik said during a Prague press conference: 'I have inquired whether there is under the Warsaw treaty any provision which would give other partners a right to station or deploy arbitrarily their units on the territories of other member-States.' Why would a person in his position have to 'inquire' into this problem? Obviously, because someone had claimed the right to do so.

His study of all the documents showed that there was no such right, that the deployment of forces was to be carried out 'ex-

clusively' for the purposes of mutual defence against an 'external
enemy' after agreement by the member-States of the Warsaw
treaty organisation. 'I emphasise,' General Prchlik added, 'after
agreement.'

His emphasis clearly implied that the Kremlin was claiming
that it was entitled to station its forces in Czechoslovakia under
the terms of the treaty without the agreement of the Prague
Government. Although the Soviet Union may have promised to
withdraw the troops it now has in Czechoslovakia, this would not
affect its claim, as disclosed by General Prchlik, to have the right
to station them there if it so wishes.

The fact that General Prchlik thought it necessary to disclose
this claim means that the Soviet Union still insists on this right.
And so long as the Soviet Union insists on it, the danger remains
that it may wish to take advantage of this 'right' by reintroducing
its troops into the country.

A Soviet military presence in Czechoslovakia would give the
Kremlin a guarantee, of sorts, that political developments would
not get out of hand. It would strengthen the hand of the more
conservative elements in Mr Dubcek's entourage and make it
possible for them to resist the reformist pressures—both from
the politicians and from the nation—by hinting at the danger of
Russian intervention.

The Kremlin might well reason that the Czechoslovaks, known
for their caution, could be deterred in this way from going too far.
And if the deterrent should fail, it could still be used to put down
quickly a limited 'anti-Socialist revolt' against which the Dubcek
leadership, left to itself, would not use force. The conservatives
could then rally the 'workers' militia' to their side and finish the
job—and finish Mr Dubcek, too, as they finished Nagy in
Hungary.

One of the main arguments against this analysis in the past was
to be found in the view that, in this day and age, the Russians
were most unlikely to risk the odium that would attach to them
for ever if they tried to drown the 'Prague spring' in blood. But
the spring has now passed into high summer and many elements
in the situation have changed.

Above all, it is clear that those Soviet leaders who previously held out against drastic action of any sort are no longer in a position to restrain their colleagues as effectively as in the past. The ups and downs of the Soviet press treatment of Czechoslovakia over the past few months, alternating between the highest invective and mild remonstrance quite unrelated to the gravity of the supposed offence, clearly reflected the Kremlin see-saw between those who advocated firm action and those who preferred to wait and see.

But in recent weeks, the tone of the Soviet press has become increasingly threatening, reflecting the changing balance in the Kremlin. The Western Powers, too, have made it clear by their studied silence that they would not move a finger to help the Czechoslovaks in case it came to blows. They have even made it clear that they do not wish to rush in with economic aid, lest this should appear to the Kremlin as an attempt to fish in troubled Communist waters.

Those Kremlin 'hawks' who argued from the start that the United States, preoccupied with Vietnam, was unlikely to risk any complications over Czechoslovakia, can now back up their claims with the evidence they have accumulated over the past six months. And the Communist regimes of East Germany and Poland, to judge from the tone of their newspapers, have made it clear to the Kremlin that if nothing is done to stop the rot in Czechoslovakia, it might spread to their own countries. Nor can the Russian leaders be sure that it would stop there.

It is in this political setting that the Warsaw Pact units entered Czechoslovakia for 'exercises' which were at first to involve only commanding staffs and marker troops, after Prague had successfully resisted a Soviet demand for large-scale manœuvres. It is now clear that the Russians must have introduced more troops into the country than they disclosed even to their reluctant hosts.

At first, official Czechoslovak spokesmen insisted that the Russian troops amounted to no more than a 'few hundred.' If this were so, the 'withdrawal' which is supposed to have begun on Saturday would have been completed long ago. Further explanations to the Czechoslovak public by officials who said that there were 'two regiments' of Soviet forces in the country now make it

MOTHER RUSSIA.

clear that these might well amount to something like six or seven thousand.

While Czechoslovakia's politicians were beginning to sound the alarm, its military leaders sought to give the impression—as did the Russians—that the crisis was got up by the press. General Dzur, the Defence Minister, declared that there was 'no delay' in the departure of Soviet troops, and that, in any case, it was 'their own business' when and how they went.

When General Prchlik, representing the politicians, declared at his own press conference that it was not 'their business,' but a question of Czechoslovakia's sovereignty, he was criticising the Prague defence establishment no less than the Russians. The Army leadership played a sinister rôle in the early attempts to keep Mr Novotny in power. The dismissal of General Lomsky, Mr Novotny's Defence Minister, was not followed by any extensive purge of the Army leadership. General Dzur, his successor, had previously been his deputy.

General Dzur has sought to put himself right with the politicians by publishing in 'Rude Pravo' an article supporting their view of the Warsaw Treaty organisation. He, too, believes, that the treaty precludes any interference by one member in the internal affairs of another. It all hinges on what is understood by 'interference.' It is already clear that the Russian view of this is quite different from the Czech, and that the Russians have the power to enforce their interpretation. All they need now is the will—and they seem well on the way to acquiring it.

VICTOR ZORZA

This article appeared on 17th July, 1968, five weeks before the Russian invasion.

At Midnight in Bratislava

Czechoslovakia goes to sleep early as a matter of habit, and Bratislava was almost deserted when the first tanks appeared in the streets around midnight.

We were munching hot dogs in the main square when a soldier near us spotted three tanks at the far corner. Something was certainly amiss; in Czechoslovakia tanks are not permitted in the streets as a matter of policy. And these particular tanks were acting most strangely.

They took up strategic positions on the street corners and threw out leaflets in Russian, calling on Czechoslovak soldiers to support their Russian brothers in their struggle to liberate Czechoslovakia from the counter revolutionaries and imperialistic elements which had taken control. The point was made. 'This is the end,' said the soldier.

In the next hour and a half all the city centre was strategically occupied, and convoys of tanks, armoured cars, and personnel carriers began to deploy to the outlying districts. A telephone call was made to the Slovak National Council, and another later to the Ministry of the Interior, but nobody knew anything. The surprise was complete.

Was Czechoslovakia's 'bloody autumn' about to begin—that prediction so feared by the people when made by a clairvoyant in July, and yet considered 'impossible' even this morning when the fact was accomplished.

For the next three hours the streets of the city were filled with the noise of the rumbling tanks, but only a few people woke and came down to watch. Czechoslovak policemen, their clothes hurriedly put on, and their brief cases swinging rather absurdly at their sides, ran or walked swiftly to work. The Russians remained quiet, simply taking up their positions in complete oblivion of the frantic scurrying, not seeming to care. The tactic was effective. 'We can do nothing,' said a bystander.

In the main square, however, things began to hot up. Long columns of Russian vehicles continued to pour through on their way to new positions beyond the city, but a sad and bitter crowd began to form. Most of the people were young, but all ages and types were represented.

One girl raised her skirts and wiggled her behind at the Russians. Then, as the main column of supply lorries came to a momentary halt, two or three young people sat down, Gandhi style, to block their path. Although the fear was great, especially as the trucks began to move again, more people joined the protestors.

The lorries stopped again. Slovaks began clawing at the door handles, locked from the inside. Headlights were broken, and a boy sat in several obscene positions on the bonnet of the leading lorry. More people joined the blockade, singing the old Slovak national anthem, the 'International' and other patriotic songs.

Many people tried to speak with the Russian soldiers, to convince them that they ought to go home; their listeners remained stonily silent. One Russian soldier, however, spoke up to a small group of Slovaks. Russian soldiers, he said, were intelligent; they sympathised with the argument of the people, but their officers and politicians were stupid and the soldiers could do nothing.

In the ensuing hissing, the soldier lost his hat, but the Slovaks gave it back to him. But the pressure point was getting ever greater. The Russians decided to move. The lorry-drivers, ordinary soldiers, began to drive but stopped—causing a minor collision—when the crowd began once again to sit down.

The tank-drivers were not so charitable. They drove straight at one boy who had stretched himself out across the road. At the last instant, he turned sideways and passed beneath the treads, scrambling to safety after it had passed over him. What relief! Nobody was in any mood for martyrs; the tragedy would have been too great.

A man of about 35 standing next to me began to sob and one could not help recalling those famous photographs of the crowds —crying, jeering, and waving their arms in despair—when the Nazis occupied Prague in 1939 or Paris in 1940. The crowd at most counted only about a hundred people, perhaps two hundred at its peak; a feeling of helplessness pervaded the atmosphere. Should they cry 'Fascist,' as some did, or should they just say 'Please go home, and leave us in peace,' as most did? At most, the acts were symbolic.

A few attempts were made to increase the resistance. Paving stones were torn up and either placed beneath the tyres of the lorries to block them—which it did only momentarily—or thrown at the tanks, along with litter bins. Like shooting elephants with cork-tipped darts!

The best opportunity came when a supply tank loaded with spare parts and oil drums drove by. Several boys managed to clamber aboard and threw two oil drums into the street, one of which was set on fire. But it did not burn well, and the tanks just brushed it aside.

By this time, the main column had already passed and people were following them up the street. Some shots rang out—about three rifle shots and two machine-gun bursts—but they were over in an instant and nobody seemed to have been injured.

Now and then a Czech army truck or jeep appeared, to be roundly cheered. Smiling, confused Czech policemen began to turn up, and the big events of the night seemed over by 4 o'clock, until the morning, at least—after a few hours for reflection, discussion, or, if one has iron nerves, sleep. In the morning, solemn faces queued up at the shops; hoarding became the order of the day. The occupation had begun.

The impossible had happened—the last death struggle, the final groping for life, of a form of communism long since relegated to the dustbin of history. Stalinism triumphant, but for how long? And for what? A military coup is one thing; a turning back of the political clock to the days of Jan Hus and the blindness of ideologically based power is another.

The Czechoslovak people have lived most of their history under some form of subjugation; their reflex mechanisms are well developed. That their efforts turn away from social productivity to personal entrenchment and self preservation on the one hand, and to intellectual and artistic endeavour on the other, is a fact of history. They are accustomed to oppression, but that does not excuse the Russians for their action. That the Czechoslovaks will endure is certain; that they *must* endure is injustice.

P. G. CERNY

Encounter with an armoured cyclops

It was eight on Friday evening when I got over the border and a steady drizzle had set in. The road wasn't all that good, but it seemed sensible to keep up a good speed to get as far into Czechoslovakia as possible.

I lurched and bumped along but saw no evidence of any Russian guards, tanks, or anything else. At the first village, however, came the first signs of the occupation. Walls were daubed with slogans and the roads were smeared with whitewash, which the rain had diluted.

A few miles farther, a group of youths was busy touching up some of the new road signs—Moscow 2,500 kilometres said most of them. All along the route I got involved in some fairly tricky navigation. Road signs had been painted out, turned round, bent over, or torn down.

Few people were about in the villages and towns, and after a Czech bus I had been following turned off, I began to feel lonelier and lonelier. On the car radio the smooth tones of the BBC told British subjects to get out of the country. An occasional car would come the other way.

One motor-cycle appeared on a long straight stretch and would not dip his light. I flashed mine angrily. Still he would not dip. I flashed him repeatedly and a large staring eye suddenly swivelled round slightly to catch me fully in its beam. At about that moment I caught the chink and rattle of tanks on asphalt.

I jammed on the brakes and waited for the shots. But cyclops merely eyes fronted again and clanked on. He was the head of a squadron of T34s and his tail man was on my side of the road. I gave an ever so gentle blip of my lights, the beam barely crawling out of its hole, and he obligingly rumbled over to his side. You could almost swear he doffed his turret as he passed.

Then the mist closed around me and I groped on, convinced that every tree was a Russian road block.

It was on the outskirts of Prague that I finally hit the Russians. Two tanks and a group of soldiers with sub-machine-guns stopped me. They searched the car perfunctorily, laughing heartily over the jerry-cans of petrol stuffed into it, accepted my assurance that I was a German tourist going back to my hotel, and wished me a good journey.

A bit farther on I picked up a Czech who turned out to be nobly and roaring drunk. But we found our way to the city centre with only the odd hiccough or two and, under the curious gaze of the five tank crews in Wenceslas Square, I banged up a hotel. It was just about midnight.

It was only later, in the snugness of the hotel room, that I heard on the radio that the Russians had threatened to shoot anyone out on the streets at night.

HAROLD JACKSON

The men in Russian tanks

In the five days I spent in Prague I did not see a single Russian soldier in the streets, let alone get a chance to speak to one. Nor did anybody tell me that one could ring the Russian HQ and have a talk to them over the phone. I heard about that only on the sixth day—my last—from a boy at the hotel reception who also found the number for me. 'Better than nothing,' he said modestly. I kissed him and grabbed the receiver.

Yes, the Kommandatura answered in a pleasant Moscow voice. I told him I was Russian by birth, but not by passport, that I was leaving Prague in a few hours, and could we have a little chat if he could spare the time?

'What about?'

There was nothing to lose, so I said recklessly: 'To tell you the truth, there is only one thing I want to know: what on earth are you people doing in Czechoslovakia?' After that I waited for the bang of the receiver at the other end, but what I heard instead was: 'How can I deal with such a question over the phone? You must come here.'

I wrote down the address he gave me, in Praha 9. 'Where's that?' He said: 'I don't know exactly. Somewhere out in the suburbs.' This was pathetic. How cut off can one be? He added hopefully: 'The taxi is sure to find us.'

The taxi did, but it took a good hour, and 35 shillings in fares. We circled endlessly in Praha 9, stopping the passers-by, and none had heard of the street, or that some Russians were stationed there.

Finally we pulled up somewhere in total darkness. One could barely distinguish the outline of a biggish house. The sentry became visible only when he came out on to the pavement. He looked Mongolian. He pointed vaguely to the far corner of the courtyard and said: 'Fourth floor.'

I groped my way up a sinister staircase. Not only did it have no lights, but it was also icy-cold. In that city of cosy overheated houses, the place felt like a cemetery vault.

At long last, there we were, around a wooden table: a major on my right, and two lieutenants facing us. The major looked solid and nice; the boys were remarkably handsome and touchingly young. The light came from a bare bulb on the ceiling.

The major began to explain: 'Our intervention here was a painful necessity. We did not enjoy it, any more than the Czechoslovaks did. Also we fully realised that we would be inflicting a bitter blow on their national pride. But . . .'

I knew it all by heart, not only from 'Pravda' but also from having heard it word by word, cliché after cliché, in East Germany where I had been the previous week. So I just waited for the right moment to interrupt him, and meanwhile rehearsed the basic rules that I had learnt in East Berlin: never attack, never make statements, never score points. Stick to questions, loaded or not. This is not to get sensible replies [you never do] but in the hope that the people you are talking to might begin to realise, however dimly, that there are things they have taken too much for granted, and facts they may have refused to face.

I did not have to wait long for a good cue: the bit about the Fascist-Imperialist elements raising their ugly heads.

'I am so glad you mentioned that,' I said. 'It happens to be my main source of puzzlement. What are these "elements"? Where? How strong? Were they just a bunch of hooligans, or did they represent a serious menace?'

The major said: 'You're ill-informed.'

'That is precisely why I'm here,' I said. 'But what about the others? The Czechoslovaks themselves—they categorically deny that they ever had such "elements" in their midst. The entire Western press? The Western Communist parties, who all protested against your intervention?'—'Cuba did not protest,' the major said hastily.

'But are you trying to tell me that apart from Cuba the entire outside world is uninformed?'—'This sounds impossible to you,' he said, 'but it's the only guess that I can honestly make.'

'What about informing me now?' I suggested. 'Just something concrete, a few names, slogans, dates—anything.'

The major replied: 'I cannot divulge the facts I know. They are military secrets.'

The 'boys' exchanged cautious glances. They must have hoped for something more convincing from their chief. One of them prompted helpfully: 'She wanted slogans. Tell her about the film.'

'Ah, yes,' the major said. 'On television here, they showed the May Day demonstration in Prague . . .'

Oh, not again . . . ! I had heard it all in Germany: allegedly, the film showed people carrying banners with Fascist slogans. I had asked 'What slogans?' and my friend in Berlin did not even seem embarrassed when he told me he had forgotten. So here at the Kommandatura I asked nothing, because they could not have possibly seen the film. In May they were in Russia. Besides, they could not speak Czech.

It was at this point, I think, that the phone rang. The major answered and to my amazement passed me the receiver. Who on earth . . . ? It was one of the receptionists at my hotel: I had been away for over two hours, and they all felt worried.

I told the major, and he said: 'You see what we are up against. Wild fantasies, idiot suspicions. What did they imagine—that we had packed you off to Siberia?'

'Now, comrade major, let's be fair. What if the Communist parties who disagree with your present line, i.e. all except Cuba and Albania, decided that you needed friendly help, redressing, normalising and so on. And then one morning you'd wake up to find the Red Square swarming with International Brigades. I bet you'd feel a bit suspicious, too.'

By now I was dangerously near missing my train back to Berlin, and stood up. I was sorry to leave (and I think the major was sincerely sorry to see me go). 'Are you sure you can't put it off? Can't you come again?' Alas, I couldn't. I had only £1 left.

'Can you show it to us?' asked the major. All he wanted to see was the picture of the Queen. He handed it round, pointing. 'This is the Queen.'

From the alacrity with which the pretty lieutenants jumped to their feet and rushed to get the jeep, one could safely conclude that a trip to the city even in their own jeep was a rare treat. They told me on the way that they hardly knew Prague as they did not have enough money for the tram. They also had great difficulty in finding my hotel, although it was bang in the centre.

They were innocent, charming, and bored. 'Bored?' I said. 'but the Czechoslovaks say you are tremendously busy, still looking for the chap who had invited you.' To my relief, they laughed.

VERA TRAILL

Festering wounds in Polish pride

'Antisemitism was really rather a small question, but very disgusting. The big question was the question of Czechoslovakia.' This is the ornate but considered opinion of an impeccably liberal figure, a man of Jewish blood and a Polish patriot, and it opens up all the awkward and important questions about what happened to Poland in 1968: antisemitism, ideology and the struggle for power, and the present temper of Polish nationalism.

Everyone I spoke to in Poland, from the crudest party-liner to the most sophisticated liberal, thought that the world outside had either misinterpreted or under-interpreted the attack on the Jews. A loud old hardliner like Henryk Tycner, editor of 'Kurier Polskiego,' will tell you that the Jews who were dismissed from university and Government jobs were all old Stalinists, just as the disaffected writers were Stalinists (Andrzejewski wrote some very enthusiastic stuff in the forties) and/or opportunists writing anti-Communist works for Western publishers' gold (his last novella was refused by his Polish publisher after March as 'inferior,' and he nervily sent it to be published by the emigré magazine 'Kultura' in Paris).

A decent Jewish writer, on the other hand, insists that the campaign was entirely artificial, drummed up in the press of General Moczar's ally, the absurdly sinister ex-Fascist Piasecki who now runs the Catholic-Communist front organisation PAX. 'Antisemitism is not endemic here now,' this good old man assures you. 'There are less than 20,000 Jews in Poland: there is no rational basis for it.'

The reality of the matter, as always in Poland, is more difficult. It is clear now that the purges were part of a complex deal, forced on the party by General Moczar before his wings were clipped last autumn. The General, who is not so much simply antisemitic, or nationalistic, or anti-Russian, as a pure power-seeker (which is why rumours about his alliances in the course of last year were so conflicting and baffling), was playing all ends against Mr Gomulka's middle.

It is a sociological fact that many members of the small pre-war Communist Party in Poland were Jewish, and an historical fact that they emerged from Moscow at the end of the war in positions of power and influence. To that extent, Judaeo-communism, Hitler's old cry, had a basis in reality in Poland; and to the same extent there has been a very particular sort of anti-semitic tinge to anticommunism in Poland during the last twenty years.

This was one of the currents which Moczar diverted to serve his purpose. It may have been swelled by residual antisemitism of a more traditional sort among some of the simpler Catholics who take the PAX press for its titbits of religious gossip; and joined by the resentment of a later generation of party men seeking change and places. For Gomulka and his more elderly allies, on the other hand, the purge offered an opportunity of getting rid of those 'revisionist' intellectuals and others who might, if left to it, infect young Poland with the virus then raging in Prague.

In the event, the purge got out of hand. There are many grim and funny stories still current in Warsaw about the worst weeks of last year, when all sorts of bodies were required to find their sacrificial Jew. In one institute, I was told, the decent people got together and firmly nominated a keen party man who they knew was not a Jew, but who was then obliged to demonstrate his Aryan-ness. Shortly afterwards he went on a scholarship to a Western capital which shall be nameless and was ostracised as a bloody Pole and therefore antisemitic—which on the whole he wasn't. A less amusing story is that of the young man who, wanting to go abroad, was at first refused, then returned with the names of his parents ringed on a copy of the old Nazi *Volkslist* and was handed his exit visa without a word.

69

Now General Moczar has lost much of his power. He has been completely cut off from influence where it counts in the Ministry of the Interior, which he formerly ruled, and an editor of one of the most influential Warsaw weeklies described him to me coolly as 'one politician among others, not a special person.' I don't know whether the first thing that meets the eye in the Polish Embassy in London is still a pile of copies of a pamphlet called 'The Tel-Aviv-Bonn Axis and Poland,' to which the Polish Institute of International Affairs with such discernment gave its first prize last May, but at any rate, the count of references to 'Zionists' in the Polish press has dropped dramatically recently.

What is left, chiefly, of the whole sordid episode is a deep trauma in the pride of decent Poles, a wound made worse by the complicated psychology of Polish attitudes to the Czech reformation and the invasion for which they feel Poland has collected more than its fair share of international odium.

One of the nastiest things that happened to me in Poland was having to listen, more than once, to virulent attacks on Czechoslovakia. A Polish diplomat told me, in rather more words, that the Czechs were virtually Germans anyway ('Look how flattered they used to be when the Germans told them that they could almost mistake them for real Germans'); and that if you left them to it they would *become* Germans. A journalist on the daily 'Standard Mlodych' spat out the word 'collaborators' again and again. They collaborated with the Nazis, he said, and they collaborated with the Stalinists—all this, with a passion that seemed above and beyond the call to party duty.

But there was trouble, too, in the attitude of some decent people whose sympathies with the politics of Czechoslovakia's 'January' couldn't be doubted. One of them summed up his feelings about the invasion in this way: 'They had their Army ready to invade us in 1956. They had no choice then; we had no choice in August.' But most Poles, he conceded, would have preferred that it had been done with the decent reticence that Kadar and the Hungarian press generally brought to the job.

One night in a student club, admittedly, someone jumped up and shouted 'Dubcek oui! Gomulka non!' and it was taken up as a toast for one of those desperately quick Polish rounds among the crowd of girls and boys at our table. But even that was more a kind of convivial swearing than a real overflow of political feeling.

It's only fair to record that some people, journalists particularly, sailed as close to the wind as they could over Czechoslovakia and others damaged their careers by what they did not write and say. It would also be fair to conclude, I think, that many Poles were wounded in their national *amour propre* when a people who historically they have tended always rather to despise seemed to achieve more with the Czechoslovak 'January' than they were able to keep after 1956.

Just as Britain suffered by being the first country to experience the industrial revolution, so now the Poles suffer as they sit among the ruins of their October revolution. Like the British, too, they are tired of the criticism of people who they feel don't understand their position (and quietly appalled at things like the brave campaign of Amis and Co. against Yevtushenko, and the political—or is it moral?—infantilism of some Western journalists). Look at the map, they say. There is our past, our present, and our future. And in the wide, raw boulevards of the rebuilt Warsaw in February you could feel the cold winds driving down that great war route, straight from Moscow to Berlin.

'If you're a natural politician,' a Polish playwright told me, 'you might find what has been happening here interesting. If not, you ignore it as best you can and try to get on with your work. And there you sometimes decide that there's something worth taking a chance on. And if it comes off you feel a fine fellow.'

Just now, with everything shelved, nothing really resolved, it seems a bad season for taking chances. So Poland waits, with one sceptical ear tuned to Radio Free Europe and the other cocked sensitively for the slightest change of tone from Moscow. But who can tell when that 'insomnia of the conscience' will become intolerable again, or another romantic epic upset the political applecart?

W. L. WEBB

Work on the human voice

For a country to have a great writer is like having another Government. The man who says this is Innokenty Volodin, a Soviet diplomat in Solzhenitsyn's new novel. But it is more than the voice of a character. It is the challenge which, more than any others, Russian writers have put to our civilisation.

The First Circle* is a major work: more important and more convincing than the version of the first part of *Cancer Ward* which was published a few weeks ago. One way of stressing its difference is to say that *Cancer Ward* could be read as, in a weak sense, literature; a particular imaginative world. In *The First Circle* the hard inner meaning of the challenge is clear: a refusal to recognise frontiers between the imaginative and the real; an insistence on the authority of a particular and contemporary truth which will of course shock Governments—it is meant to shock them—but which also, unless it is put in a special glass case called Soviet or anti-Soviet writing, shocks, or ought to shock our own assumptions about literature.

There may be hypocrites around who can damn Hochhuth and praise Solzhenitsyn, or who have an idiom for reducing Solzhenitsyn to a creative or imaginative protest against an arbitrary political power. Things like that get said, in bad faith or under pressure. But having another Government means what it says: another source of information and values; another centre of decision and truth.

The courage of Solzhenitsyn is that *The First Circle* is not, like his earlier novels, an isolated world. Its method is not to draw a line around an area of human suffering, but to make connections, from this instance to that, until a whole system is described.

This is the literary importance of *The First Circle*; an original method in the novel, which goes flat against most of our critical assumptions. It moves from character to character, in what looks at first like a string of beads, a series of cases. It tackles what we

* *The First Circle*, by Alexander Solzhenitsyn, translated by Michael Guybon (Collins/Harvill, 42s).

call external reality and internal reality in a single dimension, and another way of making the same point is to say that in describing successive individuals, apparently casually linked, it succeeds in describing a system and a society.

That the connections are arbitrary, at first only a restless shifting from this person to that, is in the end the meaning: a series of arbitrary connections which compose an arbitrary reality: a Government which operates by seeing men in this restless, serial way, and which is then necessarily opposed by the substantial relations of real men which, while literature stays with them, are always and everywhere another Government.

What can be called, in abstraction, the plot moves through this way of seeing reality. A special prison for scientists finds a way of identifying human voices on the telephone which is used to catch and condemn the diplomat who tried to warn his family doctor. This work on the human voice, on detecting it, understanding it, scrambling it, is done by men who need also to speak, to describe their common condition. But what happens in the novel is also a kind of scrambling, in which a human society (that connected community which is the ordinary form of the realist novel) is fragmented into pieces of sound which can be understood only when they are put together again in a particular way; when the series is surpassed and its real connections made clear.

The First Circle is as different as anything could be from what is known in the West as experimental literature. It is a novel in the great realistic tradition, which has transformed itself to express an altered reality. It is mercilessly accurate on the last years of Stalin (of whom it includes an extraordinary serial glimpse) but perhaps its lasting importance is that it represents a new way of writing about a contemporary reality which, like the challenge itself, crosses and annihilates frontiers.

RAYMOND WILLIAMS

Zorza

The one Kremlinological story Victor Zorza has never written is how the embryonic Journalist of the Year escaped from the Communist world in the first place. Until a couple of years ago he would not have allowed it to be published, but the death of Ilya Ehrenburg, the man who sprung the lock, now makes it safe to tell.

It was winter, 1941-2, Kuibyshev on the Volga, where the 16-year-old Zorza drifted with thousands of other refugees. The young Pole was living rough, sleeping on the concrete floor of the railway station, queueing for bread, and, inevitably, reading between the lines of the papers, where he discovered that his hero Ehrenburg was also in Kuibyshev.

Zorza found his address and presented himself—rags and all—at the novelist's flat, an admirer paying his respects. 'Which of my books do you like best, then?' Ehrenburg asked suspiciously. 'Julio Jurenito,' Zorza answered, naming a book written soon after the Russian Revolution in praise of an anarchist leader, but banned by Stalin.

Ehrenburg could not afford to be reminded of it now. He immediately changed the subject, but simultaneously his manner became warm, friendly, and helpful. Zorza was found a bed and hot meals. Ehrenburg questioned him about his literary ambitions. 'The Soviet Union is no place for you to grow up in,' he said after a few weeks. 'You must get out, or you won't survive.'

Then Ehrenburg told him what to do. Polish prisoners in Russia were being formed into an army to fight the Germans. An air contingent was due to go to England for training. Zorza must present himself at the recruiting centre, claim some familiarity with gliding and with the English language, and hope for the best. He did, and it worked.

In England Zorza stayed with the RAF until 1948, when he joined the BBC monitoring service. He was sacked in 1953 for writing for the *Guardian* on the side, and joined the staff of this paper in 1956. Zorza is an extremist and a perfectionist. He works on his terms, or not at all. He is an analyst who insists that his readers are shown the evidence as well as the conclusions. Although his week is geared now to his 'Communist World' column, he still works an 11 or 12-hour day. In the mornings he sifts a huge mass of newspapers, broadcasts and translations from Russia, China, Eastern Europe, Vietnam, and Cuba. (He speaks Russian and Polish, and has a working knowledge of most Slav languages.) In the afternoons he checks the day's news on the agency tapes.

Then the analysis begins. It is, he says, a matter of 'relating something you see to a dozen or a score of other things to which it is not obviously connected—making the logical link, then going into your files to find the evidence, if it exists.'

The Zorza method turns on the assumption that the Communist world, just like the West, has its conflicts of ideology and of interest, but that these are usually kept below the surface of a party press. More and more pieces are becoming available, but the evidence is still scanty. Just enough is let out to enable him to weave it into a pattern.

Ironically, one of Zorza's repeated themes is the liberalisation of the Soviet system, growing out of economic development. Doesn't that mean he's writing himself out of a job? 'Yes. The pace of change will be so greatly speeded up that within 15 years we shall see the Communist world adopt many of the political practices we regard as democratic. The process of decision-making will be observable on the surface. The press will be more free. And my job will be not just harder, but no longer necessary.'

Victor Zorza's scoops included the coming invasion of Czechoslovakia in 1968; the Peking power struggle, which erupted into the cultural revolution in 1966; the Kremlin challenge to Khruschev, which led to his fall in 1964; and the conflict between Russia and China more than ten years ago, long before it came out into the open.

ERIC SILVER

Storming the Kremlin walls

As always in Communist politics, it is not the public announcements that reveal the most important aspects of the world Communist conference in Moscow. Far more important than the official declaration, and even the refusal of some parties to sign it, are the deep undercurrents that swirled so far beneath the Kremlin proceedings as to be barely visible.

The debates on China, and even on Czechoslovakia, were only a smokescreen to hide from view this new and most divisive issue —the attempt to intervene in the Kremlin's internal politics and power struggles that is now being made by the leaders of some of the other parties.

The Kremlin struggle is between hawks and doves, and the intervention by other Communist leaders is, in effect, an attempt to push Soviet policy towards moderation and cooperation with the West, and to parallel this with a policy of liberalisation at home. There has been much talk of Soviet interference in the affairs of other Communist parties, but it is the other parties that are now increasingly interfering—or at least trying to interfere— in the internal affairs of the Soviet Union.

The struggle is being waged by hints and innuendo, for the parties that protest so loudly at Soviet interference in the affairs of other parties can hardly take sides openly in the Kremlin's own squabbles. They therefore do this by resorting to the time-honoured Communist debating 'code,' which provides handy formulas to hide the real issues from public view.

One such formula deals with the 'balance of forces between the Socialist and the imperialist worlds.' The foreign policy of the Soviet Union, and of the whole Communist camp, depends on whether the predominance of power lies at any one time with the West or with the East.

If the West has the greater power, then, according to Communist theory, it will act aggressively and will seek the destruction of the Soviet Union. Any such relationship of forces would therefore increase the danger of war, and would require Russia to act as if war were imminent.

In foreign policy, this would lead to the politics of confrontation and rising hostility, fed by the suspicion on each side of the other's motives, to an arms race, and therefore ultimately to a more real danger of war. The prophecy would thus tend to be self-fulfilling.

In home policy, it would lead to the politics of repression, to a more conservative attitude in ideology and in daily life, to the imposition of material sacrifices on the nation in the name of military security, to the demand for national discipline, and to the suppression of liberal trends on the grounds that these might impair the political unity and therefore the security of the State at a time of danger.

And in that intermediate area of Soviet politics that covers the satellite countries and is therefore neither home nor foreign policy, it would lead to such actions as the invasion of Czechoslovakia—and to the attempts to discipline any other 'allies' who might at any time seem like trying to follow a more independent line.

Depending therefore on the Kremlin's estimate of the balance of world forces, and of the danger of war, Soviet actions at home and abroad would be either more hawk-like or more dove-like. There has been considerable evidence in the Soviet press, from the time of Khruschev on, that the Kremlin's estimate has veered from one extreme to the other, in keeping with the course of the internal struggle in the leadership.

After a protracted struggle with his colleagues Khruschev managed to impose on them a more moderate policy, but the 'collective leadership' which succeeded him has retreated from this, gradually but by no means completely, in a series of zig-zags which bespeak a policy struggle that continues to this day.

If the other parties could influence the outcome of this struggle, which is the key to all Soviet actions, they would be helping to bring about the results they want to see on the issues on which they now disagree with the Kremlin's hawkish majority— whether in the treatment of Czechoslovakia, or the liberation of the Soviet system.

Thus the Italian delegation's complaint in Moscow that the declaration presented to the conference suffered from 'gaps on the essential aspects of the international situation' was a veiled attack on the whole underlying rationale of Soviet foreign policy. This is all that the delegation said publicly, but in refusing to endorse that section of the declaration which gave an analysis of the world situation, the Italian party demonstrated the strength of its objections to the Soviet stand.

So did a number of other delegations. Although none of them thought it wise to explain their objections in detail, and thus expose themselves to charges that they were interfering in Soviet internal affairs, some came quite close to specifying the real issue.

Mr Brezhnev, who has argued in his opening speech that it would be a 'gross error' to underrate the threat of war posed by 'imperialism,' was answered by the British delegate, Mr Gollan. Without referring directly to Mr Brezhnev, the secretary of the British Communist Party said that 'only a fool' would under-estimate the danger—but the balance of world forces showed that 'we are not in a period of an automatic relapse to the worst days of the cold war.'

Are we not? Then surely the 'gross error' imputed by Mr Brezhnev to unnamed comrades, both among foreign Communist leaders and among his own Kremlin associates, is really an error by Brezhnev himself, who over-estimates the danger of war?

Before the conference, the Italian delegate in Moscow said that his party did not accept the analysis of the international situation given in the declaration, which, he argued, failed to provide an explanation of the 'real processes' taking place in the world. At the conference itself, Mr Ceausescu, for Rumania, took up the argument, and demanded outright that the declaration should give a more objective picture of the world.

He reiterated the Khrushchevian view—now so often forgotten by the Soviet leaders—that there was a sure possibility of preventing war, and, just to show how objective he was, he deplored both the 'underestimation' and the 'over estimation' of the danger of 'imperialism.'

78

But which of these did he deplore more? Perhaps, as the signing by Rumania of the final declaration shows, Mr Ceausescu feels that he cannot at this time afford to antagonise the Russians too much. But a pre-conference article in the Rumanian press made his objections quite clear.

It spoke of the 'paramount importance' of clarifying the question of the balance of power, and of the 'inadmissible' over-estimation of 'imperialist' strength. This would lead, in its view, to 'alarmism'—that is, as the context makes clear, to panic actions of the kind seen in the invasion of Czechoslovakia or in possible future reflex actions dictated by fear. This, too, is the 'automatic relapse to the worst days of the cold war' of which the British delegate spoke at the conference.

But the Rumanian paper went further, and recalled that wrong estimates in the past had produced the view that the world was on the brink of war—thus implying that Soviet brinkmanship was the result of the Kremlin's own illusions, and that any revival of such illusions might bring back not only the cold war but something worse.

Thus the conference debate was really about the basic issues of war and peace—that is, exactly the same 'ideological' issues which lay deep under the surface of the first Sino-Soviet debates ten years ago. This became gradually entwined with a whole network of other disputes, leading to the split between Moscow and Peking.

The hidden arguments about war and peace in the present debate are at the centre of a tangle of contradictions that will end in an equally momentous split between Moscow and the Western wing of the Communist movement—unless, that is, the doves prevail in the Kremlin once again, as they did under Khrushchev.

VICTOR ZORZA

'Sit up old man, and see us'

Many people say the junta killed George Papandreou. There is no doubt that the harsh conditions of his house arrests since April 21, 1967, contributed to the deterioration of his health, particularly the last arrest which extended from April to September, 1968. He was allowed only occasional contact with his son George; his doctors visited him in the presence of guards; his trusted body-guard and confidante of twenty years was sent to island exile, and the days were passed in lonely solitude.

For George Papandreou this was the extreme in cruelty, for his life, like that of most political men, was people. Although a man of great wisdom, he was not an intellectual in the sense that books could be his companions. He needed the give and take of personal contacts, either individually or with crowds, an opportunity to express his ideas, to use powerfully and beautifully, as only he could, the Greek language he loved so well.

For me and for my children, he personified Greece, the Greece which existed before the colonels took over. Warm and generous, hospitable, dynamic, with great strengths and great weaknesses, he was basically a simple man. He grew up in the tiny mountain village of Kalentzi in the Peloponnesus, son of a village priest, and whenever he could he would take us there to enjoy a day with the villagers. He would show us his home, his room, the homes of his relatives, the hills and the trees among which he played, or sneaked off to read ancient Greek history. In one election which he lost he was more disturbed by the fact that two votes in Kalentzi had been cast against him than that he had lost his seat in Parliament.

Papandreou was a pure democrat. He fought fascism on the Right and communism on the Left. He was a romantic, and sentimental, but he had the passion of an evangelist when it came to fighting for his ideals—freedom, democracy, human dignity. It did not surprise any of us who knew him that after his first long and difficult house arrest he smuggled out under the noses of the colonels a taped message to the Greek people and the world, castigating the dictatorship and urging action on the part of the Western world against the tyrants of Greece.

In the end he gave his life for this cause. But in his death he gave them a moral victory, and the opportunity to explode the myth woven by the colonels that the Greeks have accepted their slavery. Half a million crying, shouting Greeks came to his funeral on November 3 to mourn the loss of a man, and the loss of their freedom, and to protest against their chains.

What I found in Greece the six days I was there was a Fascist atmosphere, and the people under terrible conditions of fear and intimidation. An estimated 10,000 people are in gaol, in island concentration camps, or exiled in remote villages. Arrests continue daily. Tortures have not ceased, in spite of the outcry in the Western world. Heavy taxation is combined with a 'review' of income and property taxes paid by individuals during the past five years, and retroactive payments are requested arbitrarily as a means of penalising 'wrong' ideas.

Young people whose parents have been in any way connected with the democratic movement in Greece are refused entry into the universities and at the same time refused passports to study outside of Greece so they are denied a professional career and sentenced to menial, unskilled jobs, a form of cultural genocide. Professional men themselves—doctors, lawyers, professors—are denied exit from Greece, even to attend international professional conferences which they need to keep up with modern trends. Young men and women who supported the majority party in Greece, the party of Papandreou, are called in regularly by the security police to sign statements of loyalty to the Government, and rejection of their leaders, and are mistreated and imprisoned until they do. Others who have suffered the barbaric tortures of the security police are forced to sign documents that they were never mishandled and never saw any of their fellow prisoners tortured. These statements will undoubtedly be produced for the Human Rights Commission of the European Council as 'proof' that stories of human torture are false.

The army has been purged beyond recognition and a Communist commissar system of control set up. Many well-trained N A T O officers have been thrown out. Some are in exile. It is not an army in condition for meeting an external threat, from my information there, but is well equipped to keep the people under oppression and attempt to keep the Government in power. Apart from the moral arguments against keeping dictatorial Greece in NATO, one wonders how its NATO partners can feel safe about what would happen should mobilisation against an external threat become necessary.

I do not know how Greece is going to be liberated. I know that it will be. I am merely expressing my deep sadness at what a great nation is going through. That wonderful soul of the Greek people has been torn asunder, although the spirit remains.

The funeral was political, as his life was political. That is the way he would have wanted it. The voices started with 'Pap-and-reou, Pap-and-reou' outside the church while the funeral oration was being read. After the speech of Panyiotis Cannelopoulos, leader of the Opposition party—a moving tribute to George Papandreou and democracy—the doors of the church were opened and we filed out into the sunlit day.

At the cemetery Greeks were clubbed when they kneeled and started singing the national anthem, a song of liberty, as George Papandreou's body was lowered into the grave. Thirty-six people were arrested, and with a sense of despair I read in 'Eleftheros Kosmos' of November 6 that they had summarily been given sentences: D. Triambellos, 40-year-old lawyer, four and a half years; E. Valosopoulos, 25-year-old worker, three and a half years; S. Katsoulas, 33-year-old tapestry maker, three and a half years; K. Voyiatzakis, 34-year-old insurance broker, two and a half years, and so forth. It was said that they shouted 'Andreas is coming,' 'Democracy,' and 'Down with the junta.'

The cry that touched me most was when the crowds shouted, 'Sit up old man, and see us.' They wanted him to know that they had not lost their beliefs in what he fought for, and that he did not die in vain. Freedom is part of their tradition. George Papandreou died to keep up that tradition.

MARGARET PAPANDREOU

A jaunt to Manila

On the pretext of informing myself about conditions in the Philippine Islands, of which I was wholly ignorant (and to a large extent still am), I recently accepted an invitation from KLM Royal Dutch Airlines to join their inaugural flight from Amsterdam to Manila on board a DC 8-63. This formidable aircraft, carrying between 200 and 225 passengers, will remain the largest in service until the new Boeings arrive to carry nearly 400. It provides, I must confess, a very comfortable flight, and my only regret about the journey is that I failed to strike a blow for Britain by selling KLM some Concordes to replace it. As soon as I raised the question it was evident that the company had made up its mind, and nothing I could say made any difference. Privately I would agree that the Concorde sounds a loathsome machine, but business is business, especially in the export trade.

After we had taken off from Amsterdam, and the champagne and appetisers had been offered, we received the first of many civil attentions when we were issued with bedsocks. By we I mean the first-class passengers. I cannot say whether the economy class passengers were given bedsocks, but I have no doubt that their needs would be catered for in a manner appropriate to their station. The idea of the bedsocks was presumably to suggest sleep, but both the meals and the stops were so frequent that sleep was not a serious possibility. Somewhere along the route Amsterdam-Zurich-Athens-Beirut-Kuwait-Karachi-New Delhi-Bangkok-Manila, I must have fallen unconscious. I remember puzzling to myself, as one might in bed, over the meaning of the words, 'Camlocs not captive' stencilled on all the engines. I think I finally dozed off when I had decided that this was an operational notice and not a political slogan, although I seem to have read about a tribe in the Indonesian Archipelago called the Camlocs.

Every few hours we exerted ourselves so far as to enter an airport, but this was not allowed at Kuwait. Whether through oversight or to provide a cordon sanitaire against the outside

83

world, the airport buildings at Kuwait have been built several miles from the runway. What we saw of the territory persuaded us that little had been lost by staying on board.

The oil oozes up through the sand, ignites, and lights the early morning sky, but these lights and the distant derricks are the only relief in a barren landscape. I later learned from a woman who had spent four years there, out of loyalty to her husband, that the life is equally barren. No alcohol, for example, may be imported or sold. But it is made in the kitchen, and some of the methods described to me (and I claim a passing knowledge of the subject) were perilous in the extreme. If anyone proposing to go to Kuwait will apply to me, I will do my utmost to talk him out of it.

But back on board life continued its epicurean course across thousands of miles of Asia. Everest shone magnificently 250 miles to the north, and then we looked down on Calcutta. At Bangkok airport the television news was delivered by a girl with a mellifluous voice who read from what appeared to be parchment twenty inches by fifteen, and followed every word with a fingernail. And then, after only three more dishes had been served (apart, that is, from the caviar and vodka) we arrived in Manila.

It transpired before long that as the only Englishman in the party I was expected to state the British case on the Sabah dispute, once at a press conference and again to a man holding a microphone. This presented some difficulty because I had read the Philippines argument in the plane in a booklet donated by the Philippines Embassy in The Hague. It was completely convincing, but I suspected this might be because I had not heard the Malaysian side. I therefore put up a stonewall defence and spoke, I like to think, in a thoroughly statesmanlike manner. The Foreign Office and Tunku Abdul Rahman should be thankful that they found themselves represented by someone with a certain presence of mind.

The inaugural flight proper ended in Manila, but there was still the problem of getting home. To do this, I flew, again by KLM, on the polar route from Tokio. To this day I have not worked out what happened to the time, but the journey went like this. We left Tokio at 10.30 on Thursday night and were served with 'supper,' another prodigious meal as far as I recall it. By the time the brandy glasses had been cleared away it was time to lay the tables for breakfast, and after six and a half hours' flying we arrived in Anchorage, Alaska, at 10 a.m. on Thursday morning, having crossed the international dateline. The mountains and tundra of Alaska in the early morning, seen from a few thousand feet, are a wonderful sight, but not after supper and breakfast have been thus telescoped. We took off from Alaska at 11 a.m. (Thursday), lunch was served to those interested, and darkness fell during the entrée. We did not see the shrinking icecap about which so many complaints have been received. After another 10 hours' flying we reached Amsterdam disorientated at 7 a.m. on Friday.

Yet if one has to return to Europe from the Far East one has to choose. It is either the Polar route, with lunch at six in the morning (Tokio time) just as it is going dark, or the long haul back across Asia and the Middle East. A friend who returned from Hongkong this way not long ago found that he arrived at every airport just as day was breaking, and was served seven breakfasts in a row. Either route plays havoc with the bowels, but given the choice I'm a polar man every time.

GEOFFREY TAYLOR

Lancashire hot-pot for writers and readers

Sunday. Iris Murdoch, John McGrath and I arrived Manchester 25 minutes late, hoping for and not getting lunch. Immediately whisked off to a cold, sunny Wigan non-pier to compare ourselves with Orwell, whose relevant book none of us have read. Get very cold admiring decaying industrial scenery while BBC newsmen dawdle over photographing our shivering opinions. Atmospheric shots of us admiring slag-heaps mercifully called off. Have very cold feet (literally) and slightly appalled by publicising a tour whose very form is still uncertain.

Later. Where is Adrian Henri? Champagne to celebrate opening of tour with David Pease of the North West Arts Association and

85

one of our Lancashire Intourist girls. Eat in Manchester at 'the country's only Armenian restaurant.' Adrian at last arrives: Gaiety and bearded uplift.

Monday. Iris and I got to Bolton School. Start by chatting for three quarters of an hour with the 'intelligentsia,' about twenty boys and girls. One boy thinks spontaneity in art is everything and disapproves of our confessed rewriting. Am impressed by their knowledge (how deep?) of contemporary movements—is B. S. Johnson's 'The Unfortunates' a con? Well, is it? Radio 4 arrives and sits quietly listening. Just as things are really warming up, we're marched off to the school theatre, 200 girls and boys, the headmistress firmly in the chair. What I'd like is for the students to feel free to ask and say anything, which they really can't with the headmistress there. She comments on this herself afterwards. Lunch in Sixth Form Common Room. Boy next to me is reading 'Finnegans Wake.' I am delighted and amazed and ashamed—never got through it myself.

Later. Buy orchids for Iris, carnations for John and me, a cactus for Adrian. Evening almost a total disaster, on theme 'The Poem, The Novel, The Play.' Actress from Octagon Theatre, where we are, reads Joyce and Eliot beautifully, but we flounder, blinded by lights, unable to see or feel our audience, or to keep to any one point for more than sentence or two. Finally God speaks, heavily moustached, from the gods, attacking our verbal approach to theatre—at last we get going, but by now, astoundingly, it's been an hour and a half, and we go off to the bar. This works fine—plenty of discussion and contact and warmth. But what did the people who didn't come to the bar think? 'I was very disappointed,' says a woman, patting my arm kindly, '*Very* disappointed.' Gloom. Format and physical conditions all wrong. Brood on this back at the hotel, where tense and furious actor arrives and denounces us till 2 a.m. for not giving value for money (2s 6d a head). He is particularly incensed by the flowers, and won't have a second drink on the Arts Council. I will . . .

Tuesday. Wigan Grammar School, with Adrian—100 boys. They all really want to hear Adrian read, but we talk furiously for an hour and a half before he does so—virtuoso performance of 'The

Entry of Christ into Liverpool.' Good audience—receptive, responsive, unexpected. Find wholly unexpected *new* BBC TV camera crew—from 'How Late It is.' They shine lights in our eyes. Feel I have started something now quite out of control . . .

Drive to Mayor's parlour—Mayor greets us in Mayoral chain. First Mayor I have ever met—very handsome miner, great dignity. Room full of town clerks, deputies, assistants, librarians and chairmen of committees. Sudden longing to enter local politics, give up writing, abandon solitary for community life. Mention my Manchester Collieries and NCB grandfather and uncle, feel related to whole scene, till remember these almost certainly spent lives opposing Mayor's ambitions.

Later—Back to Grammar School—250 or so, plus TV and Radio. Discussion much better than last night—first question, about working class writers and middle class critics, gets us all going. Rapport seems genuine, but problem in this sort of audience is that young people tend to be shy of asking questions. Highlight is Iris effortlessly expounding and destroying McLuhan in about four minutes flat, to deserved applause.

Wednesday. We go together to Chorley College of Education. Best audience so far—of course these are teachers and so highly articulate. To John's delight we go straight into politics and stay there for nearly two hours.

My afternoon off. Tell Iris all about my love-life which becomes, in the telling, more and more like the love-life of a character called Julian in a novel by Iris Murdoch. Why is it *always* early closing day on one's afternoon off?

Evening in Ormskirk. Completely new atmosphere—serious amateur writers trying to sell stories to the BBC. Young seem tongue-tied again, which is a pity, but we feel it is a good evening, and John is now enthusiastic again.

Iris and I go to Manchester for dinner. Tell Iris rest of my life story and become an Iris Murdoch novel in myself. Feel slightly thwarted—no, out-manoeuvred. I should be asking, not just answering. We have two bottles of Retsina, I get very romantic about Greece, we get lost in Eccles.

Thursday. Kirkham, a secondary modern, with Iris. I get the fourth form, Iris the fifth. Was worried about this, our only secondary mod, but enjoy it hugely, and end up trying to explain 'The Bacchae' as a Western movie I hope to write. Feel happy, even if they didn't understand a word, but think they understood everything. Then join Iris for another half-hour. Suddenly it's spring, and Blackpool is acres of empty beach in the sunshine.

To Poulton-le-Fylde library, expecting no one, finding 50 people. Relaxed afternoon, with tea and McLuhan again. Afterwards, back to Blackpool to find house where Iris lived during the war. She is much moved, points to her old room, talks of her imaginative life there. We walk on the sands. Iris gathers rocks, I shells; Tina, one of our Intourist girls, in a long Russian coat like Anna Karenina, comes dancing to join us. Fresh air leaves us all exhausted.

Evening, Preston. Audience, incredibly, of 400, in a huge gymnasium. Launch immediately into writers' political responsibility, John and Iris starring as revolutionary and democrat respectively. Part of audience discontented by all this, but what are we to do? Break for ten minutes, then come back for more on other topics. Most of audience stays, which is gratifying.

Friday. Worsley Wardley Grammar School with Adrian . . . One boy, obviously speaking from the heart, says I'm all wrong about the extension of one's imagination being a good thing in itself; the more you feel, he says, the more awful you see the world is. Remember feeling this myself, can't offer any hope or help. This whole tour is full of unexpected confrontations with past and present feelings—and inadequacies.

Go with John in afternoon to Leigh and get utterly lost. End up forty minutes late in cricket pavilion . . . Stay as late as possible, and discover boys' subversive use of language—'normal' means crazy, 'clean' means grotty, and 'Victor' means immature. Next stop Standish. Feel near to collapse, but John is now brimming with energy and agrees to chair. We talk about books which have influenced us and go on about our childhood reading. Smallest evening audience and very nice too.

Combination of exhaustion and not having to chair makes me listen more relaxedly to what is said, and make sudden baffling discoveries about my own motives for writing. Feel naked, un-ashamed and incoherent. Unable, when usual question about social role comes up, to answer at all, I'm too confused. Adrian's three best fans from Wigan sit in front row and giggle, which is nice. Feel near collapse in pub afterwards, where are two boys, very sharp dressers, also from Wigan, and coming to hear us for second time. They order their clothes from *Wolverhampton*, which seems not quite credible.

Saturday. Skelmersdale Library in morning with Adrian. Six people in two hours. The elaborately casual library visit doesn't seem very useful, as they found in Wales . . .

Idle afternoon except for Adrian, who visits his Wigan fans. Iris says she feels disappointed it's not all starting again next week. Can't agree—I'm worn out. But all of *us* have found it extremely enjoyable and valuable. And the idea was to benefit writers as well as readers. I've come to feel amazingly at home—though I realise how superficial my experience of the area is. But hell—north and south is all crap. The people, particularly the young, are, in Iris's Oxford phrase, 'very superior.'

Evening at Skelmersdale, Lancashire hot-pot off aluminium covered PVC at the Beacon Club, an outpost of old-fashioned eat-ing in the new town. Replete, we go to comprehensive school, audience of 75, for our final meeting. Find ourselves covering new territory—are there things we shouldn't write about? Go on for our longest yet—$2\frac{3}{4}$ hours. Then slowly back through Wigan for the last time to champagne and sandwiches and exchange of presents. The girls give me an Ordnance Survey map of Pwllheli with 'I'm lost' written in the middle of the sea. Granada producer of 'Nice Time,' whose buttons we've all been wearing, says our audience was very reverential, that we didn't really get across. Suspect him of underestimating the audience. It can't be rever-ence or Northern determination to get value for money which makes audiences stay so long, surely?

Sunday. Farewells. I distribute broken Blackpool shells to the streets of Salford. Iris near tears in the train. I am still too exhausted to feel. John talks about his new play—Iris cross-questions closely, till it sounds like an Iris play. We all do this,

I realise, remaking the world to suit ourselves. What have they all made of us? Did we make contact? Was it any use at all? London is desolate with Sunday rain, just as I'd imagined Bolton.

JULIAN MITCHELL

Pomp and circumstance for the millions

The Prince of Wales, alias the Duke of Cornwall and Rothesay, Earl of Carrick, Baron of Renfrew, Lord of the Isles, and Great Steward of Scotland, will be invested with his principality at Caernarvon Castle on Tuesday.

All these titles will stick in the gullets of thousands of Welsh Nationalists. And yet the louder they protest, the more their noises seem to sound . . . now what was that word our dear Queen used in her great television show? . . . *churlish*. It's rather like that story of George Bernard Shaw at a first night of one of his plays. The audience roared its approval, except for one little man in the gallery who booed. G.B.S. turned to address him: 'I agree with you, Sir, but who are we among so many?'

A year ago it was estimated that perhaps half of the Welsh people were at best indifferent to the investiture. Today, the pub pundits reckon that anything from 70 to 99 per cent of them favour it. If anything has won the doubting Thomases and Evanses over it is their own Welsh susceptibility to fervour.

Anybody visiting Caernarvon finds it difficult not to be caught up in the spirit of a show being prepared by the world's greatest pageant-makers. The Castle, a pile that impressed even that old curmudgeon Dr Johnson, has been tricked out with mock-medieval panoply—red dragons on rippling banners, and coats-of-arms so carefully antiquated that nobody would believe them to be made of that grand old medieval craft material, expanded polystyrene.

And within these walls there roams Lord Snowdon, Constable of Caernarvon Castle, anxiously involving himself with medieval

90

environmental studies. Is that red colour too deep on the finial? Will the heads of reporters in the press gallery obscure the castellation?

Unasked, and driven only by kindness and that old Welsh fervour, he took me on a ten-minute tour of the trappings of pageantry. He pointed to the 28ft. circular dais where the investiture will take place. 'What one tries to do,' he said, 'is to create a theatre in the round, to be watched by 500 million television viewers.' The three thrones, made of riven Welsh slate, 'could be of any date because their design is so simple—you wouldn't be surprised to see them at Stonehenge, would you?'

Do not let it be thought that Lord Snowdon has gone druidical on us. When he came to the microphones at the lectern he insisted that he was 'absolutely against' any camouflaging of modern means of communication, even in a medieval setting.

With one eye on the taxpayers, the Ministry of Public Building is offering to sell to seatholders the special red chairs they occupy at the ceremony. They should be a sell-out. Where is there a local worthy who could refuse, at £12 a time, mute evidence to stand in his front hall that he was a man of importance in Wales, 1969?

Those who are considered to be worthies get seats; those who consider themselves to be worthy still try to get into the castle, even at this late stage. Their tactics include a rather sad form of Welsh name-dropping of distant relatives. What passes in England as the old boy network seems in Wales to be the old druid and eisteddfod network.

One can find choice examples of Welsh commercial patriotism in Caernarvon. Crosville Motor Services are selling souvenir bus tickets, 3d extra, to any one who wants a bit of paper with one mention of the Prince of Wales and two of the bus company, 'proud of its long association with Caernarvon, having served the area for over 43 years.' The Wales Gas Board, having touted around the world for its showroom feature 'The world's gas men greet us,' offered in its window the message: 'On behalf of the Hong-kong and China Gas Co, I wish to extend warmest greetings to Wales Gas on this historic occasion.'

The 'souvenir' industry has flooded Caernarvon with Prince of

Wales pottery, rugs, aprons, oven mittens, and perfume. They can hardly fail to sell them when they share shop windows with cigarette cases stamped with the words 'Smoke like Helen B. Merry,' and goods stamped with 'Cymru am byth,' the legend of a thousand public lavatories.

A week is a long time in pageantry. By next Friday, Wales will have her Prince, and the shopkeepers their profits. There will still be those who rail against a Prince speaking language-laboratory Welsh, and owning just about enough Welsh blood to lurk in his left earlobe. But there will be thousands more who, over the year, have come to think of him as a likeable lad, and of the investiture as the kind of national promotion that Welsh money could not buy.

Caernarvon will return to the calm it enjoyed on July 1 last year. 'Drowned man had drunk 20 pints,' the local newspaper reported a year ago. Lovely old Mrs Owen celebrated her one hundredth birthday at Penrhyndeudraeth. Man guilty of indecent assault at Port Dinorwic and a speedy recovery is wished to Mr Griffith Williams, the farmer.

Even if one takes the cunical anti-monarchist view, Caernarvonshire will have done well out of the investiture: straightened roads, freshly painted houses and priceless publicity aimed at 500 million television viewers. Cause enough for the staple industry of North Wales, the famous Bed-and-Breakfast-25s industry, to shout 'God Bless the Prince of Wales.'

MICHAEL PARKIN

D-Day: the lonely ride

They had devised breaching teams for the assault on the beach—five tanks, a bulldozer, and a handful of sappers. The first two tanks belonged to the Royal Engineers. One carried a steel roadway to lay across the mud expected below the high water mark; the second bore a huge bundle of chestnut palings which could be dropped into an anti-tank ditch. Our three tanks were those ungainly mine-sweepers—the flails. The bulldozer and the Sappers would be left on the beach to clear obstacles.

Our instructions were explicit. The RE major who commanded the team had reduced them almost to monosyllables: 'Get up the beach, clear a lane through the mines, turn right at the road, and meet in Le Hamel 20 minutes after landing.' He was killed in the first 300 yards, and his shattered tank blocked the one behind. The flail in front of us was hit in the petrol tank—but we got through, and it was a lonely ride to the road.

I was the gunner in our crew, and to break the waterproof sealing round the turret it was necessary to do a 360-degree traverse before we started mine-sweeping. It had to be a careful traverse, but it provided an all-round view of the assault. It was slightly unreal like watching a film, as if one were set apart from the infantrymen struggling through the water or getting shot on the sand. It was obvious, too, that the opposition was not uniform. On some parts of the beach people were landing without trouble, on others they were getting a pasting, and from the number of boats still heading for the shore, it was clear that confusion would mount on chaos.

As we reached the dunes we began to flail—jogging along at less than walking speed, kicking up a tremendous cloud of sand, and banging away at the mines. This was where it would happen, we thought; this was where we were a sitting target for anybody who cared to pump shells into the dust cloud. Then we reached the road, and turned right towards Le Hamel. It seemed a good time to fire a short burst to clear the water-proofing off the machine gun. The road was deserted, but as I finished the burst, three of our infantrymen crashed through the hedge. One fell as if he had been shot, and for 25 years, on and off, I have wondered whether he was caught by one of my ricochets, or by some unseen German.

When we turned the first bend in the road, we realised that it was not the one we had been shown in aerial pictures during the briefing for the assault. That one had a narrow railway line running alongside it; the one we were on was no more than a lane, with hedges and ditches on either side. There was no time to worry about it, because immediately afterwards we plunged into a bomb

93

crater—terrified lest the minesweeping gear had been damaged, because it was supposed to be a court-martial offence if anything happened to it that could be pinned to the crew's neglect.

The invasion wasn't 10 minutes old, and men and equipment were piling up on the road behind us. From that time on for our crew at least, D-day developed into the kind of shambles familiar to anybody with experience in the front line. A furious argument began to develop among a group of officers (none of whom had anything to do with us) about the need to get our tank out of the way so that they could push on towards Le Hamel, or wherever else they had been ordered to go. We stood there, foolishly holding a tow-rope, hoping for the best, while the infantrymen—with relieved patience—flopped down at the side of the road and got their fags out.

The most senior officer decided that whatever else happened we were not going any further along that road. Once we were out of that hole we could fend for ourselves. It soon became obvious that Le Hamel—which was supposed to be held only by a German platoon—would not provide a meeting place for anybody; it was mid-afternoon before it was finally taken.

We pulled off the road and let the war go on without us. Our tank commander decided to set off on foot to try to get some new orders; we stayed with the tank, harassed by everybody from military policemen upwards who kept moving us out of the way. We were rapidly becoming an embarrassment to all.

The only thing to do was to sit in the sun and wait. It was then that we saw our colonel approaching—wearing white overalls. He was not even supposed to be in France, but had come across because he 'couldn't bear to miss the show.' He told us to stay where we were while he strode away to 'round up the stragglers.' His presence confirmed in our minds that the English upper classes were stark raving mad.

Eventually he returned with his 'stragglers.' On that crowded beachhead—where everybody must have been impressed by his whites—he had contrived to find a field and regroup his forces, three runnable tanks out of 13; his other squadron was 20 miles away on the easternmost beach.

That night I went on guard with him. He insisted on flinging a hand grenade into the bedroom of a house which he thought contained a sniper. The grenade hit the window-frame and bounced back. We were unhurt, and he was obviously so relieved about it that he excused me for losing my revolver earlier in the day. 'Damned stupid to walk about unarmed,' he said.

And that's how it was. We always felt a bit aggrieved in our crew about D-day. Our tank commander got a mention in dispatches out of it; the rest of the crew got nothing except abuse from people who wanted us to get out of their way. It had been a long, noisy, confusing day, and we had spent most of it hanging about, never more than half a mile inland. But it had not been entirely wasted, and at least we were on land again—and alive, in spite of the unspoken fear that our orders covered only the first 20 minutes because nobody expected us to survive much longer than that.

JOSEPH MINOGUE, 7962283, Trooper (retd.)

Before the sunset fades

A week ago on 'Stir up' Sunday, at evensong in Christ Church Cathedral, Port Stanley, the congregation of 50 burst into that rousing evening hymn: 'The day thou gavest, Lord is ended.' The churchgoers included a Minister of the Crown, the Governor of the colony, a number of naval officers and ratings from HMS *Endurance*, and a few of the windbeaten inhabitants of Stanley. Maybe the vicar, in choosing the hymn, thought that his tiny flock would be comforted by its closing words, which proclaim defiantly:

> 'So be it, Lord, thy throne shall never
> Like earth's proud empires pass away.'

For, with a politeness worthy of a better cause, the Right Honourable the Lord Chalfont (as his baggage tags proclaim) had come to inform the inhabitants of the Falkland Islands that

95

the proud empire that had sustained them for so long was in the process of following the western sun beneath the horizon. He did not put it quite so bluntly, of course. He told them of a Britain which had no plans to maintain strategic responsibilities in the South Atlantic, of a Britain where the top rate of income tax is not (as in the Falklands) five and ninepence in the pound, and of a Britain which sees no economic future for woolgathering islands in a world of synthetics.

The islanders loved him. So palpably honest, so dashing and debonair, he melted the suspicion from all hearts. Even the terrible old gang of sheepowners who have misruled the colony for years had to admit that they had more than met their match, prompting the irreverent thought that if they are going to be sold down the river the islanders would prefer it to be done by a lord.

For they live very far back in the past. The Falkland Islands is probably the only place in the world where Edwardian Britain is maintained intact. The population of two thousand boasts a Governor, a Colonial Secretary, a cathedral—built in the 1890s with bricks brought from England—and even a flag-flying London taxi that serves as the gubernatorial car. On the day of our arrival there was a sherry party on the lawns of Government House, a rambling building reminiscent of a Victorian rectory. The Stanley ladies paraded in their finery, one of Her Majesty's ships stood anchored in the bay, and with the exotic flowers in the conservatory, one could be forgiven for thinking that the British Empire was still in existence and that Britannia still ruled the waves.

It is a reflection of the appalling neglect in which imperial England left its most distant colonies that only now is there enough general interest for a Minister and five journalists to arrive and discover what really goes on in the Falkland Islands. Rummaging through some old parish magazines I found that lack of concern in Britain appears to have been a constant complaint throughout the colony's history. Even in 1914, when it was in its heyday, at the time of the Battle of the Falklands when Churchill packed off a fleet of ships to defend the colony and to avenge the defeat at Coronel, the islanders found it hard to excuse the ignorance of the outside world.

'It seems a most extraordinary thing,' wrote the *Falklands Islands Magazine* in March, 1915, 'that our poor little Islands should be so unknown in the Old Country, let alone in our Colonial Empire. It is a well-known fact that not only a few, but even great numbers of people many of whom are supposed to be fully educated, have not the slightest idea of our whereabouts, and those who have come out from Home know how true it is that nearly every other person one meets asks you, "Where are the Falkland Islands and what colour are the natives?" '

No newspaper in those days aroused the anger of the islanders more than the *Daily Express* which had printed a 'scurrilous' article depicting the inhabitants of the islands as uncivilised natives. Then, as today, they took pride in the fact that, unique among British colonies, they were entirely British and white. Hence their current disgust with Britain for giving aid to the 'blacks' of Africa and not to the white Falklands.

More than anything else, however, a reading of the history of the Falklands since the 1830s when Britain took over reveals that the islanders were always uncertain about what the future would hold. There were always doubts as to whether the islands could provide a living for the next generation. The present highly unsatisfactory situation in which emigration has caused an absolute decline in population is not without parallel in the past. I found, talking to young people in Stanley, that most of the brighter ones were already making plans to leave, not because of British Government equivocations but simply because they did not see an economic future for the islands.

The real problem is not in Stanley, but out in what the islanders call the Camp—the moor and grasslands where the sheep that provide the colony with its livelihood are left to graze. Few young islanders today want to be shepherds, and the labour shortage is so acute that on two farms I visited more than 50 per cent of the labour force had come under a short term contract from abroad. This figure probably applies to the rest of the Camp, where about half the population lives. So the islands are in no sense a self-sustaining community. Apart from the need to import farm workers, doctors and teachers also have to be brought in from outside.

Under normal circumstances a British Government might have been able to ignore the Falklands. In essence this is what the Conservative Governments of the 1950s did. One now gets the feeling that it is too late to do anything to safeguard the economic future of the colony. In the late 1940s various efforts were made to diversify the economy. The ill-fated Colonial Development Corporation provided money for two schemes, one to do with seals, and the other designed to freeze 50,000 sheep a year. Both collapsed after two years, and the second cost the British Government just under half a million pounds. From the efforts that were made then, and from the lack of ideas that have emerged since, it is clear that diversification is no solution The future of the island can only lie in improving the quality of the grassland and thereby increasing the number of sheep that can graze on it Only by offsetting the decline in the price of wool by a dramatic increase in production can the colony hope to survive.

The question is, is it worth it? Most of the companies have shown little enthusiasm to plough back their profits into grassland development, nor have the inhabitants enthused themselves over the prospect of paying income tax at the United Kingdom rate. If the Government of the colony removed their perks, their cheap drink and easy money, it is legitimate to inquire how many of the islanders would remain.

Curiously enough, if only the islanders knew it, they are much closer to the South American mainland than they think. Native-born children are called 'Che'—not a reference to Guevara but to the Argentine nickname that he made world famous. The Camp is a corruption of 'el campo,' the Spanish for the countryside. And everywhere place names testify to the Spanish influence. Sailing into Falkland Sound that divides the two main islands, we passed Chanco Point. On the port bow lies Rincon de los Tres Picos, and beyond is Paloma Pond. Homelier names like Hill Cover and Pebble Island also abound, but Spanish names crop up with sufficient frequency to remind one that only 30 years ago contact between the island and the mainland was much closer. Islanders went to work in Patagonia and farm managers would send their sons to the snob English schools in Buenos Aires.

Politically, too, the islanders have much in common with the

Argentines. One prominent figure, who would fight to the **death** to resist an Argentine take-over, told me of his admiration for the way General Ongania had dealt with labour troubles. More detailed probing revealed that he preferred Ongania's methods to those of Harold Wilson. Many islanders would find themselves at home—and equally out of touch with reality—with the 20,000-odd Anglo-Argentines who live on the mainland.

But perhaps the closest parallel is the economy. Like many a Latin-American country, the Falklands is a monoculture effectively sewn up by two or three companies. It is not inconceivable that the chief companies, seeing the possibility of losing their capital through a collapse in the wool market, might decide that their future would look rosier in cahoots with the Argentines. One can rest assured that the farm managers and the shareholders (most of whom live in Britain) will not lose much sleep over the changeover. The people one feels sorry for are the poor ignorant shepherds out in the Camp who have been led to believe that to be British is to be owed a living. As an Empire collapses, it seems almost inevitable that some people will go to the wall. If anyone deserves the crocodile tears being shed in Britain about the fate of the Falkland Islands, it is these innocent victims of a cruel and essentially irresponsible system.

RICHARD GOTT

The Queen's man

There is a Garter available. Sir Humphrey Gibbs should have it. No man living has served his Queen so gallantly, so unselfishly, and with such elegance, modesty, and style. Only his closest friends and family know how much pain and embarrassment that service cost him and his family.

Sir Humphrey came through the last $3\frac{1}{2}$ years with an unsullied, even enhanced reputation. No other Queen's Governor in history has been so humiliated and insulted in his person and his office.

The Smith regime really declared its authoritarian little republic the day they cut off Sir Humphrey's telephones (his secretary had to go to a call box to phone the doctor); removed his guards; drove off his official Rolls for the use of the usurper 'governor', Clifford Dupont; sent in a bill for the rent, which he defiantly never paid; cut off his salary and gave it to Dupont.

Gibbs, at 67, is the Queen's most perfect gentle knight, who did battle for her honour in the lists of Cecil Square, Salisbury. Being a modest man he would laugh at this blushmaking concept, mutter 'absolute nonsense' into his evening whisky and water. The Queen writes to him regularly. He writes back. Some say that without those letters of encouragement he could not have carried on.

What makes the republic harder for him to take is that he feels himself the Queen's representative among her 4½ million African subjects, now to be deprived without any form of consultation.

Sir Humphrey's friends called him 'Gibbs SR.' At one time supporters stuck packets from toothpaste tubes on their car windows. It seemed appropriate, for legally Rhodesia is still 'Southern Rhodesia.' His enemies called him 'traitor,' 'sell-out,' 'Communist.' He received appallingly virulent poison pen letters.

Gibbs, the son of a peer, 30 years a Rhodesian farmer, is a quiet man, says little, but listens a lot. Millions of words have been expended since UDI. Few of them were uttered by the Governor. His public utterances could be fitted into two quarto pages.

He scrupulously and correctly followed the convention of the constitutional head of state not to take part in political controversy. The Queen does not take sides in political issues. In Rhodesia he was the Queen's man. This attitude maddened many opponents of the Smith regime who wanted him to become the focus of militant opposition.

His enemies argued that by staying put at Government House, refusing to retire from his post, he was behaving politically anyway. But he only behaved constitutionally, for his job was to uphold the legal constitution which the regime had overthrown. His saddest day was when the judges, who had taken their oaths before him as the Queen's representative, went over to the regime. In a rare outburst of anger he promptly threw the Chief Justice,

Sir Hugh Beadle, out of Government House where he was a house guest.

It was not Gibbs's style to attract the limelight of an international crisis. He was unfitted by his upbringing as a gentleman farmer, by his unassuming nature, for a star rôle in this kind of drama. This obscure Governor of a self-governing colony was accustomed for years to do nothing but act on the advice of his ministers, sign documents, open schools and bazaars, do good works and entertain visiting dignitaries.

On November 11 all this changed. Performing his first and last executive act he publicly sacked Smith and his ministers, openly clashed with the rebels. Because he had authority without power the regime took no notice. They have gone on taking no notice.

Journalists interviewing Gibbs are in great difficulty. He gives you a drink, or tea poured in crown stamped cups, asks you 'What's going on in the world?' but reveals little. What he does reveal you cannot quote.

One fear has always haunted Gibbs. This was that the regime might take over Government House in Salisbury for the use of Clifford Dupont. Long ago they took over the Governor's second residence in Bulawayo. To Gibbs, his residence in his beautiful, patrician house with its lush tropical gardens, was symbolic of his post. Over the door hung the Governor's blue flag with the gold crown. The Union Jack still flies in the garden.

So, except on those two air trips to Gibraltar for the Tiger and Fearless talks, Gibbs never went away, not even for a weekend, during the whole three and a half years of UDI. He did sometimes go out to dinner with friends, or to the Salisbury Club for a game of snooker.

Gibbs played a vital part in the parleys which followed UDI. He was Britain's only link with Smith, and the British Residual Mission was accredited to him. Because Whitehall preferred to keep up the pretence that it did not deal direct with Smith, negotiations were carried on under his aegis, though he was never present at the conference table. Without him the Tiger and the Fearless talks could not have taken place.

He often saw Smith, who used to pop across the road from his own residence. He arranged secret meetings between Wilson emissaries and Smith. There was a time when he really believed Smith wanted an agreement on the Tiger and Fearless lines. He even believed that an agreement was possible. Without that belief he could not possibly have carried on until now.

One of his recent utterances summed up the rôle which he saw himself playing: 'I still properly regard it as my duty to the Queen and to my country Rhodesia to continue to serve, as I believe that by doing so I may yet assist in bringing about an honourable settlement between Britain and Rhodesia.'

That he has failed is no fault of Gibbs, a man who did his plain duty, perhaps rather more than would have been expected from a lesser man.

JOHN WORRALL

Chinese on the right track

'*Why cannot the West realise that Africa is more important to the West than is Asia? The dangers of communism in this continent are insufficiently appreciated.*' Dr Marcelo Caetano, Prime Minister of Portugal, January, 1969.

'What is the *quid pro quo* for China? When does Chairman Mao present his IOU?' This is the Chinese puzzle in Africa today. These are the two questions one constantly encounters in Addis, Nairobi, Dar, Lusaka and the other capitals where the full impact of China's 'forward policy' is now being felt.

It is a circular puzzle with no obvious answer. It rattles about in the subconscious mind as one travels the bush roads of Zambia and Tanzania, in the terrain where the prospective Zamtan Railway is to be built: £115 millions, 1,042 miles of steel, operational by 1975.

'The Chinese think long: finish the railway five years from now; finish the guerrilla war in twenty.' The speaker had been a Western diplomat who gave me lunch in Dar-es-Salaam; one of the many China watchers among the men who staff forty-seven diplomatic missions in the Tanzanian capital. His words came back to me as I slowed the car to glance at a neat, inconspicuous signboard where there was a break in the elephant grass and two tyre tracks led away under the thorn trees. Beneath the Chinese characters were a few words in English, stating that this was the Zambia-Tanzania rail survey, People's Republic of China. Thirty yards away, jutting above the tall grass, was a cluster of bamboo poles topped with bulging plastic lanterns looking like red pumpkins. The same bright mandarin red they use for the book jackets for the Thoughts of Chairman Mao.

I was far inland from the Indian Ocean, on the route that runs up over the spine of Africa at Mbeya at 5,600ft.—higher than the main pass on the Canadian Pacific in the Rockies, and often as cool if not cooler. All told, more than 1,000 miles of track to be laid through baking scrubland, the Mikumi flood plain, the fortress wall of the Rift valley and on through the malarial zone that killed David Livingstone, to Zambia's railhead in the Copper Belt.

The equivalent stretch on the CPR took the Canadians 10 years; the Chinese propose to drive their last spike in five. The comparison may be unfair; China will have modern equipment, road access, and a work force of 4,000 men who are unlikely to complain.

But no one who has seen the enormous Friendship Textile Mill near Dar-es-Salaam doubts that the railway can be built on schedule on simple, rugged lines suited to African conditions.

Western visitors strove to conceal polite smiles for two reasons when the Friendship Mill was opened for inspection after the dedication ceremony. First, the machinery—obviously new— looked as if it had been ordered from some sepia catalogue of the 1920s. Secondly, wherever you would expect to find a tabulator or cash register the Chinese had installed a simple abacus.

A year later the smirks are forgotten. Harassed African managers, used to the holdups when a machine from the West breaks down and you queue up for a technician, find to their relief that almost any handyman can keep the Chinese machines in good order. As for the abacus, it proves to be both speedy and unbreakable.

I thought of the diplomat's words again—'the Chinese think long'—when I encountered a British engineer who knows the Mtwara zone like the back of his hand, though our conversation took place a thousand miles inland from there. 'Drive through there today,' he said—'if you can get a permit, which I doubt—and the Chinese instructors will pick you up on their walkie-talkie network and track you all the way: round through Newala, up to Masasi and Nachingwea, and back across to the Lindi junction. It's good practice for their pupils.'

What strikes the traveller like myself most forcibly of all, on returning to Europe, is the bland insouciance—one could almost describe it as wilful ignorance—about what China's aims are in Africa and how effectively she is pursuing these goals under the new diplomatic policy that began in 1966.

The Zamtan Railway is the textbook example. The myth that obstinately persists in London and the other capitals in the West goes like this: the Chinese are heavy-handed; they are extracting absolute allegiance to the Peking line as the pre-condition to any aid they actually give; they are not serious about Zamtan, which remains pie-in-the-sky and is useful simply to keep the African governments in a client rôle and for fending off the Russians. The facts are the opposite.

Quite simply the explanation seems to be that the Chinese burned their fingers in the affair of the Algiers Summit in 1965, learned their lesson about the ultra-sensitivity of Africans, and made a diplomatic *volte-face* soon afterwards. The Algiers affair was the proposed 'Second Bandung' that never came off. But so insistent was Premier Chou about China's friends agreeing to take their places at the table—part of the policy for outflanking the Russians—that Chinese diplomats were made to crack the whip with clumsy urgency that failed to work.

Ultimately, in a shake-out that ruffled the OAU and drove Algeria and Egypt into the Moscow camp, the Algiers summit collapsed. Peking lost face badly; and after a minor démarche in November the Chinese pulled back and reconsidered their whole Africa policy.

Other events forced the process on. Nkrumah fell while actually visiting Peking in February, 1966. In Ghana, the legendary 'Chinese training camp' at Obinimasi, in the bush north of Accra, proved to be a reality and Col. Yen Leng and his instructing staff were asked to leave.

Later when Formosa's deputy Foreign Minister, Mr Yang, was passing through Accra Airport and members of the Red China mission went out as a team to heckle and boo him, the Ghana Government asked Peking to withdraw its mission. This reduced mainland China to 13 missions in Africa against 19 for Chiang Kai-shek's Nationalists.

The Chinese rethink appears to have ended in a decision in 1966 to concentrate on the part of Africa where offers of economic and military aid would inevitably be received with gratitude rather than suspicion. In retrospect, it is obvious enough: Peking would move in on the Zambesi belt where the black-white confrontation had sharpened with Ian Smith's UDI and talk of guerrilla war.

A Russian gaffe strengthened the Chinese position as the true friends of black Africa. Portugal invited two members of the editorial board of 'Pravda' to visit Mozambique for a tour of the 'terrorist zones' and this was accepted in principle. (An unofficial Soviet mission was in Portugal in February this year, supposedly paving the way for the embassy that Dr Caetano has invited them to open in Lisbon.)

Britain's failure to respond effectively to UDI provided another opening. When Tanzania broke with Britain over the failure to bring down Smith, Dr Nyerere sacrificed £7 millions of new aid money still in the pipeline from Britain. Mr Wilson suspended (and later cancelled) the loan. Peking, after a short interval, announced a new interest-free loan to help bridge the gap, bringing Chinese total aid to £16 millions.

When, a year after UDI, President Nyerere spoke the first words at the opening of a 100-kilowatt transmitter, the most powerful in Eastern Africa, which is now the main voice of black Africa in the propaganda war with Salisbury and Pretoria, Mr Ho and Mr Chou were guests of honour. For China, as they remind you in Dar-es-Salaam, had built and equipped the transmitter and paid the bill.

Four Chinese experts were reported to have arrived in Tanzania last month to start the surveys for a new cement works and a brick factory. These projects were merely the latest in an endless list of state farms, rice projects, a sports stadium, a shoe factory and so on. There is the army barracks at Nachingwea, the new training course at Moshi for police field force units, the un-chronicled list of guerrilla camps, and the tanks—sufficient for two squadrons, with reserves—which can be glimpsed as one passes the main army barracks at Calito.

Both in Tanzania and Zambia there are extensive teams of Chinese doctors, orderlies and medical technicians who may be connected with the guerrilla programme, but also carry out an impressive 'meet-the-people' campaign in the villages.

President Nyerere has a sharp retort for those from the West who offer unsolicited advice about China. He says, simply: 'We will never allow our friends to choose our enemies for us. Our independence is not for sale to the East any more than the West.'

On the South Africa-Rhodesia problem, President Nyerere said in May, at the opening of the new textile mill at Mwanza, built with French aid: 'Only the Western world can help solve the problem of Southern Africa with the minimum of violence. We still appeal for that. It can be seen in the recent Lusaka Manifesto. If all this fails we shall be compelled to take arms from the East, and we shall be accused of being Communists.

'To us China is a friend in need. Take, for example, the railway between Tanzania and Zambia. We tried very hard to get it built by the Western world. But we failed. The Chinese are ready to build it for us. But the West, now, does not want China to build it. So, should we go without a railway?'

As for this project being a lot of airy politics, the thing that emerges from talks at Ministries in Dar and Lusaka is the hard, specific nature of the agreements. These began with Presidents Nyerere and Kaunda making separate visits to Peking, continued with the setting up of a corporate body to manage the project— the Zambia-Tanzania Railway Authority—and continued with talks in Peking, where the signing ceremony, on September 5, 1967, was attended by Chou En-lai.

Apparently oblivious of these facts, the director of the AID

106

office in Washington, Peter Straus, said in September, 1967: 'We are now engaged in a survey of Middle Africa transportation. The study obviously will include the proposed Zambia railroad.' The American agency carrying this report quoted 'Washington sources' on the Zamtan project: 'Non-Communist countries do not take the Chinese offer very seriously.'

On September 10 the leader of the Zambian team, Mr Soko, arrived home from Peking and said: 'I am fully satisfied the railway will now go ahead.' On December 26 that year eight Chinese experts arrived quietly in Dar, led by a Mr Liu Chi-fu. They had talks in Lusaka on December 30. The moment when the die was finally cast came on April 1 last year with ministerial talks between the three Governments at Dar. This resulted in the 'Tripartite Agreement' of April 8 which was then taken away for legal drafting to the three capitals. The formal signing ceremony followed on April 28, 1968.

I gather the agreement provides for the survey and design stage that is now running well ahead of schedule, on a route of 1,042 miles between existing railheads at Kidatu in Tanzania and Katanino in Zambia. And although there has yet to be a final summit session on the long-term finance, the 1968 document sets out the general terms of the interest-free loan to the value of 200 million Zambian kwachas, which is roughly £115 millions.

On April 12, 1968, amid hoots of sirens, the 20,000-ton liner MV Yao Hua slid into Dar harbour with the advance party of 154 surveyors lining the rails. Each clasped his little red book, and the banner above their heads proclaimed: 'Long Live the Invincible Thoughts of Mao Tse-tung.'

The West may continue to scoff, but I am sure Mr Vorster in Pretoria takes China very seriously indeed.

PATRICK KEATLEY

More Tory foibles

Gerald Nabarro isn't the only 'propagandist' in the Tory ranks. Nor, it seems, are they restricted to the back benches. Geoffrey Rippon, Ted Heath's rising shadow Defence Minister, was cantering through party policy and Labour failures for the Conservative students' conference at Hoddesdon in Hertfordshire yesterday, and came at length to Aldabra.

Britain, he said, had finally found a staging post in the Indian Ocean, when presto, 'with the aid of Soviet funds all the wildlife conservationists came out and said that the British would kill the turtles.'

A curious charge, coming weirdly and late from an official spokesman. So Miscellany's scout, freely invited to a public conference, bearded him about it. What was his evidence? 'I have no evidence,' Rippon replied. 'I can't substantiate the charge. I withdraw it. I didn't know there were any press present.'

MISCELLANY

Caution: Strauss at work

Ten days ago, Franz-Josef Strauss was the belligerent German Finance Minister who refused, in spite of enormous diplomatic and speculative pressure, to revalue the mark—and thus, according to Economics Minister, Professor Schiller, to 'play the game according to the international rules.' This week he has appeared as the genial would-be Chancellor, eager on Germany's behalf to help Britain into a federal Europe. These two figures are the same, consistent man, and the conjuncture is a little sinister. The economics of Herr Strauss's Europe are worth examining with some suspicion.

He set out the ground rules plainly enough. He wants a federal, not a confederal, Europe, with one currency—he was polite enough in London to call it a Euro-pound—and one monetary authority. It would thus have to possess one central economic policy.

There is no need to assume that Herr Strauss would have the running of that policy to find the prospect a little forbidding. There is no need even to look ahead as far as a federal Europe. The very tentative steps toward centralisation already taken in the Common Market are already beginning to show up not only the rewards but the dangers inherent in a united European economy. The problems are not insoluble, but it would certainly be much better to face them before we join, and there is very little sign that they are being faced.

The danger is the loss of independence which has long worried the Left, and the possibility that this would cause regional decline on a scale never seen in Europe. To put it into rather over-stated national terms, Britain could wind up as the Ulster of a federal Europe.

The reasons are familiar enough. Primitive market economists like Herr Strauss and our own Enoch Powell imagine that they live in a world where economic forces, left to themselves, attain a balance. But there are some situations known to more sophisticated economists as being in unstable equilibrium, where the ball sits on top of a hillock, and will simply gain momentum in one direction or another as soon as it starts to roll.

One direction is the competition between national economics: the economy which gains a lead also gains a wider competitive advantage just because it is growing faster. The other direction is the health of industrially specialised regions: technical change can push a region into a decline which soon spreads to other trades in the region as they lose their local markets.

The problem of national competition inside Europe is the immediate cause of the present world financial crisis. The French wage-cost inflation set off by the troubles of last May has thrown the whole system out of balance. A change in exchange rates would restore the old competitive balance between French and German industry, but it is very difficult to accommodate within a common price system for farm produce.

Herr Strauss, who considers the competitive advantage conferred by resisting inflation as the just reward for virtue (he calls Government spending 'frivolous'), would probably have resisted a change even if it did not threaten his farming constituents. If the French prove equally obstinate, their future economic growth is threatened, as ours has been for a decade: if Europe had a common currency, there would be no way out except to wait for a German wage revolt, or to fight French costs down again.

All the same, the French were able until last May to pursue the General's expensive rearmament policy without suffering competitively. This is partly because their 1958 devaluation—the one on the way into the Common Market—gave them something in hand; but it is mainly because the value-added tax, which is not charged on exports, does give Common Market Governments some freedom to fix their total tax burden where they like.

So far, this argument means simply that the Strauss programme is a strictly realistic one: if a united Europe means a united currency and a central monetary authority, then the surrender of sovereignty involved in joining it is a very real one. Economics will see to that. National Governments, in the Strauss scheme of things, would have about the freedom of action of very strong local authorities, and that sounds about right.

But how would the regional problem then be solved? Local authorities in England were not able to solve it; would a British Government with strictly local powers do any better?

The fact is that continuing change is bound to produce regional problems: we will suffer at least our share of them, and possibly more. So the question that has to be asked is whether we are sure that we and our partners are prepared to think on a sufficiently European scale to tackle them as European problems.

If so, they can be solved; but if, in Euro-elections, the Germans grumble at being taxed to help British problem regions, or if we resent paying out to help the Sicilians, then the problems of change will not be tackled. We cannot risk a future where British separatists—or Irish or Italian or Danish separatists—queue to draw their dole in Euro-marks.

ANTHONY HARRIS

How it must look to gnomes

The fuss the Government has been making about strikes must have led many an awestruck foreign observer to conclude that the only way to make the British do any work at all is to send strikers to prison. This is not what Mr Wilson and Mrs Castle have been saying. But messages become simplified on their way to IMF headquarters, Basle, Zurich, and beyond. The foreign observers cannot be blamed. While the fuss lasted every day was St Crispin's day, Mrs Castle fought seven Agincourts a week, and the nation's fate appeared to be perpetually at stake.

The Government now must try to dispel these illusions as best it can. The true situation is that the pledge the TUC gave on Wednesday will deal more effectively with unofficial strikes than penal clauses could have done and that, in any case, Britain's strike record probably is better than that of any other industrial country except West Germany. British strikes may be sillier than those that occur in other countries but they are less frequent and (as the Montague Burton Professor of Industrial Relations at Cambridge, Professor Turner, has shown) they do not harm the economy much.

When the Government now tries to describe this true situation to a foreign creditor the creditor can be forgiven for saying that he does not believe in unicorns either. After a full century of non-intervention the TUC must prove that its pledge was real. After five months' apparent hysteria about strikes the Government must now prove the opposite of what Mrs Castle seemed to be saying. Which is that British workers (according to Professor Turner) go on strike about once every 20 years at a cost that amounts to less than 0.001 per cent of the annual national product.

LEADER

Boardrooms selling Britain short

In the economic doldrums of May, HELLA PICK interviewed Charles Levinson, Secretary-General of the International Federation of Chemical and General Workers' Unions in Geneva, who argued that existing concepts of managing trade and balance of payments were obsolete—

What do you see wrong with the conventional British approach of trying to get the balance of payments right through increasing exports and decreasing imports; through deflation at home and making British exports more competitive abroad?

This is no longer valid because the world economy is undergoing very important structural changes which introduce a whole series of new dimensions to trade. These stem from the fact that the multi-national corporation has modified the basic structure of modern trade. In the old days trade took place exclusively as a result of production and products going across frontiers. This is less and less the case today. Instead, production is now taking place directly in the foreign market through subsidiaries, and export trade in manufactured goods is less important. This invalidates much of the established theory and policies in the field of foreign trade.

You argue that the United Kingdom balance of payments is affected by the price policies pursued by the international corporations. Can you explain your argument?

This aspect of the multi-national corporation has an effect which has not yet been sufficiently examined, and is not taken sufficiently into account in formulating Government policies. 'Transfer prices' is a technique which multi-national corporations use in transactions between their own plants in different countries. It is a system of bookkeeping entries. They are not subject to the competition of market prices. The companies are free to set prices pretty much as they wish in response to the strategy of the company aimed at maximising profits. One of the primary objectives of 'transfer pricing' is to minimise tax payments. This is achieved by pricing as low as possible parts, materials, etc., transferred from a corporation plant in a country where taxes are high to another plant in another country.

The aim is to make the least possible profit with the object of minimising taxation. In return, corporations will fix prices as high as possible in countries with low income taxes or profits taxes. Ultimately, this can end up in the collection or accumulation of profit in tax-havens where profits can usually be hidden tax free. Utilisation of tax-havens is one of the real spurs to the spread of the multi-national corporations. Increasingly these global corporations, like Shell of United Kingdom, are utilising tax-havens to accumulate profits and escape the taxation of the higher tax countries like Britain and the United States. It means that a large part of the real value of exports are not recorded in the nation's official balances.

It is estimated that almost 25 per cent of British exports are now accounted for by intra-company transactions and subject to 'transfer pricing.' Because Britain is a high tax country, something like a quarter of its trade is now entered in the book at distorted values. This could easily represent a loss in foreign exchange receipts which more than account for Britain's trade deficit.

Germany is a different example of this thesis. The German trade surplus in 1968 was around $4 billions. The main reason for this is that Germany has very little overseas investment and that only a very small network of international corporations radiate from it. Germany's overseas investments were seized in 1914 and 1946. The postwar reconstruction in Germany involved mainly concentration on the national market, complemented by direct exports, rather than capital investment. Overseas manufacturing by German subsidiaries last year amounted to only $3 billions, a very small proportion of the total value of its export trade. Transfer prices do not therefore prominently affect German trade figures. This more than anything else has contributed to Germany's favourable balance of trade. The same situation is also shown up by the case of Japan which has virtually no important multi-national companies, and consequently concentrates on physical exports and has a tremendous trade surplus.

What can be done?

There must be a fundamental rethinking and a recasting of trade policies. There are various instruments available to Governments once the facts are grasped. It should not be impossible to adopt measures to compensate for the negative effect of transfer pricing in the same way that the British Labour Government recently set up an import compensation to France. Transactions made through transfer pricing could very well be taxed on the basis of prevailing prices with the international corporations paying the differential in foreign currency. That alone could mitigate the negative trade balances of both Britain and the US to a considerable extent—certainly more than devaluation. Other devices could impose on the multi-national corporation the obligation of accounting to the national economy and for the national account for the advantages it is deriving by its being a multi-national corporation in an international economy. Once the principle has been accepted that foreign trade today has undergone a very profound structural modification and that old measures and policies no longer apply then I think new approaches become available.

What should the trade unions' response be to the international corporations?

Trade unions must also modify their policies and structure to take account of the multi-national companies. I believe that within 25 years some 300 corporations will dominate Western trade and our Western nation States. Trade unions have also got to become international in their bargaining. There has got to be a counter-vailing union force to confront this new global power. But unions have got to understand very quickly that they can only solve the economic problem created by the multi-national corporations by themselves becoming truly international. Politicians no longer have the real power of resolving these problems. The jargon is out-moded which claims that productivity has got to increase, but wages must not outstrip worker efficiency, that higher money wages will cause inflation, that inflation will adversely affect exports and the money go down the drain when replying to workers' demands. Those who continue to perpetuate such nonsense have become very dangerous. They impede the formulation of modern solutions to modern problems.

British workers and their trade unions are in no way responsible for the problem of the pound or Britain's balance of trade. I think Mr Jenkins's problem is that he has to respond to pressures from the International Monetary Fund and the central bankers who have neither the means nor the power to move against the international corporations who in a real sense control and dominate them. Because of this lack of effective power, the monetary managers always end up by saying the same thing, and always come up with solutions, such as deflation, that do not work. As a result they go from crisis to crisis.

In your assessment of the multi-national corporation, what do you consider is its influence on speculation in currencies?

The speculation of the multi-national corporations consists of hedging or forward buying of currencies in order to protect themselves against devaluation. Because they have gigantic forward-going global investment programmes, they cannot afford to get caught in a weak national currency whether it is pounds, French francs, or dollars. They therefore protect themselves either by borrowing a maximum amount in a shaky currency so that if there is a devaluation they can repay the loan in cheaper money (Amercan companies did this in France during the recent crisis to protect their French investment programme). Another way is to keep balances in different currencies and switch them as the interest rate changes. But by far the most expensive method is forward buying or hedging in which the company buys or sells a relatively stable currency such as the German mark, to be delivered at a future date.

This hedging involves billions of dollars and exercises the greatest amount of pressure on foreign exchange rates. Multi-national corporation money management has become a major aspect of their international policy. The Ford Motor Company, for example, has a department exclusively concerned with such operations. Because of the vast amount involved this has become virtually another area of banking, and as the multi-national company grows it will increase in the exercise a dominant influence on exchange rates and speculation. Such activities by some of the major British companies like ICI, Dunlop, Bowater, etc., have contributed much more to the recurring weakness of sterling than any amount of strikes or consumer buying could possibly exert.

HELLA PICK

The thoughts of Francis B. Willmott

Every morning, close on 9 o'clock, River Street, in foundry choked Birmingham 5, is startled by the spectacle of a Pickwickian-proportioned gent in spats, brocade waistcoat depicting frenzied plant life, and a buttonhole-rose flown fresh from the Continent. Alighting from his personalised number-plated Rover 3-litre, the sartorially bold gentleman draws a veil over the sulphurous scene which Birmingham 5 presents, and enters the front door of his personal empire where, in a mahogany-lined setting reminiscent of a reading lounge in a thirties cruise liner, he is welcomed by a portrait of himself in oils, with rose, and a bust of himself in bronze, with rose. Francis B. Willmott, philosopher, industrialist, and champion letter writer, has arrived at the Forward Works, hub and powerhouse of the Francis B. Willmott Group, incorporating Francis B. Willmott, Ltd., and Roderoid (shrunk-on), Ltd.

Mr. Willmott is remarkable on many scores. He is a demi-millionaire who was a bicycle factory labourer at the age of 12; and an employer who, at 75, works a nine-hour day for six days a week, and looks in on Sundays; a philanthropist who buys huts for underprivileged Africans, and makes a point of employing abandoned workers in his own age-bracket (20 per cent of his staff are past retiring age); a frustrated doctor, cleric, musician, and lawyer, who has sublimated his untrained energies in the publication of four books; an industrial sociologist at the head of an anti-trade union, paternalistic New Lanark; and an unbridled reasoner, who unsaddles his gems of wisdom on the British press at the rate of 3,500 letters a year.

Every night, after he has spoken at a dinner party, opened a Salvation Army hostel, or simply spent the day considering the heartache and the thousand natural shocks that shrunk-on ring gear is heir to, Francis B. puts pen to paper and has a shot at nailing some of the flashes of insight which have pierced the overall maelstrom of the day's reasoning. Ten letters later, the urge is spent and he rests up to face another day of applying The Human Touch in Industry.

The Human Touch in Industry (title of one of his four basic works on industrial philosophy) is a way of living and working which contains something of Owenism, a soupçon of Dewey, an attitude to interpersonal relations which is pure Buber, and a practical history which savours unmistakably of Hoffnung. The purpose of the Forward Works, Roderoid (shrunk-on), et al, is to provide employment for men and women, to allow them a share in profits, to give them pretty much a free hand in the running of the work, to uplift retired and redundant souls, to loan capital sums to the workers, and to encourage them to realise and voice their individuality and worth. The purpose, is in brief, to establish the little Utopia of River Street.

And to be fair, things appear to run much according to the superoptimistic plan. Quaint secretaries in their seventies, humming fragments from *King's Rhapsody*, beam as they grapple with new Pitman outlines; the works decorator stalks about the place looking for extra jobs he could be doing; the chauffeur takes his coat off and marches purposefully into the foundry, where he is cordially accepted by the operatives, who take home more than any union rate, and don't jib at overlooking four machines at the same time; wiry ladies sling white hot steel alongside men; and Mr Willmott attaches little importance to growing rich, and addresses himself to the task of penning encouraging notes to his team.

Letter writing is all part of the plan. If a Forward Works man, in passing, expresses some mild personal worry, he is apt to receive a copperplate riposte of 1,000 words from Francis B. If he is off colour, his doctor is apt to receive a diagnosis, and more than a hint of a likely cure, from the same source. Typical examples of helpful correspondence are cited in Mr Willmott's book, under the heading: 'The Human Touch in Practice,' from which the following extracts are culled:

Employer to doctor: 'In an endeavour to help the Medical Profession in their arduous duties of today, especially since the advent of the National Health Service, I presume to approach you in regard to Miss B, a senior stenographer . . . She gets a period of very noticeable tremor affecting the hands . . . to the layman this is an obvious nervous condition and aggravated, one would think, by symptoms observed by other members of my staff, who have noticed a distinct clamminess, even during the hottest weather, and a huddled position, over an electric fire, suggestive again, one would think, of a starved condition inherent in some complaint of which Miss B is a victim . . . These observations are made deliberately to help you in your diagnosis: and yet it is apparent that you would require nothing of the kind, as Miss B is your patient.'

(In this case, Mr Willmott concluded that the unfortunate

stenographer was overtaxing her strength, and after she had broken down and gone away for a long rest, he took the liberty of writing to her previous employers, suggesting that they might like to take her back. They acceded, and informing the woman of this new turn in her affairs, Mr Willmott was obliged to rebuke her for complaining that she was being 'thrown on the labour market at the age of 47,' and to mention that she was likely to forfeit her pension rights.)

Employer to employee executive: 'This is inspired by your own admission the other day of experiencing a sense of loneliness . . . it is the penalty of accepting responsibility . . . you have, I think, aggravated or developed the detached attitude by visiting, eating, and drinking at places located in town, in lieu of local places, and there you have met and intermingled with some middle-class people, and thereby experienced an added sense of loneliness . . .

'I have promised to help you a little by seeing what can be done to help you to become a member of the Institute of Managers . . . one helpful attribute you have is that you have made a study of drinking . . . I do not mean this in any unpleasant way . . . you will find that even you, as everyone else, including myself too, have our limitations . . . there is another background, however to your own life, which I realise is not a helpful one, and that is your domestic set-up . . . you have gone a long way since I "fathered" you . . . I know you will take this communication kindly.'

There is indeed an enlightened despot in a boardroom where a list of incentives to increased productivity includes: '5. Companionship; 6. Cheery good morning from the management and the "boss"; 8. Sing and whistle and listen to the workers' playtime music; 9. To have permission to go to a mid-week football match.'

Mr Willmott, who contested Wednesbury as a Liberal in 1958, after three years as a Conservative representative on Birmingham City Council, attributes his eccentricity as an employer to having a philosophical turn of mind. 'When I was a young man, I was sensitive, like you—no, more than you. The violin was my sweetheart. I wanted to be a musician, or a lawyer, or a doctor, or to enter the Church. But circumstances didn't allow, and so, since I was always thinking on a serious plane, the abilities I had were given an outlet in concentrating on the philosophical approach to everything. That's why I've written more than 10,000 letters to the press on everything that occurs to me.'

One week's letters to the *Guardian*, prepared by his full-time press secretary (aged 74), will include speculation about the space race, and congratulations to Prince Charles: 'The radio recording gave a delightful impression of a young man at ease and typically alike to his father in tone and delivery. This revelation is a sure sign of the Prince's popularity among the populace reminiscent of the Duke of Windsor when Prince of Wales, and yet a likely reminder of the moment of time when a new King abdicated from the Throne.'

The next week, he will write about the unions, and branch off on the subject of rowdyism in sport: 'What can be the real cause of it all? Is it frenzy and a state of mind like madness, or violent excitement, which is of course possibly due to emotional re-action? Even so, there must be an added reason likely to be side effects of drug taking or strong drink. Such are human failings which, if taken in excess, can mean loss of control and ability to apply self-discipline. The future for any peaceful game is likely to be very remote.'

And it is the philosophical approach which prompts Mr Willmott to publish every year the company report, without stating a single figure of profit, loss, or holding. His latest annual report as chairman and managing director, says more than figures could convey:

'The fall in profits during a year of exceptional activity in which the demand for our products was the highest on record was foreshadowed in the context of rising costs and reduced static prices. This has meant the development of a paradoxical situation difficult to overcome. That we measured up to the need has aroused in us the knowledge of a sustained reputation for quality and dependability. It is fitting, too, to mention that 40 per cent of the personnel have more than 20 years' service, and are privileged wearers of an engraved watch of their own choosing.'

JOHN HALL

Today's thought

Sir,—That the Government has willed the intention to impose

the decimal currency system on to the country, it is no secret to learn of their determination not to allow compensation, even to any deserving cases.

Surely it is fundamentally unsound and unwise to contradict participation, without which there can be no conciliation or acceptance of any new scheme compulsorily imposed, devoid of compensation. it is to the credit of the Opposition to have attempted to gain this concession.

Surely no new system should entirely cast out our own currency; provision should be made for continuing it to those who need to do so.

Fifty years ahead is time enough to think of adopting every facet of European life, if ever.

Yours truly,

Francis B. Willmott.

Forward Works,
River Street,
Birmingham, 5

The Chancellor's fortunes

Exit Mrs Castle pursued by a carthorse. Enter Mr Jenkins bearing a missive. With these brief stage instructions our drama continues and it is time to return to the fortunes of our Prince.

In one of his occasional writings Mr Roy Jenkins repeats the probably apocryphal story of the conversations between Attlee and Bevan in 1951. Bevan wanted the Foreign Office for himself. Attlee expressed surprise, warning him 'it very seldom leads to Number 10 Downing Street.' 'In that case,' Bevan said, 'I suggest you offer it to Herbert Morrison.'

Attlee did. Later he recorded: 'He seemed to want it so badly and turned down every other suggestion I made to him, so in the end I appointed him. Rather bad luck for him as it turned out. It brought him a pack of troubles.'

There is a strong hint of pleasure in this pipe-sucking comment. Something very similar may one day appear in the Wilson memoirs. For the Treasury these days very seldom leads to Number 10 Downing Street. In Mr Jenkins's favourite period of history it nearly always did. But more recently Chancellors of the Exchequer have tended to experience what Attlee called 'rather bad luck.'

Roy Jenkins is the exception to many rules but not yet to this one. After 18 months at the Treasury he is not the glowing prospect he seemed when the sought-after job dropped into his waiting lap. To a very great extent it was inevitable that his career would be checked. Having adopted his post-devaluation strategy there was only one thing to do and that was to stick to it; he could not expect to be very popular. There has been no scope for spectacular innovation: it is not possible to slog hard and be effortlessly superior at the same time.

Nevertheless there is a feeling around that Mr Jenkins's reputation has been dented deeper than can be explained by collision with unavoidable obstacles. There are three heads of complaint: the first is that his judgment has been less than sure; the second is that he has gone the way of previous Chancellors and too readily accepted the orthodoxy of Treasury officialdom; the third is that he has shown reluctance to take sides and show fight on issues that extend beyond his departmental responsibilities.

The errors of judgment will be forgotten quickly enough if the underlying judgment is vindicated. There was the too slow start; then the laborious public expenditure review of January 1968; and the lost psychological impact through postponing the post-devaluation fiscal package until March. There was the uncertainty, verging upon panic, shown by official policy at the time of the monetary crisis last November. There was the decision, a boomerang this week, to announce the plans for immediate and urgent trade union reform in this year's Budget speech —a decision, it is now said, which was not requested by Mrs Castle.

However, in spite of these stumbles, the Chancellor will be able to give a reasonably optimistic account of his strategy's progress when he takes part in tomorrow's debate. The providential discovery of error in the recording of exports means that on current account the balance of payments is in the black for this year.

However puny it is of prime psychological importance. Mr Jenkins now has a chance to alter the tone of the Government's presentation at home and abroad; he can try to do what some have argued he should have tried to do before: that is to stop making such a drama of the balance of payments.

The second charge is more serious for a man who went to the Treasury with a reputation for independence of mind, indeed an attractive streak of arrogance, backed up by a grasp of economic matters. Already, scarcely 18 months after devaluation, there is a depressing air of *plus ça change* about the policy coming from the Treasury. There is, at least, a tendency towards restraining growth beyond the restraints of productive potential. That was the self-immolating policy from which devaluation was supposed to provide the escape.

There is the hastily placed emphasis on the unproven theory of the money supply. There is the suspicion that the Chancellor and his officials were on the point of signing a Letter of Intent with trigger clauses, now removed, which would have been politically disastrous as well as an act of economic folly. Treasury and Bank officials break Chancellors, they seldom make them.

The third complaint suggests that Mr Jenkins sometimes prefers to remain on the fringes of common political brawls. For example, we learn that he was most sceptical about the great invasion of Anguilla but we do not learn that he used his position and ability to oppose it either in the overseas and defence committee or in full Cabinet.

It was not until the argument was effectively over in last week's historic Cabinet meeting that he, as it was described to me, 'slid elegantly off the fence'; that is to say he maintained his loyal support of Mr Wilson and Mrs Castle but his rôle in the battle seems to have consisted of holding their coats.

The same sort of complaints was made by his closest political friends before he succeeded to the Treasury: why did he not more often speak up in Cabinet for his known views; why did he always seem to wait for greatness to be thrust upon him? Is he, some now wonder, a case of the deponent politician—active in meaning but passive in form?

His historical writings are filled with tempting clues to the man, for although sociable he is elusive in person. He has noticed and admired in the politicians he has written about 'that persistent desire to wield power,' 'that combination of long life and persistent ambition which, allied with adequate political talents, is the best recipe for leaving a big imprint on events.' Yet he also admires the civilised virtues, the sense of humour, and urbane lack of earnestness which are present in his heroes.

In Asquith and in Attlee he notes a 'fixed radical purpose' at variance with other aspects of their lives and outlooks. He concludes this to have been for fifty years the best recipe for a Left-of-Centre Prime Minister.

How much of this ambivalence is in himself? The more jealously inclined of his colleagues are quick to recognise in him the 'persistent ambition.' The adequate political talents, the urbanity and sense of humour, the civilised virtues, are there for all to see. But is there a 'fixed radical purpose'? After 18 months of Mr Jenkins at the Treasury his desire for power is more apparent than the shape of the imprint he seeks to leave upon events.

PETER JENKINS

Magistrate at the test bench

One reason why Mrs Bette Bell has no intention of resigning from the Bench is that she thinks she will be a better magistrate now she knows what it is like to be locked in a cell for sixteen hours with a bucket of excrement in the corner.

As it happens, Mrs Bell, gaoled for her part in a demonstration over increased admission charges to a park near her home in Havant, has never sent a woman to prison. She has been on the Havant Bench for just over a year, one of the new working-class magistrates that the Labour Government's Justices of the Peace Act aimed to bring in as a leaven to the Establishment lump.

'But I've sent men,' she said yesterday, 'and now I'll know what I'm sending them to. I'll put it this way: when you've experienced a thing, you're not doing it in the abstract.'

Of Holloway, Mrs Bell says: 'There are things that happen in there that I never dreamed could happen. It has opened my eyes I can tell you . . . People are always saying magistrates should visit prisons more, but when they go, they go on a conducted tour. They see nothing, and I mean nothing.' Mrs Bell was unwilling to talk about it, but one of the things that clearly had shocked her most was the amount of open Lesbianism she saw in only two days in Holloway.

The 'abstract' for Mrs Bell was knowing that ordinary remand prisoners were not separated from other prisoners, but not quite realising what this means: knowing that there is a shortage of prison staff, but not grasping the human consequences; knowing that there are no men in women's prisons, but not that this automatically leads to homosexuality; knowing that prison work was not interesting, but not how boring and worthless it is to have to do it.

'I didn't properly realise what a shortage of prison staff there is. This must be the reason why the girls are locked up for 19 hours, which is a dreadful thing. How can this kind of appalling boredom help anybody?

'And what more nebulous work than putting spoons in a bag,' Mrs Bell said, with a sudden access of anger. 'That's the work at Holloway, that and jam making. And if you're on jam making you're lucky. . . . All this does, all it can do, is make more trouble. . . . I couldn't believe it.

'The prisoners hated magistrates. When I went out on my first morning for the exercise and we sat on the grass—only a little bit of grass that they were allowed to sit on—some of them asked what are you in for. I told them I was in for a principle, that I had refused to be bound over. They didn't understand. Then somebody came out with the punchline and said who's the so-and-so magistrate. I've always wanted to get my hands on a magistrate. I thought, crumbs, here's my lot. The warden was away on the other side and I thought I was going to get it. But they didn't. . . . In the end they were quite sympathetic.

'The girls tried to force me to eat and stop my hunger strike, and they were quite angry when I wouldn't, because they thought I was doing myself harm. They're having a rough time in there, I can tell you, and I thought they were going to give me a rough ride.'

Mrs Bell is from a country town and has served on a country bench for only a year. She describes herself as a Christian Socialist, and although not naïve, could hardly be described as worldly. Some might ask what she expected a prison to be like and why she is surprised that prisoners get a 'rough time,' and that prison society is drug oriented, sexually twisted and revolves around boredom. But, apart from her social class, Mrs Bell is probably pretty close to the average of magistrates—feeding people into a system about the nature of which they usually have only the most distant notions.

'Down in Havant we get very little in the way of drug cases,' she said, 'I think we've had two that I can remember. But in Holloway all of them, well, the majority were boasting about taking drugs, about the kicks . . . about things like the rolling of a bloke—I learnt the lingo, you see.

'Sixteen hours stuck in a cell with a bucket. That was the only toilet facility. It was horrible. I was lucky. I had a bed. . . . A lot of the girls in that wing were just sleeping on the floor. A lot of the girls had just smashed their beds out of the frustration.'

Before her weekend in Holloway, Mrs Bell rather prided herself on being able to understand the problems of some of those who came before her. 'My husband is like almost everyone else in Leigh Park, skint . . . we haven't even got a full carpet in our main room. You know, we're skint. So anybody who comes before the bench who is skint, I can understand how they feel. . . . I think that makes me a good magistrate.' Now she thinks that, if the Lord Chancellor will let her, she can be a better one because she also knows what it's like to be in gaol.

Mrs Bell could end up in Holloway again if she is once again asked to agree to be bound over to keep the peace. 'I will refuse and I'll go to Holloway,' she said. 'Don't think I'm treating this as a joke. Holloway is no joke.'

If she does return to the bench, Mrs Bell said, 'obviously I'd still have to send people to prison. . . . But I wonder now whether prisons are the answer. They can't be the answer in the future.'

MARTIN WOOLLACOTT

Mosley: the bison in waiting

The way things are shaping Orsay could soon be a place of pilgrimage. For 17 years Sir Oswald Mosley has been in a kind of retreat here, where the electricity pylons from Paris go striding across the market gardens of Villebon and Orsay. He has patiently waited until we should recognise him for what he has always known himself to be—part soldier, part politician, and all visionary. He has written his autobiography, which is going to clear the old bogey that he wanted to be a dictator; and with it he is himself prepared to bury the hatchet after the years of hatred and abuse. This morning he is a man quietly ready for acclaim.

It has already begun. Sir Oswald Mosley is the only living Englishman who could perfectly well have been either Conservative or Labour Prime Minister: we have Mr Muggeridge's word for that. He might have been a very great Prime Minister, according to Lord Boothby. He was the outstanding politician of his generation . . . spurned by Whitehall, Fleet Street, and every party leader at Westminster simply and solely because he was right: that is Mr Crossman speaking. And Sir Hugh Carleton Greene's organisation is spending much valuable time on him tonight, though it is a very few years since Sir Hugh said that Sir Oswald would appear on BBC television only over his dead body.

A man was meant to come into his own in this house with its Classical front, its landscaped lawns and its lake set among trees. Napoleon built it for General Moreau as a present after Hohenlinden and called it Le Temple de la Gloire. Sir Oswald grins at that one; but he bears it easily. He has logs spitting in his fireplace,

127

an Irish retainer for a chauffeur, and, facing him across his dining-room table, a bust of Chatham to remind him how glory is sometimes delayed. He does not fail to remark that Pitt was excluded from affairs until a crisis befell the nation.

He plays the host magnificently. He is attentive, considerate, and infinitely courteous. He wonders twice whether Mr Lehane, the chauffeur, managed to obtain food during a long wait at the airport. When a telephone call from London interrupts conversation he does not ask to be excused: he says 'Forgive me.' You would have to be quite frantically hostile not to be charmed off your chair by Sir Oswald Mosley in private.

He talks like a statesman who may be in the wilderness but who knows he is not finished yet. The heavy bison head, with the blotches of age staining its cheeks, is held motionless, looking straight to the front. That husky voice—a bit like Macmillan's—is not really answering questions. It is reciting policies which have been worked out and refined beyond all shadow of doubt and which are presented with all the caste marks of reason. It is utterly persuasive. But there is an unsettling way of flashing the eyes in aside to emphasise a point; the lids flick back without the brows shifting at all. In its time this trick, or birthright, must have mesmerised thousands.

The past, it seems, is a thing that is over and done with. Sir Oswald has only one regret about his Fascist years and that is putting his men into a para-military uniform, which frightened people who thought he had something to do with Hitler, though Sir Oswald can see why; they were hysterical at happenings on the Continent. There is, though, a residue from the past that ought to be cleared. Sir Oswald believes in consensus government, with people from the parties, the universities, public life, and the Army. The two parties are only a couple of moneybags with two or three hundred paid agents and they can't prevail for ever. But then he remembers that in the rank and file of the parties are some of the earth's salt. For Sir Oswald would go to the stake for Britain and her people.

He would still do this in spite of deliberately setting out, 17 years ago, to make himself a European. Beyond Great Britain's greatness Europe A Nation is a prospect more dazzling still. And in it there is room for men like Herr von Thadden, who is not a Nazi and whose supporters (pure soldiers and passionate patriots) are strong Europeans, driven back into nationalism because they have seen their country put into an inferior position.

Great Britain first, though. 'I staked,' says Sir Oswald, 'the whole of my political life on the belief that there would be a major economic collapse in Britain.' Those flashing eyes can still see this on the horizon and they are ready for it. Sir Oswald does not now want to be Prime Minister, though he can see himself as a servant of the people in Europe. 'But the British people must express their desire if they want me.'

The recitation goes on for a couple of hours. 'Once England was awake we could have a foreign policy that would astonish the world . . . the genius of India and Japan promoted by British and European thinking . . . if the parties continue to frustrate reasonable opinion there would be reason to start a grass-roots movement.' And in London there is an office run by five old friends, testing opinion in local elections against the day when it may be necessary to organise for a general election at tremendous speed.

Sir Oswald has kept himself, he says, like an athlete in light training. He walks in the Orsay woods an hour each day and he swims a lot. He touches no sugar and he sleeps a little every afternoon. He is 71 years old and he looks a very rugged 55. He is about to read Che Guevara because one must know one's enemy. And in the new year he will embark on a trip round the world which may take him face to face with Mao Tse-tung himself. If this happens he has a proposition to make. It is that Mao confines himself and his experiments to the mainland of South-east Asia and leaves the rest of us alone.

Lady Mosley comes in and, with something very Mitford that lies between a giggle and a shrug, announces a postcard that has just arrived from Broadmoor. It invites Sir Oswald to take himself off to San Marino with his friend Harold Wilson. Sir Oswald is merely curious. He is wondering how the writer got on to his home address when the office run by the old friends in London usually manages to filter the cranky mail.

A little stiffly, for he has an honourable old war wound in one leg, he moves courteously off into the night to keep a dinner appointment in Paris. One day another invitation may come out of England. He is ready and waiting for it in his Temple of Glory.

GEOFFREY MOORHOUSE

The noble anachronism

Why did he do it? We may never have a satisfactory answer to the problem of what drove General de Gaulle to pledge his mandate on the result of a referendum when the general election of last June had given him an unexampled majority in the National Assembly and when members of his Government, notably the Prime Minister, Mr Couve de Murville, are known to have advised strongly against it. Perhaps, as some have suggested, the General felt the election victory was not his alone because it owed so much to his then Prime Minister, Mr Georges Pompidou. Or, as others think, he may have come to feel the need of a popular reconsecration at regular intervals. At this moment one can see only the classic, if tragic, appropriateness of the fact that the General's 11-year reign should be ended, as it was begun, by his own hand.

It was just short of 11 years ago, on May 15, 1958, two days after the beginning of the Algerian putsch, that General de Gaulle issued a statement to assure the country—which, in the past, 'from its very depths' had entrusted him with the task of 'leading it to salvation' and was now facing new ordeals—that he was 'ready to assume the powers of the Republic.' At that time France had a legally elected President (René Coty) and a legally elected Government, headed by Pierre Pflimlin. If the first was less than a man of iron, and the second almost pathetic in its handling of the Algerian situation, those powers were not vacant. There are still stubborn Republicans in the National Assembly and elsewhere, who maintain that General de Gaulle came to power as the result of a coup d'état which he accepted even if he did not directly instigate it.

He came at all events to a country quivering on the edge of civil war, whose Government was so fragmented by party divisions that it had become a laughing stock. He began his term in a climate of violence created by the Algerian extremists. He ends it in the shadow of last year's Latin Quarter barricade. He built up to a record total the country's reserves which, in 1960, were something less than $20 millions.

Today they are running out so fast that it has been estimated that they will be exhausted by the end of 12 or at most 18 months. By pursuing a policy of independence for France and by putting prestige before pragmatism he has left the country isolated and, if not bankrupt, at least in the position of those families who hang damask curtains in the front windows while they are eating kippers in the kitchen. In more prosaic terms, while the *force de frappe* was paid for on the home front, the housing programmes were persistently inadequate and the poor got progressively poorer, though national living standards rose.

Is the bill then negative? It would not be that if General de Gaulle had no more to his credit than the Algerian settlement and the decolonisation of black Africa, though the seed of the latter had been planted before the General came to power. The major achievement, which is not diminished by the General's own frequent references to it, is that he gave France political stability. It has not been a Ministerial stability. Abroad, there is a tendency to overlook the fact that the Fifth Republic has got through three Prime Ministers, six Ministers of Finance, five Ministers of Agriculture, and eight Ministers of Education. But the régime held. Politics, in the opinion of the public, became once more a tolerably respectable occupation, if not for gentlemen at least for citizens, and within that stability the authors and executants of the successive national plans got on with the task, still in progress, of dragging France from the edge of agriculture to that of atomic power and aeronautics.

With luck the managerial aspects of Gaullism will prove viable without de Gaulle, particularly if his immediate successor is Georges Pompidou.

Grave charges rest against the General. He has devalued the National Assembly, which now has less and less chance of exercising its proper function of controlling the Government. He has, particularly in recent years, divided the nation into those who support him and those who oppose him, and by doing so forfeit their right to call themselves Frenchmen. Possibly the most fitting epitaph was written some years ago when Alexander Werth described General de Gaulle as 'a noble anachronism.'

NESTA ROBERTS

Pouvoir de lycée

Created by Napoleon to turn out a young ruling class imbibed with the 'classical virtues' (submit to your superiors and repress your inferiors) the French lycées since May have become a place of desperation for both pupil and teacher. A 'happy' high school in France these days is one where if the teacher is not actually making any headway pedagogically at least he is in no real danger of getting a poke in the eye from a 16-year-old.

The headmaster, once a god in his own fief, has now to live with the excruciating humiliation of being treated with indifference—or worse—by his pupils and impatience by his teachers. The mediocre teacher, whose only skill was that of using his rigid authority to make students ingurgitate lessons parrot-fashion is now stripped of his authoritarian camouflage and treated with contempt (the incidence of nervous breakdowns and resignations has increased dramatically); the docile young student is distressed and resentful because the smooth path leading to a pensionable job on to which his parents had urged him no longer seems to lead anywhere; and the adventurous young reformers of May have found that the heady break-through from martinet discipline to self-discipline has landed them in bewildering country where everyone has lost control.

'We cannot function any longer,' one teacher said, 'and the

young people are realising that it is a slow and painful business learning how to use your liberty constructively.'

Thirty years ago, A. S. Neill in his celebrated experimental school, Summerhill, discovered that it was the 'trained puppies' from the traditional authoritarian school who experienced the most difficulty in adjusting to a free system of education—that is one which made demands on a pupil's capacity for responsibility and initiative. The French lycées are now paying the price of at least two generations of refusal to adapt to the realities of modern education.

The first real challenge was in the thirties when secondary education became free and mass education became a reality. Successive Ministries of Education have made innumerable recommendations for a more imaginative approach to education, but while the record can seem quite enlightened on paper, in reality conservative thinking blocked new methods.

Educators felt, plausibly enough, that it was sufficient to provide the same system of learning for all. So youths of totally different social and cultural backgrounds were put through the same drill. There was no effort to cultivate an individual's imagination or initiative if he did not seem to be able to keep up with the pedagogical trot.

In the early fifties the Government had to cope with the enormous increase in pupils, a result of the jump in the postwar birth rate. In 10 years the schools took on nearly 400,000 teachers, fresh material which could have been persuaded, as the old professors could not, to approach teaching in a new way. The opportunity was thrown away; it took the revolt of May to reveal how many mistakes had been made.

Not surprisingly the young revolutionaries who crashed through at least a generation of mismanagement find themselves unable to cope. The *Nouvel Observateur* the other day published a revealing account from a young, revolutionary professor, who finds he can no longer go on.

Aged 29, Professor of English in a lycée in a workers' suburb, he has always—from the students' point of view—been on the right side. From the first days of May he was one of the few teachers who co-operated in the occupation of his lycée and tried to make direct democracy work; he was with his pupils on the barricades; was arrested with them, and has never lost their respect. But he too finds it impossible to function with pupils intoxicated with liberty or those disheartened with the results of the whole business. He wrote:

'I saw those boys and girls of 15 discovering the reality of politics, the reality of their own social condition and of their relationships—these beings without memory opening dazzled eyes on a world to be conquered. That I cannot ever forget, yet I cannot function any more as a teacher.'

The students' ambivalent attitude to authority and freedom was illustrated by a 16-year-old who, when challenged on the length of his hair by a dean of discipline, remarked cheekily, 'When it grows longer I'll put it up in a *chignon*.' Next day the same student exclaimed to the same dean: 'I got an 18 in history; mama won't be so annoyed with me this week.'

A young woman teacher was howled down on her first day in class when she proposed a dissertation on Montaigne and Pascal. 'We want the three Ma's!' roared the class. 'Don't do anything to upset them,' the headmaster warned. So she had to swot up on Marx, Mao, and Marcuse.

But whatever the confusion, indecision, or deception there is no going back; the French educational system got a jolt which reverberated all the way back to Bonaparte.

PETER LENNON

Universities of the future

When Cardinal Newman wrote *The Idea of a University* in 1852, the University was still something that might have an Idea behind it. For Newman, the University was there so that the mind could be cultivated for its own sake, this disinterested self-cultivation being the only justification that a liberal education needed.

When Dr F. R. Leavis wrote his *Education and the University* in 1943, the Idea behind the University was not less noble: total attention to the best that has been written and thought, a kind of arduous self-purification to be carried on in the refining fire of English Literature.

But now, in 1969, it seems to be no longer a question of how we can define the Idea of a University, but rather more a question of how we can justify it at all. And this intensely radical critique is coming from the students themselves. It is becoming monthly and weekly more clear that the students would eliminate far more aspects of the traditional University than they would keep. The students seem to be saying: the University no longer exists. We have to build another University. The University is dead. Long live the University.

'Student unrest' is an improper nomenclature for what is going on. The students are not expressing unrest. They are expressing rejection, pure and total, of the greater part of all that the University has ever stood for.

The history of the great European universities—from the Platonic Academy through the medieval traditions of Padua and of Bologna, of Paris, Lund, Oxford and Cambridge—this tradition seems no longer to impress them. Whatever it may be that the students do positively want and admire it would certainly not seem to be the tradition of disinterested and patient scholarship which we associate with the universities of the past 800 years. The modern student remains unimpressed by the great name, the great critics, scholars, poets, historians, and philosophers. It is not that he absolutely rejects them, so much as that he is for the most part profoundly disinterested in them. Past work, however great in its time, is now judged according to the standards of to-day and of today alone.

If one asks one's own students what the University is there for, the answer will, surprisingly, come back readily enough. The University is there to experiment in, to use, to be submitted to various tests as to its integrity and value, to offer a playground for the free expression of ideas, to have certain arsenals of 'facts' at the disposal of any students who might one day want to know one or two of them. ('Facts' are much-despised lower-order munitions of the universities, as out of date as the rifles of the

Crimean War.) These arsenals of facts should be kept discreetly in the background and the University should not 'impose' them upon the students if they don't want to be told about them. The University should watch, wait, and serve. In fact it would seem to resemble nothing so much as a forgiving mistress, who may be much abused and much deceived, but who will wait, loving as ever, until the experimenting lover should care to return to her arms.

One pursues a little further: 'What is so wrong with facts?'

'Oh, facts . . . facts are dead things, belong to the past . . .'

'But is the University not there precisely to study and evaluate the past?'

One could not have committed a greater blunder. Of course not! The University is there to study the future. What students really want are facts about the future, and teachers are judged harshly if they cannot supply them. Those who have studied the past so much are expected, by some subtle internal torsion of logic, to know about the future.

The University is thus defined by the students as a forward-looking, projective, creative instrument which is, however, failing abysmally in its task due to the lamentable hanging on to outdated facts and subjects, to outdated theories and attitudes—those which have to do with the past. The University's Idea should be to study the present moment, whose creativity is alleged to be colossal, and yet the University persists in wasting its time on studying out-of-date botchy attempts to do what is being done by our contemporaries much better.

Poetry? Who needs the Odes of Horace, of Marvell, of Keats? The absolute effective model of beat poetry or guitar poetry has made their pretended virtues only too relative. The new poetry has replaced the old. It follows from this that the teacher of poetry should himself be first and foremost a poet. His concern, as far as literature is concerned, is with the immediate present. He does not exist as a teacher, for there is, strictly speaking, nothing to learn.

It is the English Department which takes the brunt of this. Despised by its scientific colleagues as being unscientific and despised by its artistic inhabitants as being unartistic, the English Department may be said to be in a parlous state.

'Why did you come to an English Department?' one asks the students. The answer once again is, of course, simple. 'I don't know. I am disappointed in it. I hoped for better things. I wouldn't ever do it again. It has no real applied usefulness.'

'But what would be the purpose of an English Department, according to you?'

'Well, I don't think it could have one really, could it?'

Down for the count. The English Departments have been judged and found wanting. There is nothing further for them to do but to retreat in shame and find a quiet place to die. The English Departments produced no poets, no prophecies. All their teachers exist in a false temporality.

Students in the English Departments also have a new attitude, which is all their own, to the text as such. Just as the historical tradition of the great universities is not respected in itself, so too the principal occupation of the universities for nearly a millennium now (exegesis of, and commentary upon, received texts of significance) is also refused. The modern student stares upon any text as if it had just sprung from the press. Classical, foreign, home-grown, all's one to him: it's just a text.

What does he want to do with this text? What he does *not* want to do, at any rate, is to comment upon it. That is a kind of sacrilege. The text is there to be *felt*, to be *experienced*, in *the here and now*. Historical comment upon it is valueless.

We thus come to the nub of the problem, the essence of the problem which is one of two conflicting attitudes to time. We constantly misunderstand the students because we do not really believe them when they tell us what they want, and this may be because we are too flabbergasted to comprehend fully what they say. The students want the University to be futural, of the coming age, of the twenty-first century. At the very least, it must be of the here and now.

But a University, of its very nature, cannot be that. It cannot be ahead of its time (except in the speculative work of one or two of its most brilliant thinkers). No, its nature is to be of the past, to teach the past and to get the students to agree to study and evaluate the past, to take the past seriously as an immense fund of richness which we cannot, in the nature of the case, have today.

But the modern student will not do this. He does not want any more of the past. He wants the future. For the modern student, the University is quite simply there to study, and even to create, the future.

But that is just what a University cannot do. That runs against its entire Idea, which is essentially concerned with Tradition. The new University of the students would be without tradition. It would be a pure study of potentiality. For this reason, the students have no sympathy for the present Universities, which they consider as wilful and as betraying the true *gnosis*, which is a *gnosis* of the present and the future. And no teaching academic who does not try to understand the amazing up-side-downness of this logic has the slightest chance of understanding the students whom he has under him, nor the general public of comprehending its errant sons and daughters.

ROGER POOLE

Back to front

The misprint man is older than we thought. The August *Encounter* contains two 'hitherto unknown pieces' by D. H. Lawrence. One is an unsigned review of German poetry, the other a backpage feature published in the *Manchester Guardian* on August 18, 1914. A searing, sombre piece on the folly of war, for which the great man was paid two guineas (care of Gilbert Cannan, a Manchester-born novelist, who seems to have been acting as Lawrence's post box, or perhaps agent).

But why, after all these years of Lawrentian scholarship, has the article stayed 'hitherto unknown'? The answer is simple: the byline to the article, 'With the Guns,' reads 'By H. D. Lawrence.' And the librarian in the *Guardian* Manchester office has at last dredged the 1914 account book, which clinches the identification.

The money was sent to D. H. Lawrence. Why then, was he by-lined H. D.? No one knows. Some of us can guess.

Welcome home from the gentlemen of the press

Gerald Brooke's return to capitalist society was dominated by a three-ring press circus of the most old-fashioned kind, and one not without a certain period charm—although the Brookes probably didn't think so.

The press put on a first-class show for the Brookes which began quietly, even decorously, with some balletic jostling at the airport before the interviews. It developed brilliantly with a breakneck car chase through London, and culminated in a major affray on the Brookes' tiny front lawn in North Finchley.

After a break for refreshments, the company tried to keep things going by delivering a number of letters to the Brookes' home, each rumoured to contain an even huger bid for Mr Brooke's prison diary—top offer was £40,000—and by ringing the doorbell at half-hour intervals.

The Brookes—at least Mrs Brooke seemed more amused than enraged by this fairly gruelling programme. It was a next-door neighbour who descended furiously on the pack shouting 'Get away, just get away!'

The cavalcade, which wild-eyed photographers claimed had at times done 90 mph through North London suburbs, hit Highwood Avenue at around 1 p.m. The score of photographers waiting there had, after discussion, agreed to range themselves in a neat line around the Brookes' front door. But their colleagues in the following cars knew nothing of this: they leapt from their vehicles like commandos jumping from the ramps of landing craft, and ran low and fast, cameras at the ready. Within seconds total confusion reigned.

Mr Brooke, grey-faced, looked like somebody who had just

returned from an unsuccessful camping holiday during which there had been a lot of rain. He and his wife were led to the front door of their home by the formidable Mrs Brooke senior. 'Give me a day or two to get over it,' Mr Brooke said over the shouts of reporters. Somehow, as about sixty people tried to get near the couple, the garden gate was broken and the little front lawn more than slightly bruised.

Mr Brooke opened the front door himself, with a certain relish. Then he turned in the doorway to the milling people: 'Thanks very much for all you've done.' A reporter shouted: 'Give him a nice kiss, love.' Mrs Brooke wouldn't, so Mr Brooke kissed her instead. Then the door closed.

MARTIN WOOLLACOTT

French press in Revolt

With the two revolutions envisaged for the press—in printing and distribution—by Mr Hugh Cudlipp, there is a third, not very discernible in Britain, but apparently inevitable in France. This, in the words of M. Jean Couvreur, writing this week in *Le Monde*, is the determination of journalists 'reacting against an evolution which tends to make of the press just another industrial and commercial activity . . . to reassert the proposition that a newspaper is above all an instrument of information, above all the affair of the journalists.'

The French journalists want to have a say in who is appointed to run their newspaper, and direct participation in the management of the newspaper and in the major decisions which affect the life of the enterprise. They want to redress the balance which has resulted in advertising too often having the final word. In short, a showdown between the mission of informing and (albeit valid) preoccupations with profit.

Writing in a newspaper which has for a long time admirably demonstrated the success of such an approach, M. Couvreur goes to some pains to soothe the fears of newspaper proprietors about the possible 'revolutionary' nature of this movement which has begun to affect the provinces (*Paris-Normandie, Courier de l'Ouest,* and *Ouest-France*) as well as Paris (even *Elle* flirted with the idea in revolutionary May).

'It is not,' M. Couvreur declares, 'a revolt in the brutal sense of the word.' It is simply a logical development of the right of participation which is now generally accepted, in principle at least, as the first condition of progress and social peace. (This remarkable change of attitude in all walks of life in France gives the lie to those who, judging only on the results of an election, insistently claim that the May revolt was a total failure.)

The timing of *Le Monde*'s articles cannot but have been deliberate, coinciding as they do with a crisis in *Le Figaro.* Unless an agreement could be reached on these issues of participation, and on that of a moral right to veto the appointment of an editor not acceptable to the majority, the staff and illustrious contributors (three of them are members of the Académie Française) of this sedate newspaper had fixed a strike date: next Tuesday.

Yesterday the foreign editor told me that contact made early this week made it unlikely that they would have to resort to such an extreme measure. So we will probably be deprived of the experience of seeing M. François Mauriac in the rôle of a strike leader.

Le Figaro is owned by a textile and popular magazine 'king,' M. Jean Prouvost, aged 83, and a paper and sugar industrialist, M. Ferdinand Beghin, aged 66, both of whom could not without difficulty adjust to the proposition that journalists—traditionally simple employees at the mercy of the caprice of the proprietor—should be entitled to a say in the management of the newspaper, traditionally considered a purely financial preoccupation. But journalists know from experience that managerial policy has a direct bearing on the liberty of the press.

The death, four years ago, of M. Pierre Brisson, an editor capable of exerting a certain measure of influence on the management, and the impending expiration next May of a contract which allowed the journalists a say in management, made it imperative for the staff of *Le Figaro* to take a stand.

Since so many of the contributors are people of considerable influence an agreement is almost inevitable: but what *Le Figaro* may settle with discretion, other newspapers will eventually have a more troubling task to achieve.

France is facing a dramatic decline in the number of its daily newspapers. There were more than two hundred dailies in 1945; now there are less than a hundred, and it is accepted that the inevitable advent of computerised newspapers will drastically increase the concentration of newspapers into a few hands, since not one in ten have the financial resources to adapt to modern methods.

Already French newspapers are becoming less political in an effort to reach as wide an audience as possible. The recent remark of a provincial newspaper's 'baron' is illuminating: 'Me an editor? I run a factory.'

The sinister truth that newspapermen are turning into factory workers producing a carefully commercially blended product, coupled with the irony of being told constantly by everyone from sociologists to the Pope that they are 'the educators of modern times' has provoked a crisis of conscience among journalists. This crisis could provoke a profound change in newspaper practice.

As M. Jean Schwoebel declared in his recent book, 'La presse, le pouvoir et L'argent,' journalists are 'tired of being considered at best as amiable nuts, or more frequently, people willing to write anything about anyone: who will report any news, partial, tendentious, or even false . . . to please their all-powerful directors.'

PETER LENNON

Writing on the wall

'Klotterplank' is an enticing enough name for Stockholm's graphic Speakers' Corner. It turns out to be a white board, some 30 feet by 10, at the core of the main shopping area. The citizenry is invited to scrawl whatever it likes with impunity. It is distempered every morning, so that the panaceas fade slowly into oblivion.

The emphasis this week has been on betrayal: 'Jesus was the first Socialist—the Church betrayed him,' and 'to the memory of a man who was betrayed—Vladimir I. Lenin.' These are flanked in red, blue, green, and black (bring your own paint) with a memorable thesis on the evils of inflation and Bank Power, a tantalising one in English, 'I love somebody you don't know,' and a timely reminder that 'All tempest has in its middle a hole like a navel through which a gull may fly in silence.'

And, almost gone now, in a small black hand on the far left: 'Congratulations Palme, you put Frost in his place.' David Frost was here last weekend for Swedish television, interviewing Olaf Palme, heir-presumptive to the Premiership falling vacant in September. Frost was billed as the fiercest man-eater this side of Bengal, but gave Palme a winsomely easy ride ('All I am looking forward to is a very pleasant conversation in, indeed, very pleasant chairs that they must have picked to make me feel at home because I have these in my lounge', etc.).

The kindest comment came from an evening paper critic, who said Frost must be a brilliant interviewer to have drawn so many platitudes from Sweden's most exciting politician.

Palme's admirers prefer to present him as a budding Kennedy rather than a Scandinavian Trudeau. At 42 he is a very professional politician, who makes no bones about his taste for power and what can be done with it. Palme, short, sharp-faced, with imperious blue eyes, is not as flamboyant as the Canadian Premier, but has the same zest for polemic and a fight (which was why Hugh Gaitskell was the British politician he most admired).

If the lines have stayed open between the Social Democratic Government and the dissident young, it is mostly Palme's achievement. He speaks their language, even down to accusing them of élitism. As Minister of Education, he subsidises their art, if he can't stomach its politics.

To the students (as perhaps to the Americans) Palme will always be the Minister who not only marched against the Vietnam war, but also embraced the North Vietnamese Ambassador. Like John Kennedy, he has marked himself as anti-Establishment in spite of an Establishment background—in Palme's case a family of Conservative politicians, priests, and civil servants, university education here and in the United States, and a reserve commission in a cavalry regiment.

A lineage, none the less, already streaked with radicalism. Palme Dutt, the half-Swedish, half-Indian Guru of British Communism, and Olaf Palme's father were cousins.

MISCELLANY

After the Games are over

The troubles of Mexico were never far below the surface. The brutality used by the police in July to break up an argument which developed into a fight between two university groups merely ripped off the paper that covered so many cracks and holes in the façade of Mexican life. The facts behind the fighting that occurred while I was in Mexico for the Olympic Games were of such a nature that I was unable to write them while I was still in Mexico City.

The one outstanding achievement of the I R P, the only political party, is a highly developed educational system at university and polytechnic level. It has produced a community which is conscious of the vast gulf between rich and poor and the corruption that maintains it. In the past three years, steeply rising prices which have mainly affected the working classes, have caused the country to simmer. The students have merely blown the lid off.

Without the Olympic Games the Government could probably have crushed the student movement in their own effective manner without any nasty publicity. But, as the pictures of tanks and troops opposite the main Olympic Stadium were published throughout the world with stories of deaths in the riots, the Government became trapped.

To ensure the peace of the Games they have had to expose

their ruthless oppression to the world. October 2 shocked the world and stunned Mexico. The fifteen days of the Games created a curious sort of vacuum which allowed thought and discussion between the sections of the community that would not have otherwise occurred. 'The people of Mexico City are all on edge,' an Englishwoman who has lived here for many years told me. 'Even our servants are talking about the movement and that has never happened before. We all know that something must happen but we don't know what it is going to be.'

The conflict has long ceased to be just a student uprising. When the students make their demands to President Diaz the professors and the teachers are behind them on the one side, and on the other are the peasants, who find things are more easily gained by turning to the student movement.

This can best be seen in the repercussions of a bus crash at Topilejo, not far from Mexico City. Many buses in Mexico are unsafe; this one went over a slope and 26 people died. The relatives, knowing that it could take seven years to go through the courts for compensation, with the strong chance that they would lose their case at the end, turned to the students. They got the company to increase the compensation from 1,000 to 25,000 pesos per person, and they got some new buses.

Then again, just before the Games the police rounded up the pedlars in one of the main squares of Mexico City. Two who managed to elude this sortie turned to the students, who freed the others and discovered that the 'inspector' who made the arrest was a police constable who had bought an inspector's uniform. This sort of action is going to win popular support more quickly than speeches in town squares about freedom and liberty.

The army does not make or destroy governments. It is made up of conscripts, most of whom learn to read and write—as well as doing useful work such as building roads—during their military service. The students can probably influence them through that background of poverty.

The pressure the students have already exerted is bound to affect the Left wing of the political party. The Government has learned this time that its control of politicians is insufficient to meet this crisis.

The great worry for the intellectual is the background of Ordaz, who was Minister of the Interior in 1958-9 when the railway workers' union was brutally suppressed. It is widely believed that he ruthlessly dealt with disturbances in the sugar industry at about the same time.

A month after the massacre in Tlateloco, enough facts have filtered through to put the affair in perspective. I am convinced that the army attack was ordered by the President to crush any ideas that the students may have had of taking their cause into the Olympic arena.

If it was clumsily executed as a military operation it was wholly successful in attaining its object—a peaceful Games. It was, I suspect, the bloodiest massacre of civilians in the last quarter of a century in a country not involved in war or civil war. An accurate figure of deaths will never be known but the 500 I reported on the following day is not likely to be far off the mark.

The United Press International correspondent counted 25 bodies at one point on the roadside and a flat in the square contained another 25 bodies on the day after the massacre. The magazine *Pour Que* has pictures in which I estimate there are 31 bodies.

Ten thousand people fleeing from this open forum under fire from troops coming into the square on three sides (they were probably shooting at one another at one point) could not all escape. There were also many deaths among people living in the flats, some of whom were harbouring students armed with rifles and machine-guns. In some instances when troops got into a flat they just mowed down anyone in sight.

An Italian woman journalist who was injured (Oriana Fallacci), did not get a bullet in the leg as was first thought. It was shrapnel from a grenade. The magnitude of the massacre is muffled because families of students who are missing have been threatened by the police. Those who do make inquiries about their offspring usually get a piece of paper with a large red cross, a double warning—a cross of the grave and a red cross of the hospital.

In Europe this might sound fantasy. So too might the burning

of bodies, the stripping of others and replacing their clothes with
army uniforms to boost the military casualty lists. But Mexico is
a corrupt country in which the secret agent is a crucial arm of
government power. This is the challenge that the newly educated
face.

JOHN RODDA

Alcatraz garden suburb

'In this neighbourhood, your wife will be able to visit next door
at 1 a.m. and you won't have to worry about it.' Not the usual
estate agent's blurb but then the newest, smartest, maximum
security residence for Washingtonians is a rather unusual place.

Plans for a 6ft.-high electrified wire-mesh fence stretching
around a 167-acre enclave, electronic surveyance devices in the

shrubbery, and guard houses manned 24 hours a day are designed to give residents a feeling of security, albeit at $200,000-plus, that only Alcatraz can rival.

'It's regrettable that times are such that we have to retreat into this type of operation,' said Mr C. Edward Nicholson, a pillar of the Montgomery County Crime Commission, who is acting as lawyer for the developers. 'We are going to give people safety— something they can't get anywhere else. We'll make it as burglar proof, as trespass proof, and as vandalism proof as possible. Security is the thrust and theme of the development.'

Many of the high-rise apartment buildings in downtown Washington in recent years have gone in for permanently locked doors and guards to combat the highest crime rate in the nation, but none has yet taken the concept of security quite so far. There will be only two entrances to the enclave, $8\frac{1}{2}$ miles north-west of Washington overlooking the Potomac. One will be closed at night, the other will be manned 24 hours a day, and residents will be stopped by guards for identification papers. Nonresidents will have to wait at the 'rustic guard house' while the guard telephones the home being visited for permission to admit.

Schoolchildren will be picked up at their homes by a private minibus and brought to the guard entrance where they will board the ordinary school bus. An original plan, however, to build a 6ft. brick wall around the outskirts of the property had to be dropped because of objections by local residents that it would spoil the view of the rolling Virginia Hills—excellent hunting country.

Imprisonment like this, of course, does not come cheap—sales of the first 67 plots are to begin this autumn at $50,000 for a minimum of two acres with a requirement in the contract that another $150,000 has to be spent on building the house. Then there are the extra costs of feeding the guards and the guard dogs. 'Anybody who can afford a $200,000 home' said Mr Nicholson, 'shouldn't worry about little items like this.'

The security costs—termed politely 'maintenance charges'— are likely to run at about $5,000 a year. So far that hasn't put off potential buyers, who range from foreign diplomats to Government officials. 'Where else,' said Mr Nicholson, 'can you get the Potomac, all this, and security?'

To allow the residents to have as little contact with the outside world as possible there is to be a private club in the grounds, membership of which is to be restricted to property owners. After the project is under way the club will also screen new buyers who wish to purchase homes in the enclave.

To ensure the right tone the streets, circles, and squares in the enclave are to be named after prominent literary figures including Frost, Hemingway, Melville, Thurber, Whitman, and Thoreau. The 'New Yorker' pointed out in an acid aside that perhaps a plaque should go up in Thoreau Circle bearing his advice to potential home makers: 'If one deigns to construct a dwelling, it beholds him to exercise a little Yankee shrewdness, lest after all he find himself in a workhouse, a labyrinth without a clue, a museum, an almshouse, a prison, or a splendid mausoleum instead.'

Thoreau's homespun philosophising is appropriate in more ways than one. The main developers of this maximum security bliss where you don't have to worry about your wife at 1 a.m., are led by the widow of the late Albert H. (real estate) Smith who was convicted of bribery and tax evasion concerning his gambling activities a few years before his death.

ADAM RAPHAEL

Savage heart

Sometimes I think we see too much of America on television. Almost every night Alan Whicker or someone like him is spilling it all over our living-room carpet and we all know it so well by now. There are the fat ladies in Florida who want to be thin, the dead people in California who want to be frozen so they can be thawed out later on, there is Norman Mailer and the violent blacks, and the breast beating intellectual liberals—and it is all so very familiar that I am sometimes surprised that I could have lived there for 25 years and have missed it all. Naturally, fat women in Florida and frozen people in California do exist, but what one misses on television is anything that looks genuinely familiar, authentically common.

With this in mind it was something to see Eric Hoffer, the Californian long shoreman philosopher, on BBC 2 last night. He is, of course, unusual; philosophising dockers are a dime a dozen, or 6d a dozen, or a kopek a dozen, but they are usually only talk, while Hoffer has written some excellent books, most notably *The True Believer* a study of mass psychology written in the style of Montaigne's *Essays*.

He is typical, however, of a sort of American; the sort we do not hear from or see; he is not a tourist type, nor rich, nor glamorous enough for 'Whicker's World.' But you will find him all over the country in bar rooms, at lunch counters or working at any sort of job. You will also find him in Liverpool or driving a taxi in London. He is the common man and because of poets like Whitman, Sandburg, and Vachel Lindsay perhaps this is more of a tradition in America than in Britain. Hoffer was discovered by CBS TV's Eric Sevareid a year ago and since has become famous, been invited to Johnson's White House, and now teaches part-time at a university.

On camera Hoffer is very different from the Montaigne in-fluenced man on the credit page. He speaks with a heavy German accent and is given to shouting when he is carried away. But it is lovely to hear this authentic voice of the people ripping into accepted images and intellectual convention. The avant garde artists remind him of Yoko trying to start a new religion. He is disgusted by architects who make Man secondary to nature. Intellectuals, he says, love an élite. He sees the violence of America's decaying cities but he says cities are what made Man human. He is a democrat but he is not afraid of offending Left-wing opinion by saying injustice is better than disorder because injustices can be rectified.

I was pleased to see Hoffer again, he did something to balance the Norman Mailer America we have been seeing so much of lately on television, but all through the programme I wondered why we do not see more of Britain's own uncommon common man. No one ever did, for example, Jack Common, the author of *Kidder's Luck* who died last year, and every time the Liverpool sculptor Arthur Dooley is allowed on television someone like Eamonn Andrews or Joan Bakewell is keening away in the corner of the studio fretting about him saying something wrong and ready to throw the switch. But, of course, our television is largely run by people who love a self-perpetuating cultural élite.

STANLEY REYNOLDS

The Church cries revolution

'*The Christian Church preaches non-violence. We, too, are the advocates of the abolition of violence. We do not want violence. But to abolish violence it is sometimes necessary to practise violence. And to abolish the need for the gun, it is sometimes necessary to pick up the gun. Peace be unto you, Christians.*'—Mr. George Black, American Negro field-worker for the Students Non-Violent Co-ordinating Committee.

'*The consultation (on racialism) calls upon the World Council of Churches to take the following steps: . . . that all else failing, the Church and the Churches support resistance movements, including revolutions, which are aimed at the elimination of political or economic tyranny which makes racialism possible.*'

The five-day 'consultation' of the World Council of Churches on racialism, which ended on Saturday, was part teach-in, part penitence, part act of redemption, and part morality play with unscripted episodes from Black Power.

Delegates were harangued and challenged in four-letter words and in the tones of academic theology; they were forced to recognise the hollowness of much white liberalism and the justice of many bitter black claims; they confessed the sins of the Churches and grasped the nettle of action and revolution.

The astonishing result is that the World Council of Churches, which might easily be regarded as a genial, cumbersome, mainstream body, is being asked to approve some of the most radical recommendations ever put before an international organisation.

151

And approval could come at Canterbury in August when the policy-making body of the World Council of Churches, the central committee, meets to give directives to its 220 member churches of the Protestant, Anglican, Orthodox, and Old Catholic confessions.

The consultation was no lightweight gathering. Senator George McGovern of South Dakota, who sought the Democratic nomination for President last year, was in the chair as an active Methodism layman with Dr Eugene Carson Blake, general secretary of the World Council, alongside him. The 40 invited participants, all Christians, included the Rt. Rev. Trevor Huddleston, Bishop of Stepney, the Rev. Michael Scott from Zambia, the Rev. Channing Phillips from Washington, and clergymen and laymen of similar calibre from all over the world.

The 30 invited consultants, not necessarily Christians, deliberately included some of the harshest critics of racialism and the most active workers in the field. The World Council's first truly international consultation on an international problem was bound to produce fireworks. But no one could have forecast the strength of the recommendations that emerged.

Strongest of all was the recommendation on support for resistance movements and revolution, quoted above. The point to be noted here is that economic tyranny may be judged to exist in a political democracy: support is, therefore, to be extended not merely to pariah countries like South Africa.

Next, consultation recommended the use of economic sanctions 'against corporations and institutions which practise blatant racialism' (an example quoted was Church investments).

The resolution on Rhodesia calls on Britain 'to withdraw her earlier assurance that force will not be used in resolving the Rhodesian conflict'; urges tougher sanctions; and asks the United Nations 'to ensure that members of guerilla forces who are captured in Rhodesia are treated as prisoners of war according to international law.'

There can be no doubt about the humility with which the consultation drafted its final demands. The preamble to the recommendations stated bluntly:

'The consultation clearly revealed that the Church and the world are filled with the insidious and blatant institutional racism that is producing increased polarisation and threatening an escalation of the struggle for power between white and coloured races into violent conflict. More than once the consultation itself was exposed to the pervasiveness of stereotypes, paternalism, and, in the final result, attitudes of racial superiority that have developed over centuries. And the Churches reflect the world.'

The mood of the consultation was deeply influenced by a series of confrontations and observations which daily increased self-scrutiny and self-consciousness. Mr Roy Shaw, a Black Power leader in Britain and an invited consultant, walked out after a brush with the Archbishop of Canterbury and left the Archbishop to deal with wounding criticisms of his chairmanship.

Mr George Black, field-worker for the Student Non-Violent Co-ordinating Committee, came as an uninvited speaker and demanded immediate reparations from the Churches of millions of pounds for oppressed races.

A British junior Minister, Mr Merlyn Rees of the Home Office, brought dismissive smiles from American Negroes when he quoted Salvation Army humanitarianism in the nineteenth century in the context of current race problems; and a member of the British Race Relations Board, Mrs Lena Townsend, was criticised for 'a racialist presentation' which put immigrants into special categories and saw them as the culturally deprived.

After the unscheduled demand for reparations on Friday evening, it was Dr Carson Blake who insisted on one group staying up to 4 a.m. on Saturday to draft the promised reply. 'I am not going to sign anything just to get off the hook,' he told his colleagues.

The reply repudiated 'any shred of paternalism' in reparations which were 'intended to be wholly controlled by those to whom they were given.' And it stated that present economic structures 'utterly fail to meet this standard (of economic justice), and it must be confessed that the churches have to a scandalous degree not only tolerated but profited from their relation to economic injustice. Nevertheless, it is sin and not paralysis from which the Churches suffer.'

Different perspectives were offered earlier in the consultation by an Indian layman who reminded the delegates that brown and black were as guilty in their relationships as black and white, and by a British social anthropologist who pointed out that racialist ideas were available to both sides and gave the example of 'negritude,' which assigned special qualities to black people, as a racialist idea on the black side.

But the conference chose an urgent response to an urgent challenge after its early acceptance that the Churches were largely white racialist institutions. The recommendations did not satisfy the Negro militants' demand for 'action,' but they guarantee a fundamental reappraisal of the Churches' attitudes.

CAMPBELL PAGE

The anti-pig movement

AN ESSAY ON LIBERATION, by Herbert Marcuse (Allen Lane, The Penguin Press, 25s).

Marcuse, like Nietzsche, is an alarming writer, it is not so much what he says as what others will make of him. He has the prophet's sense of enormity—the enormity of the way we live, the greater enormity of thinking such ways of living good or natural. He is also deeply and sensitively in touch with his times. That is what a prophet presumably is: one who voices the conscience and the discontents of those who feel but cannot wholly express them.

This rôle tells, to some extent, against Marcuse's own argument: that the pig-society makes us love our chains and cling to them. Dissatisfaction over the irrational and the immoral in society and politics seems to me deeper and more far-reaching in Britain and America than his thesis implies—in fact, the students and the ghetto in their several ways already speak for more of us than his eschatology predicts—which means only that the process he describes is moving faster than even he suggests.

It is a hazardous process but necessary. Marcuse's fusion of Marxism with psychoanalysis is increasingly weighted towards the Marxist side. Its weakest point, perhaps, is its failure to come directly to terms with the irrationalities of political power: apart from a footnote that a true participating democracy is not feasible today (why?) he is still vague about the institutional expression of the anti-pig movement. Socialism on the Dubcek model? A Socialist society must be anti-Puritan—'light, pretty, playful,' psychedelic not Stalinist: but how? In some of its aspects it must be puritan—in its sense of moral obligation, for example.

There are traps which could open to readmit our old guilt and new rulers. Marcuse suggests that in an order poisoned by its own irrationality it will be necessary to deal not only with frank and committed pig-people, but with misguided workers and intellectuals so intoxicated by the kitsch-consumer ethic that they prefer it. He avoids the trap—a free society will be 'incapable of any repression other than that required for the protection and amelioration of life'—but puritanism is strong, and we need equally to suppress new Robespierres.

One would have more confidence in his analysis if he contrasted the constructive rôle of figures like Castro and Ho-Chi Minh more sharply with their unconstructive and frankly terrorist activities. To an anarchist they look uncommonly like with-it and intelligent old-style politicians carried on a tide of popular courage which, like all revolutionary leaders, they use for their own purposes. Gaols, conscripts and executions are not confined to the Friworld; pig-people appear in any situation which permits command.

The strength of Marcuse is not in his declamatory argument but in his grasp of a major point, that the tide of sentiment has changed. The Labour politician who cannot see why students are more interested in Biafra than the balance of payments has been left behind by the tide (this has been the Labour Government's biggest failure—a moral and aesthetic one). The moral and aesthetic tone of the 70s in science, politics and art will differ as profoundly from that of the post-1900 era as the Romantic movement did from the eighteenth century. For all but the in-educable, life and living feel and are seen to be different, and this

155

change is itself moral and aesthetic. This is a revolution as great as that of the Romantic movement. It involves a wholly new view of life—conservation in place of 'enterprise,' inner space replacing outer space, old values suddenly seen as repellent. It is an in-depth change extending from art and biology to politics.

That political revolutions follow changes in sensibility was Herbert Read's teaching. Precisely because Marcuse is in touch with it, his book is an obligatory text for those who do not know how the new spirit 'feels' (or how it feels to be young now). Even the shouting of obscenities at politicians and the mixture of buffoonery with high moral seriousness fall into place here. Politicians are obscene: how does one meet cruel buffoons except by crazier buffoonery? Who is dirtier, the bemedalled napalm expert or the hippie?

Disturbing stuff, but revolution is a disturbing business. My confidence that Marcuse won't fall into Ludditism, Maoism or any of the other feedback loops back into pig-politics or mob-politics grows with the appearance in this book of a recognition of means. Pig-politics is to be overthrown, not by a revolutionary clique or an irrational mob, but by the weapon of 'Irish democracy'—the withdrawal, resistance and ennui of the ordinary person—in other words by rational, dogged human bloodymindedness. We shall vote with our feet. It is a good hope and one which should address us all.

ALEX COMFORT

Lament for Suez

The chill spell of the Sinai Desert still wove itself around me as we drove down through Bir Gafgafa. The bodies have been cleared away now—though it seemed to take a long time—and even the wreckage of tanks, guns, trucks is less densely scattered. But the menace of the swirling rock prominences, the pathetic thinness of the road back to civilisation, the memories of those hideous days of the June war, all combined to settle a deep gloom over the drive. The very ludicrousness of the signal gantry thus came as a real relief.

It stood in the middle of this wasteland, set at 'Go,' bidding Lord knows what imperial ghost trains to chug on. And around it was nothing, absolutely nothing. Five months ago the rails were still there, rusting and careworn admittedly, a hangover from those far off days when you could board the train at Victoria and rattle endlessly down through the Balkans and round to Cairo.

Now there is just a snaking hummock of sand, a few piles of wooden sleepers here and there, and those mysterious levers that always clutter the trackside. But the rails have long since been torn up and they now serve as part of the elaborate fortifications the Israelis have constructed since the huge artillery bombardment across the Suez Canal in October.

They must have ripped up about 150 miles of track, all the way from El Arish to Kantara and then southwards down to Port Taufik. It now adorns the roof of bunker after bunker, elaborately woven into a canopy which is said to be able to withstand the direct impact of a 120mm shell. It is easy enough to believe.

The bunkers nestle into the east bank of the canal, an easy rifle shot away from the Egyptians. Inside them curved corrugated iron sheet rests against a stout metal framework reinforced with planks. Occasionally a fireman's pole is installed for quick entry. Overhead, layers of sandbags are sandwiched with the rails and the whole lot topped with more sandbags. Some of the 15ft. lengths of rail have been cut and welded into a simple locking device which ensures that the whole mass remains as one, reducing to near impossibility the chance of collapse through blast.

There is astonishingly little evidence of last week's rain of shellfire from the other bank. Just now and then one has to dodge round a crater in the road that runs parallel to the canal and occasionally the endless scrubby desert is pock-marked. But it might have happened any time in the past two thousand years.

Perhaps the most remarkable thing to be seen, apart from the fortifications, is the blank horizons. Last time I passed this way

157

there was the usual clutter of an army in the field—the jeeps, trucks, artillery, and the Centurion tanks, their 105mm guns pointing up over the sandbanks. (De Lesseps turns out to have been pro-Israeli: he usefully threw all the dirt dug out of the canal on to the eastern bank where it formed a handy barricade.)

Now there is none of this. All has either been dispersed or dug invisibly into the desert. Just the occasional radio aerial shows. What at first looked like an endless trench running alongside the road turned out to be where the Israelis had apparently dug up some sort of pipeline, presumably as further reinforcing material.

The emerald waters of the canal look temptingly accessible. A quick plunge and a few strokes would easily get you to the other side. Standing in the tattered ruins of Kantara, its 10,000 people now scattered and the shells of their homes left to two neurotic dogs, one can clearly see the Egyptian troops on the other bank. They seem as interested in us as we in them but no one makes any signals.

On the Great Bitter Lake, however, there are no signs of life on the ships bobbing gently among the whitecaps. One or two are much nearer than you expect and the streaks of rust down them stand out in the harsh light. They, perhaps, will act as the memorial for foundering the commercial dream which is the Suez Canal.

More than all the artillery shells that whistle across, more than the million wrangling words that have been exchanged since the canal was closed, they must represent the harsh realities of the waterway's future. For what shipowner will ever risk his vessels or their cargoes here again? The route may be short but these ships have so far passed nearly two years travelling it. The very silence of their engines is surely the death-knell of the place that holds them.

At Ismailia, in what is left of the railway signal box just by the great swing bridge that used to span the canal, two sleepy but cheerful representatives of world order stick their heads out for a brief chat. An Austrian and a Burman, they are the UN observers whose job is to cry 'foul' at whichever side contravenes the ceasefire agreement. They have been having a rough time lately and the shelter at the back of their quarters has clearly been well used.

Above them another signal gantry points its absurd finger over the non-existent permanent way. It, too, is set at 'Go.' Clearly no one is likely even to try setting it at 'Stop.'

HAROLD JACKSON

Sweet Shirley

They tried to tempt Miss Shirley MacLaine out into the gardens behind the Savoy by saying 'Flowers.' She wouldn't go—at first at least—because her eyes wrinkled up in the sun ('psychological') and she didn't want to look ugly.

The cry of 'Flowers' was shrewdly calculated, however. There has to be some other reason for Shirley MacLaine to go out into gardens than that people want photographs, and flowers is the sort of reason that might appeal.

Miss MacLaine, who is in England to see her daughter Sachi back to boarding school at Bexhill, is unnervingly bright and unswervingly utopian. The abolition of war, the end of marriage as we know it, the demolition of the institutional framework of society so that 'people, who are inherently free flowing, can be allowed to pursue what they want'; these are all things she likes to talk about.

She has plans, after finishing her current film *Two Mules for Sister Sara* in Mexico, to do a lecture tour of American colleges. She has yet to write the lectures, which will be about how society should be changed 'as it needs to be changed.' She cannot say what she will talk about. 'I want to communicate . . . it will be more of a dialogue.'

All this had a slight derailing effect on some reporters. 'When did you last see your husband?' one asked, meaningly. 'Four days ago,' said the sprightly Miss MacLaine, 'Surprise!'

Why was her family scattered all over the world, with one

159

daughter in Sussex, son and husband in Japan, and herself mainly in America—and was that any way to bring up kids?

'You mean we should all live in Sussex at the boarding school?' Miss MacLaine asked the mumbling reporter, adding educatively: 'This whole psychology of internationalism seems to escape people.'

Miss MacLaine seems to have sent her daughter to an English school as an antidote to the girl's 'predominant Asian psychology and approach on life.' Phrases like 'Asian psychology,' 'her school is her syndrome' and 'diffused futility' spring readily to Miss MacLaine's lips. She is almost aggressively at the ready with every symptom of mental health and maturity.

The press conference got on to drugs. She had sampled pot but 'I am not particularly addicted to anything except being alive.' Would she take it again? 'That's like saying will you have another Martini tomorrow? What's the big deal?'

But Miss MacLaine is 'Primarily interested in young people. Politics is not relevant to me any more.' What matters is 'social revolution' in the West. In that, almost anything can go—war, of course, our 'practically fascistic' morality, monogamy ('not one of the inherent natural forces') and any or all institutions which set limits on the far-soaring human soul.

Shirley, aged 34, with a red-head's pale freckled skin, wearing a leather hat and a powder blue coat dress, looked just as good— better—as in her films. I thought I ought to slip that in.

The press conference was, naturally, devised with some thought that the publicity might help Miss MacLaine's last film, *Sweet Charity*, on general release all over Britain this week. But Universal did not push it and Miss MacLaine said: 'I never go out and sell. I hate that hard-sell stuff I think it's old fashioned. I think it puts people off.'

The details of Shirley MacLaine's hopeful programme for the world may be a bit befogged with syndromes and psychologies, but the basic message is clear 'I guess I don't do a lot of anything,' she told a pot-seeking reporter: 'I don't eat much, drink much, smoke much . . . I love a lot . . . that's something to get high on.'

MARTIN WOOLLACOTT

Grisly game to play

The scene, a riverbank winding through summer fields which an old man calmly tills, is pastoral. It could almost have been shot by Renoir, except that there's a desultory sort of chase going on—riders against men on foot. A cavalry ensign rides up to a surrendering infantryman. His tone is matter-of-fact, almost off-hand. 'Where do you come from, Armenia . . . Georgia?' 'I'm Hungarian,' says the prisoner. 'Okay,' says the ensign, 'get in the river.' He brings out his pistol. 'What are you staring at—do you think you'll ruin my aim?' He fires. The prisoner plops backwards into the water. It is hardly as memorable as swotting a fly.

This is war, as seen by Miklos Jancso, in *The Red and the White*. The coolness and lack of emotion is a device, of course—a trick even. But it succeeds in driving home the humiliation and dreadfulness of battle better than a hundred bloodier screen massacres. Like *My Way Home* and *The Round-up*, its predecessors, the film often has this aspect of seeming like a grisly game, filmed with chilly, but eloquent precision.

Some Hungarians, fighting for the reds in the Russia of 1917, are systematically hunted down. They counterattack but are outnumbered, in the end advancing, singing as they go, towards serried rows of motionless opponents. In between we see a group of nurses forced to dress up and dance for White officers in a woodland glade; the White ensign noted earlier is himself shot for trying to rape a peasant girl (it was not on his order papers); prisoners on both sides are constantly told to strip (shirts are more valuable than men in these circumstances). The camera always records but is never involved. There is no need for comment.

Considering that the film was made with Russian money to celebrate the fiftieth anniversary of the Revolution, Jancso's consistent refusal to take sides, even with his own Hungarians, must have looked to some like patent dereliction of duty. But it is of course nothing of the sort. He is simply on the side of humanity, while recognising what it can become when corrupted by war.

Possibly his almost choreographic manipulations, his fondness for understatement on an epic scale, his brilliance in weaving distant patterns on the skyline will cause some to doubt the heart behind the mind. But his aloofness makes its point very powerfully, both cinematically and as an appeal for us to face our illusions. One can readily understand why he is compared by some to Eisenstein.

DEREK MALCOLM

Midwinter's drag

O'erweening ambition was the keynote of most of this week's films—and we all know what that leads to. Peter Hall, I suppose, was the most ambitious: he set out, in *Midsummer Night's Dream* to do the impossible: to keep all the words, and yet to film on location, thus letting himself in for a plethora of pleonasms. He uses a hand-held camera, for 'spontaneity's sake,' and yet by entirely post-synching the sound, destroys whatever realistic effects the camera had achieved.

So far, we are still in the realm of the theoretical problems of Shakespeare adaptation. These can be argued, discussed, rejected. Unfortunately, the film he has made, all Shakespearean considerations aside, is just damn silly.

You can't paint your fairies green, leaving them looking as if they had all come down with a case of pink-eye. You can't use Tom-and-Jerry cartoon sound-effects to make your fairies appear and disappear. You can't again, have your 'human' characters dressed in some kind of vague swinging gear wandering through the woods with their faces picturesquely muddied without making the actors (Derek Godfrey, Barbara Jefford, David Warner, Diana Rigg, Ian Richardson, Judi Dench though they may be) look like amateurs. But I'm afraid amateur, in the less complimentary sense, is what the film as a whole must be labelled.

Maybe on American television, for which the film was made, it will look better. At least the commercials will break up the tedium.

RICHARD ROUD

Sound of dog-fights

Sir William Walton, O.M., has been cribbing tunes from Wagner. Twenty-five years after he celebrated the birth of the Spitfire in film music for *The First of the Few*, he has returned to the film world, writing the score for Spitfire Productions' new 'epic' (their word) *The Battle of Britain*, due for release on Battle of Britain Day. Wagner comes into it in the German scenes. Sir William was fascinated by the Nazis' *Nibelungenmarsch*, and, following them, lifted ideas from *The Ring*.

Asked how as an elder musical statesman he was persuaded to do the job, he explains laconically: 'Sense of duty.' A little embarrassed, he mumbles something under his breath about 'Where would we be without them?' but then in the passion of the resulting music, he has no need for explanations.

I attend a recording session in studios at Denham. The scene is the culminating dog-fight of the Battle of Britain, the date September 15, 1940. Where earlier dog-fights have direct sound-effects for accompaniment , the aim here is to heighten the scene with Sir William's music, a sustained Allegro of over five minutes, longer than anything for *Henry V*, in which (as he reminds me) the Agincourt charge lasted a mere 90 seconds.

A rival composer is conducting—Malcolm Arnold, flattered, he says, when Sir William asked him to cooperate. In the studio a whole wall opposite the conductor takes the wide-screen projection of the film, with the timing in seconds flickering along on one side like an Olympic bobsleigh transmission. Arnold, a beacon of sweat, whips up the orchestra furiously. ('Ad hoc.' explains Sir William: 'That's why they play so well.') First time through Arnold overruns by 15 seconds: 'My God, I've got to get a

163

move on!' And get a move on he does, so that on the third go it is the other way round: 'I was so excited, I got to the Heinkel too soon.'

The music fizzes. This is very much the prewar Walton of the First Symphony, uninhibited, youthful, exciting. The ominous opening tremolo (Trevor Howard as Air Vice-Marshal Park pacing the control room) has an echo of Agincourt, but then to vapour trails in the sky Walton creates an utterly original sound. I fail to identify even which instruments are playing. Sir William points to the score where violas and 'cellos are instructed to play arpeggios in glissando harmonics on the fourth string, a nice lesson in instrumentation. Then begins the Allegro proper, 'with a loop in it,' Sir William explains, 'to give some musical shape.' Twitching themes to twitching close-ups, tearing orchestral agonies to alternating panic and exhilaration. 'There's the re-capitulation, you see,' Sir William notes coolly at a moment of almost unbearable tension.

The job was rather forced on him at the last minute. He had a mere ten days to write the dog-fight sequence, a hard job for a composer who has the reputation of being inhibited. 'You just have to throw it off, and either it works or it doesn't.' Professional that he is, he wrote with a sharp eye on the stopwatch, timing his music against salient changes of shot.

He had already seen the 'rough-cut' version of the film, and knew exactly what he was about. His personal involvement is plain in every bar.

The fourth take is perfectly timed. Arnold comes to the Heinkels at exactly the right moment, and crashes the last German into the sea on the right chord precisely. We watch the playback in colour, and Arnold asks with a hint of modest uncertainty: 'That was the best one, wasn't it?'

There is one more sequence to record, and Arnold whispers in Sir William's ear. It is a grand super-dambusting march, and for this Arnold insists on handing over the baton to the composer himself. 'A piece of cake,' he says. Walton is warmly received by the players, flattered by the descent from Olympus. Back in the control room a film-man turns and asks Arnold: 'Got your assistant on, Malcolm?'

No troubles of synchronisation this time (the march comes at the end over the credits) and after the jagged syncopations of the dog-fight, the plain 4/4 time is restful for everyone. There are the usual Waltonian clearings-of-throat, and then with an outrageous whooping on the horns comes a grand patriotic tune to out-hope and out-glory any that Sir William has yet written, whether for films or coronations. We hug ourselves at the barefacedness of it, Arnold laughing out loud in admiration.

The first three notes may be a blatant crib from the opening of Elgar's Second Symphony, but they turn at once into the purplest Walton. Afterwards, as tactfully as I can, I mention something about the Elgar similarity, and Sir William gives a pointed look at Arnold. As Vaughan Williams used to say, it is perfectly all right for a composer to do any amount of cribbing, as long as he knows where it comes from. Sir William is no fool.

EDWARD GREENFIELD

Pancho wins the longest match

After the longest singles contest ever played at Wimbledon, the old man had triumphed in one of the finest and most emotional matches on the Centre Court since the war.

Pancho Gonzales, aged 41, and former champion of the world but never at Wimbledon, beat time, weariness, and expectation in defeating Charlie Pasarell, the best first-day player in the tournament, as both Santana and Rosewall remember, 22-24, 1-6, 16-14, 6-3, 11-9. Overnight he had been two sets down, and altogether he played for 5 hours and 20 minutes, and for a total of 112 games—19 more than Jaroslav Drobny played against Budge Patty in Wimbledon's previous longest match 16 years ago.

It was a match that cannot be discussed in ordinary lawn tennis terms. Here was Gonzales, gaunt and greying, the great player, fighting desperately. On Tuesday night, complaining bitterly about being forced to play on in semi-darkness, he had been booed by sections of the crowd. Yesterday, there was only cheering. Pasarell, younger and stronger, challenged him all the way, and reached match point seven times. Gonzales was so tired that he could scarcely hold his racket, but he saved himself—twice from 0-40—and went on to win the match. It was the kind of match that took your breath away, and moved you to tears at the same time.

For a long time it seemed that Pasarell must win. When Gonzales, taking the last 11 points, finally beat him, it was absolutely the right result. The crowd had watched Gonzales hold on and crawl uphill until, finally, stricken with cramp in the final set, and moving only when necessary, he reached the winning post. In the end he had to win. Any other result would have been emotionally wrong.

The tremors of Tuesday night's argument about whether or not Captain Mike Gibson, the referee, was right to allow the second set to be played in the fading light had scarcely died away when they went on to the court, and the crowd was clearly divided into pro—and anti—Gonzales sections. In the first half of the third set he drifted close to danger. Around the eighth game there were signs that his service was shortening, and all the pressure was coming from Pasarell.

The change began four games later when, at 6-5, he held the first of his nine points for the set. There Pasarell produced a service of the utmost ferocity into his stomach, which made him double up defensively. Oddly, Pasarell was using fewer and fewer of the lobs which had served him so well in the first set. When chances came his way he tended to hit his forehand nervously, and missed two crucial chances of breaking service at 8-8 and 10-10. At 13-14, Pasarell served three aces, one of them saving Gonzales's seventh set point, but at 14-15 he served two disastrous double faults.

Once Pasarell's service had gone, his confidence followed. As he said afterwards, he found Gonzales difficult to play because Gonzales had coached him and knew his weaknesses and had earned his respect. Gonzales, who had always moved as economically as possible, attacked with swifter purpose as he saw Pasarell wilting mentally. The fourth set hung on its seventh game, which was a disaster for Pasarell. Gonzales left him looking forlorn with an angled lob and by producing as many angles as Euclid in one rally. Pasarell finally lost it with a double fault.

By now the match was rather like the end of a marathon. Bruce Tulloh, having run across America, can hardly have looked more exhausted than Gonzales at the start of the last set. Time and again he leant on his racket. He regarded every good shot that Pasarell hit with a kind of dismal death's-head face.

The fascinating thing at this point was to see that both men were still capable of using every possible variation of service—spin, flow, short, deep, fast, cut, angle, or straight—to suit the situation, and in the rallies they were stroking the ball rather than hitting it. If bodies were tiring, brains were still alert. At 4-5, after three tired points, Gonzales was 0-40 on his service and Pasarell was beginning to lob again. But two lobs went inches out, and Gonzales saved his third match point with a centre line service. This agonising game went to deuce seven times.

At 5-6 he was down at 0-40 again and the crowd became wilder as, with a smash, a sweetly angled volley, and a service, he destroyed every one of Pasarell's chances. Could he last any longer? All the time Pasarell seemed to be getting closer. He missed his seventh match point at 8-7 when he lobbed out.

By this time it looked as though Gonzales could only serve. When Pasarell served, the older man seemed to have lost control of his racket. Yet suddenly he used his last reserves of energy. Pasarell cracked, and lost 11 successive points for the match. To Wimbledon, Gonzales has always been a world champion by repute. His great matches have been played elsewhere. Yesterday he showed the centre court what it has missed in the years when he had been unable to play there.

DAVID GRAY

Bernac's master class

Apart from the confessional, dentistry and psychoanalysis, the teaching of singing must be one of the most private and taxing of all practices. The voice (as we learn when films are dubbed into other languages) is the essence of the person. This fashion for master classes before an audience may well disconcert the nervous: like those pregnant or delivered ladies who write complaining about Commonwealth trainees in teaching hospitals. But the wonder is that pupils are so devoted they will accept the ordeal with gratitude: that is how musicians are.

Pierre Bernac—a wonderful interpreter of Gounod, Poulenc and all in between, well remembered here—is over in London giving master classes for some days. The last is at Wigmore Hall on Thursday. There was one last night at the British Institute of Recorded Sound (which is a name which would have pleased Macbeth and has its home in 29 Exhibition Road, SW 7). 'Exhibition' is of the essence. A plucky young person in pink essays Duparc's song 'Phidylé,' which probably needs a whole series of broken hearts behind you and a degree in literature at the Sorbonne to get into focus. Mr Bernac compliments, urges the correct pronunciation of the last syllable ('of recorded time,' adds Macbeth) and chides the singer for singing 'soor' when she ought to sing 'sur.' (But will she ever make that French 'u'—how are we to know?)

He who can does: he who cannot teaches, says the glib Shaw. But no one teaches like the man who could once but 'can' no longer. Bernac's singing even now sounded, if slightly tremulous, so authentic that one wished he would chime in more often. There's a way of teaching which is simply twisting a wrist into the right position. It was all very interesting and the 'victims' were splendidly game (if that old silly word is allowed).

PHILIP HOPE-WALLACE

Stage fright

Vanessa Redgrave is returning to the stage for the world première of *Daniel Deronda* by George Eliot at the University Theatre, Manchester, after three years of making films such as *Camelot* and *Isadora*. In doing so, she will be conquering a fear of the stage which has held her since she played Jean Brodie.

Watching Miss Redgrave rehearse one readily understands her saying she has 'the kind of physique that lends itself to demanding attention.' Her six foot, bone simple figure was intensified by having an uncompromisingly taut shawl swaddled over it; her dark blonde hair is dragged harshly back from her face, her eyes obscured by thick little gold-rimmed glasses. No make-up is allowed to soften or colour the effect which is impressively stark.

Members of the acting profession almost invariably possess a kind of ready-to-wear public persona, the image which they assume for interviews and personal appearances. But Miss Redgrave strikes no attitude, makes no jokes, tells no illustrative anecdotes about or against herself. Rather she is remote, reflective to the point of being abstracted, and probably an extremely honest woman because of it.

It had been an enormous decision, she said, to come back into the theatre, and after three years' absence she seemed to want to explain why it was that she had this fear.

'Jean Brodie absolutely terrified me. She split me up because of the kind of part it was. I had worked on it in the way in which I don't usually work—really out of necessity. I had to construct the entire part round the outside with me somewhere lost in the middle and I *did* construct it with great difficulty and time. I constructed an absolutely perfect façade. There wasn't a hole in it anywhere . . . the gestures, the voice, and when I finally got there I was thrilled by it. I got a great kick out of turning her on, which isn't the way I work at all.

'It wasn't done perfunctorily but it ran like a machine. I had constructed a perfect machine which ran perfectly. No, I wasn't appalled by it, rather pleased with myself because I had thought desperately that I wouldn't be able to do it. Indeed I tried to back out three days before it opened because when it came to it I thought it was a very bad play. I didn't believe in it at all but there was a certain pride in forcing oneself to work in something which one didn't feel any inner impulse to do.

'I lost myself in a very literal sense in the part and one night about six weeks before I was due to come off I was just split right open with panic. It took the form of my being terrified I would forget all my words. It happened just before I went on and that fear never left me until I had finished, not for one second. My great fear was that I would actually go mad on stage.

'I CAN just about laugh about it now but it was horrible then; being completely lost like a horrible little satellite having to go round in space until it got the word to come down.

'It frightened me so much that had I not had the film of *Camelot* lined up I don't know what I would have done. I had such a total fear of the stage that I couldn't even bear to go into a theatre unless I knew that the actors were going to be brilliant.

'I've never had a terrible physical thing happen to me like being burned, but this gave me what I imagine to be a similar kind of reaction in not daring to do something again. And it has taken a long time to get over this.

'It was only Michael Elliott who could have made me want to come back into the theatre and I shouldn't ever now want to work in it again unless it was with someone whom I know, like Michael.' (Michael Elliott, who is directing her in *Daniel Deronda*, also directed her as Rosalind in *As You Like It* at Stratford in 1960.)

'Michael is the only person with whom I felt safe to make myself go through what I feared to be an absolutely equivalent situation—because of him and because *Daniel Deronda* is a play that has a deep centre and because anything that grows will come from that centre. It is not constructed work, which I must never do again.'

MISS REDGRAVE thinks she is only just rediscovering why she wants to act—'I always wanted to act because I wanted to make believe . . . and the plays one was lucky enough to do all had a kernel of something beyond oneself that one aspires to but falls short of. You have to know why you are acting or you are just doing it to show yourself off. Previously I was never afraid, acting, because I loved it so much I wanted to share it. But in Jean Brodie I grew to hate the audience because I thought they would be the witnesses to my downfall.

'When I started on this play I found the old fears came pouring back but I told Michael Elliott everything and we talked it over, and more positively, we talked about taking your centre from the centre of the play and it growing outwards and then it being inevitable that you want to reach it out to the people who are watching it . . . and that way fear goes because fear is fear of oneself.'

She says that for a long time now she has been interested in work that involves the body to a greater extent, with words having less importance. 'Usually the script is constructed on words. Perhaps, stretching it very far, you could do a whole play without saying any words at all. Not because you mime but because you would have group movement or individual movement as expression: words will come perhaps, when only words will do. Peter Brook does quite a lot of movement, and although I approve enormously of any work in this direction I don't think his goal is high enough. There was a bit of mime movement in *Royal Hunt of the Sun* but that was pathetic.

'With the part of Gwendoline in this play I want my body to show things about her that my face and voice won't do, perhaps because that is what one can do on the stage. I think, oddly, that television is the place for the word. The theatre, as I see it, is the place for the body . . .'

Until Manchester, she has always taken her three- and five-year-old daughters with her when she was working but feels that this is such a turning point in her life that she is actually glad to be a bit alone and not to have her mind split with other preoccupations. Divorced from Tony Richardson she finds it difficult being mother and father.

'Difficult in the sense that one very much wishes to talk to someone else about the things that go on in the house and about the children, to discuss them in that way with someone who has an equal involvement. That is the problem of being a working ex-wife.

'The working mother problems are one's own of remorse and guilt and worry that the children should lack anything because I am so absorbed in my work. It is difficult at the moment. The children are involved in my work in an ambivalent way—they are enchanted and fascinated by it all but at the same time there is something they dislike very much about my work. If I ever start acting or dancing at home they tell me to stop it, because it overshadows them; it presses very strongly on them. They expect me to watch them when I am at home.

'Actually, truthfully, I'm glad I haven't got them at the moment.'

CATHERINE STOTT

Barrault girls

Jean-Louis Barrault arrived at the Old Vic yesterday, dwarfed by his burly administrator, Monsieur Leonard, by his long, brown silk scarf, and by Laurence Olivier's blue Rolls-Royce, to survey the scene for his production of *Rabelais* in the autumn.

The show has been an enormous success in Paris, playing to more than 110,000 (mostly young) people in a boxing and wrestling arena in Montmartre. Barrault was in London to discuss details with the National Theatre's Frank Dunlop (a gallant interpreter) and consider necessary adjustments to the stage for his production. In the Montmartre sports palace there is plenty of room for the audience to stand and wander, and Barrault is hoping for the same over here to give it the fairground atmosphere.

The production has a couple of wrestlers and a troupe of girls from the Crazy Horse Saloon—all promised for London. 'They are very interested and excited to play in London, which is famous for its beautiful girls,' he said. 'It will be a great . . .'

'Challenge,' said Frank Dunlop.

'This is a very important thing for us,' Barrault said. 'It was under the auspicies of Larry that we first came over here in 1951 to the St James's Theatre. Since then there has been great great love between Laurence Olivier and us. It was a symbolic act to invite us.' Olivier was one of the first to protest when Malraux dismissed Barrault from the Théatre de France last year after his observations on the May revolution.

Rabelais, said Barrault, was 'The modern mind throughout the ages,' a linguist, the representation of the Renaissance spirit. He dissected corpses when it was forbidden by the Roman Catholic Church: 'he had the sort of mind of Dr Barnard.' And, finally: 'He was an evangelist anarchist.'

What other plans does Barrault have? Something to do with the problems and ideas of young people, he hinted. But he is in no hurry. 'I am keeping my eyes open and my ears . . .'

'Cocked,' said Frank Dunlop.

MISCELLANY

Soaked in the actor's art

Wilfrid Lawson, as everybody knows, was an actor whose career was destroyed by drink—or perhaps it would be better to say that he was a drinker with a genius for acting, to which he brought the pity and terror of his condition. I don't know why he drank or indeed how much (when I met him it only needed a pint or so to inflame the alcohol already in his system) and these are merely piecemeal reminiscences of the two occasions on which I worked with him. One was my first television play in the early spring of 1960, when Wilfrid's face was the familiar squinting stubbly battlefield, and his voice had all its wheedling, roaring mannerisms (some due to the fact that the drink had destroyed his control over them); physically, although he was a bit hunched and shambling, he exuded enormous strength and cunning. He swayed a bit, and would turn his head slowly and erratically. He was dangerous. He could destroy a rehearsal in two minutes, and several times did so.

Our floor manager, a chunky, rolling little man named Bobby Ash, had been a circus acrobat, and Wilfrid liked him and would go more or less quietly, but it was still impossible to work with him in the afternoons. One drink at lunchtime would shatter his timing and so he would clown about and try to shatter everybody else.

One day as he was leaving about noon he swept me with him and took me to the pub (where all the old men knew him—I suppose they must have seen his Doolittle in the film *Pygmalion*) and told me very gently what was wrong with the play. He asked me what actors I liked and told me in a rambling fashion about his days in North Country rep and how he came to London. He said that his Antony had been a humiliating disaster and that he had always believed that he would be a great actor when the London critics called him one. They never did. They used every flattering word but never actually said that he was great. I was too young and too afraid of him to remember more. My play itself was a portentous effort in which an unhappy wife threw herself in the canal but was rescued and taken to the police station where she met Wilfrid, a tramp trying to get arrested because he'd nowhere to sleep. He did one marvellous thing when, talking about suicide, he drew out the 's' of 'gas' so that it was like the hissing of the tap. The final shot was of him walking away to the cells.

On the dress rehearsal he allowed his trousers to fall down as he walked, an effect that we should have had the courage and humour to retain because it was a classic Wilfrid comment—on the solemnity of the play, on himself, and on the character he was playing. He then went out and had a drink (which marred his actual performance) and when he returned there took place the legendary confrontation in which the Granada commissionaire refused to admit him on the grounds that he was a drunken tramp. Bobby Ash had to go to the rescue.

Five years later, in the summer of 1965, I worked with the same director (Herbert Wise) on a large historical piece called *The Siege of Manchester*, which had many flaws in construction but some virtues in characterisation, among them a one-scene cameo written with Wilfrid in mind of an old Puritan preacher who exhorted parliamentary soldiers at their barricades. He was frightened of the bombardment and wet himself, yet still continued to preach about Christ being an ordinary working man. One hoped that Wilfrid would transform it with his humour, his rhetoric and his sudden crazed illumination of worlds that most of us never see, and so he did. He brought also his rebelliousness, and the tenderness that in such a ruined man was always most moving. He brought echoes of the chapel preachers of his childhood, and (what one could not have known) he brought his nearness to death; for although he subsequently played the dormouse in *Alice*, this preacher was the last classic Wilfrid Lawson part of his life.

He had aged very much. He was thin and round-shouldered. The terrible danger in his eye had become a flicker of mischief. His breathing was difficult but he was sober and in his good moments sprightly. There was now an accepted clause in his contracts that a car (always referred to by Wilfrid as 'the ambulance') brought him to rehearsal and took him home as soon as his bit was finished. One morning he lured the driver indoors for a drink and they never reappeared but apart from that he was well-behaved. I think he was too tired to be otherwise, which is not to say that he did not continue to polish his bitterly comic portrayal of Wilfrid Lawson, the actor too difficult to work with.

One day at the studios a make-up woman had her handbag and jewellery stolen. Wilfrid waited in the chair, protective sheet round his shoulders, his tragic face in the mirror, while instead of making him up she recounted her loss. The trinkets brought a tearful crescendo. 'My mother gave them to me on her deathbed.' Wilfrid could stomach no more. 'Don't worry about her,' he groaned, 'worry about me.' That was one's last glimpse of the old Wilfrid. For the rest he had the energy only to act, and he would appear for a few minutes every other morning or so.

We were rehearsing in a drill hall in South London. It was difficult to work in because there was a bad echo and sun came boiling through the skylights. There were various rooms off, one with coffee and pin tables, and since the play had a large cast in short scenes the actors soon got bored and the ones not actually working spent their time in the side room. When Wilfrid appeared they would drift in to watch him, not just once out of curiosity, but regularly, every time he rehearsed. The extras to whom he preached his sermon were only hired for the studio days so in one sense he worked alone, but in another there was always a lounging crowd. He had one piece of business where his hat fell off during the bombardment and he had to walk back to pick it up. For the hat he used his spectacle case, and the way in which he contrived to jerk it out of his top pocket showed the mastery of a lifetime. Occasionally he'd stop and say 'no,' and hold his head in his hands and the director would say: 'What's wrong?' Wilfrid would say: 'It's not . . .' and wave his arms, and the director would say: 'Show me.' Wilfrid would then produce a gesture, or a new way of saying the line. His instinct was so true that he would know almost at once. If his idea was wrong he would shake his head like a boxer who has taken a punch, but if it felt natural he would nod decisively. Then he'd take a deep, wheezing breath and mumble his way into the scene again.

He would suddenly alter words, with great delicacy of meaning, smiling at me, and one moment he'd make you laugh and the next make your scalp tingle as he talked of Jesus and looked up at the drill hall skylight. Then he would finish and shamble right out of his acting area, still muttering, and throw off the odd comic line and inquire about the ambulance. His form was uneven, I suppose, and in the actual recording he was too tired to hit his peak. Things went raggedly. He got in the wrong position for the cameras so that you couldn't see his face all the time, but when you did the magic worked again.

There are very few living English actors as great as Wilfrid was (and by great I mean a comparable ability to illuminate life) and if one of them, the golden Ernest Milton, has been scandalously neglected, at least there is the air of a grand seigneur about him. The others are rich, knighted and famous. Wilfrid was scruffy, humble, and disreputable, and the almost casual homage of the actors who watched him in the rehearsal room was of the sort that fame cannot command nor pomp envisage, for they came not to praise him, but to gaze with gratitude upon the mystery of their art, and to have their pride in it renewed.

KEITH DEWHURST

The drama of talking heads

For the writer one of the assets of television is the size of the audience. David Mercer, speaking in 1962, said 'the living reality of a 12 million audience is absolutely compelling. How can one not want passionately to write for it?' But that audience sees only one performance. The heartbreak of television writing is in this evanescence. An Equity agreement prevents repeats even of award-winning plays after two years. Out of nine of Mercer's BBC plays, four of the video tapes have already been wiped—a saving of £117 from budgets of £10,000 upwards. 'No one has ever let me know they are about to go, or offered me the chance of paying for a private print. Obviously they have to safeguard their copyrights, but at least one might keep some private record of all that work. With *A Suitable Case for Treatment* they had wiped it within days and then found they'd got an award on their hands.'

'What's important to me about writing for television, is that it is a very psychologically intense medium, or it can be, and it will bear a much much more solid text. I know there has been for years a whole school of television directors who oppose the idea of words and so on. But to me this is an arbitrary dispute. What is going to determine the course of television, or the theatre, or films, is the best of what is actually being written: I think things begin with the writer. You have a kind of visual flexibility in television which you can combine with a solid text, which produces something very different from film. But it isn't necessarily a defining difference. There are also people who write television plays which are more like film than anything else. But I think some of the best television drama that's been made is "talking heads." Television drama allows a writer to explore words and relationships and confrontations in a much more profound way than is permitted in film.

'In the case of my own plays I think the BBC have been quite courageous. They've done plays which wouldn't have been done on commercial television or as films. The very first play that I wrote, *Where the Difference Begins*, which was about socialism, as it happened was quite successful with all sorts of classes, and the BBC said in effect "what you write we'll do." They've kept that promise, they've never turned down a play of mine, and I've stayed in television drama because of this freedom. What I write for the BBC usually goes onto the screen, with the exception of a word here and there, out of their silly censoring. That varies, depending on how much pressure there is on the Board of Governors at any one time.'

David Mercer has just come back from the Soviet Union, and has also visited Cuba and Czechoslovakia this year. His political commitment has been one of the main themes of his writing. 'But I think it's becoming less important for me as a writer. Political commitment is not something that I'm concerned with in the foreground of my preoccupations as a writer, and I think that in those plays where it was very overt, it was probably a defect not a virtue.

'*On the Eve of Publication* does still contain a lot which really belongs to me as a committed person. It's a play about death and memory, and the central old man reveals himself in political terms. He's asking: "What did we ever give the young but cynicism and pessimism really?" Because everything that's attempted is so visibly a perversion and deformation of social endeavour. It's a rather sad, valedictory play I suppose. But there is a real connection between things that I have felt as someone politically involved and as a human being. It might be the last instance of this sort of thing in my work, something I've attempted in different ways three or four times, like the trilogy, and *Morgan, A Suitable Case for Treatment. Morgan* did have a kind of popular success, which means it says less to more people. It exemplifies the choice really: to do that or, to be like Bergman, say, and spend one's life saying a great deal to a very few people.'

Writing for films is more precarious than for television. David Mercer is writing a script for Losey now, after doing an adaptation of *Women in Love*: 'A huge job which has since been put away, one of those abysmal film industry experiences that happen to everyone. You feel your life drifting past doing all this film work and you have to ask "What the hell does it all mean if they're not going to get made?"

'There's one clear reason: producers want serious and established writers, they want the best writers, and the kind of work they get from the best writers turns their hair white. They all tell themselves fairy stories, like the old one "you can be art and be commercial." But the fact is that if you want to write a film that is art, for want of a better word, as like as not you won't get it made. One first step would be to clamour for some genuine national British film industry. Of course the Americans are to some extent pulling out of Britain now, they've cut their investment by 25 per cent, they're very nervous about investing in what they themselves blew up into "the Renaissance of the British cinema."

'From the point of view of American backers, what a good writer produces is either too obscure or too exacting for a mass audience; or the subject is something they can't take, true to life or no. Quite recently an American producer said to me—apropos of a script in which a man commits a gratuitous killing and gets away with it—that he didn't think that in America in 1968 he could get away with a film in which a man gets away with murder. And he didn't like it when I said that, actually, there seem to be quite a lot of people getting away with murder in America this year.'

STACY WADDY

The real thing

Sir,—In the articles and discussions I have seen on the topic of public copulation as art form I have not seen any mention of the fact that (so far as I am aware) the last recorded examples of this kind of realism come from Roman civilisation. When Nero had the *Pasiphae* performed, and when Heliogabalus acted as his own stage-manager, the actors (who were, of course, slaves) had to perform acts of adultery on the stage ('in mimicis adulteriis, ea quae solent simulatio fierie effici ad verum iussit'—i.e., no pretence about it this time).

It is perhaps curious that playwrights, producers, and critics of our time who mostly hold the same standard Left-wing progressive views as the writer of 'How far is far enough' appear not to be aware of possible implications for the wage-slavery of members of the acting profession.

The argument may be carried one stage further. In 53 BC Crassus, a colleague of Caesar and Pompey, was killed in Syria. Greek strolling players happened to be acting the *Bacchae* at the time; and used Crassus's head for Pentheus's, to celebrate the Greek victory over the Romans. Of course, Crassus was already dead, so did not need to be decapitated on the stage. But Domitian took the logical next step, and had a mime devised to include a genuine crucifixion.

If the interests of realism require genuine sperm,—why not genuine blood?—Yours truly,

(Rev. Fr.) MARTIN JARRET-KERR,
Hostel of the Resurrection,
Springfield Mt.
Leeds.

Sir,—May I suggest that the National Theatre shortly stage a production of *Hamlet*, Mr Kenneth Tynan be cast as Polonius, and, in the interests of realism, he be run through with sharp sword while hiding behind the arras at Act III, Scene iv, Line 25. —Yours faithfully,

JOHN R. DAVIDSON

Flat 9,
6 Elvaston Place,
London, SW 7.

Games people play

This is in some sense a serious novel about obscene behaviour and decadent people, but I'm afraid it is also an obscene and decadent novel. *Couples* by John Updike (Deutsch, 30s). It describes a year's activities, from spring 1963 to spring 1964, of a circle of upper middle-class couples in Tarbox, a town near Boston. They give parties all the time, play various games with each other, talk sex to each other and then act it out, betray each other and themselves to each other.

There is much religious symbolism— a five-foot cock on the steeple of the Congregational church dominating the town, which burns down at the end of the novel—a symbol relevant to the naturalistic and sociological reading of the story; because for these couples sex is a cult, and pleasure is an ethic. Freddie Thorne, the town's dentist and the cult's priest, a Tiresias figure, says that they are a sect like the early Christians, only they are trying to break *into* a hedonistic Eden, instead of the reverse. And the main action is the driving out of the circle of Piet Hanema, the only naturally erotic man there, the saint and scapegoat of the cult. But the novel is a comedy, and he is not only driven out, he also escapes. He not only loses the wife and children he loves, he also wins a new, more dangerous, more heroic erotic partner.

Because this is the subject of the novel, its method also is naturally obscene. Many sexual scenes, involving many kinds of sexual activity, are described in great detail; everyone's personality is presented in terms of his body, and his body is seen as sexual object and agent; while their talk is full of references to body functions, both literal and pornographic-fantastic. One visualises each figure as a constellation of enlarged body orifices.

This alone would make one call the novel obscene, even if it were as serious as *The Golden Notebook*, as brilliant as *Lolita*. I mean I would have to call both of those obscene, even though I think so highly of them. A society as decadent as ours, in these social and sexual areas, forces its artists to deal with the obscene. It is our truth. But Updike's book is obscene in two more ways.

First, in the fairly technical sense that it profanes what it holds sacred; it makes sex the source of all meaning but itself meaningless, the source of all beauty but itself ugly, and so on. Secondly, in the large sense that the obsessive interest in sex corrupts the author's taste, enfeebles his artistic control—that it is a decadent novel too.

I hope I am not being stupidly moralistic. I can see that the novel intends to be serious. It is artistically ambitious, and I have always thought Updike a remarkably gifted writer—in some ways the most *gifted* writer on the scene. His narrative tricks, his games with imagery, his connoisseurship with language, are dazzling; and he describes human behaviour like someone who understands it. And the subject is certainly a serious one. Such circles do exist in our society: they are both religiously and pornographically erotic: and, our artists must face this for us. Moreover, Updike's picture of their manners and motives is convincing and informative. It is not a book to be read without profit.

What goes wrong in the writing is what goes wrong in the life described. Sexuality becomes an obsession. Every other interest —political, moral, aesthetic—becomes an aspect of sexuality, and seems a disguise for, an evasion of, the real issue. Mr Updike is an intelligent and serious man, but the expressions of that in the book are all undermined by the imminent expectation of more pornography. Kennedy's career, for instance, is used ingeniously as a point of reference for the group; and the book does say something about the Kennedy era; but the assassination as it occurs in their lives is quite emptied of its significance—I mean the novel does not lead you back to that significance. Piet Hanema is another Oliver Mellors, but Updike's sexuality has nothing in common with Lawrence's. It is sexual *curiosity* which is the dominant motive here—the itch to keep your eyes open just when other people's naturally close—and the author's long curving nose, photographed on the back of the cover, can be seen, lifted, sniffing, between the lines of every page.

A British author with whom Updike does have something in common is Anthony Burgess. Both men are quite extraordinarily gifted, and notably ventriloquial. It is always easy for them to let their favourite author (Joyce) take over their pens. And though both are intellectuals, seriosly troubled by problems of religion and ethics, neither can save his voice from ringing badly false on such subjects. But whereas Burgess (polarised perhaps by Amis) has worked out an intricately self-deprecating aesthetic, mocking his own ambitions and diminishing his own gifts even in employing them, Updike (like Salinger) swells himself out to include everything, aims at the highest marks against all sensations of self-doubt.

Let no one think that this is—for a WASP writer today—an easy and natural thing to do in America. But clearly this difference between the two writers *does* relate to the difference between the two cultures. It makes the reader realise which side of the Atlantic he belongs to.

MARTIN GREEN

The distant smile of JPD

It's a long time now since that first Donleavy hero poked among his landlady's most private toilet articles in pursuit of 'Mum for the pits.' The Ginger Man was no barbarian: he sought for himself a personal elegance that down the years has become increasingly refined in his successors and appears to have achieved purity in the person of Balthazar B.*

Born in Paris of 'a mother blonde and beautiful,' educated principally at an English preparatory school and in the bed of his governess, Balthazar smiles distantly on the world that the rest of us occupy. He is rich: money floats to him through a firm of solicitors known as Bother, Kritson, Horn, Pleader and Hoot. He does what he likes: he occupies himself with the governess at the age of 12, he chooses that pleasantly undemanding academy, Trinity College, Dublin, as a suitable loitering place from which to attend local racecourses and the beds of local girls. He has the good fortune to have a faithful friend, Beefy, whose passion for the flesh mirrors his own. In London Balthazar marries voluptuous Millicent, is left, finds solace with French Alphonsine; while Beefy settles for Angelica Violet Infanta.

The novel is haunted by the same surrealist mood that turned *Fairy Tales of New York* into a memorable theatrical entertainment. Outrageous yet credible, Donleavy's writing is technically ingenious. He is a master of exaggeration; he can whip together fact and fantasy; he can imbue smut with charm. I recommend his new novel, but I must add that his capabilities are not always apparent in it and that it never actually becomes as fascinating as constantly it promises to be. It's the sort of book that slips into the comic novel category, yet it doesn't make you laugh. Wit is there in profusion, but funniness is stifled by prose like this:

'Balthazar B. in Manx checked tweed. Cream silk shirted and dark tied as one's tutor. With the antique links of one diamond

THE BEASTLY BEATITUDES OF BALTHAZAR B, by J. P. Donleavy (Eyre and Spottiswoode, 35s).

set in mother of pearl laid in gold to join cuffs. Hold the socks against the turf embers. The steam rises.'

Even at its most frolicsome, the going tends to be hard, and different levels of writing occasionally cancel one another out. At the end of each chapter there's a poetic summing-up, such as: 'Hello/Now/To any/Wondrous/Little Men' or 'Under/The wild/Hair/Of the trees.'

But Uncle Edouard in Paris, English nannies wheeling out to the Bois and cane-carrying heroes gazing at the ceilings of the Ritz bring to mind a very different kind of writer. One is left in the end with the bizarre conclusion that if Nancy Mitford and Joyce had collaborated the result might have been quite a little like the adventures of Beefy and Balthazar B. The mixture may not be to everyone's taste and the unevenness and difficulties of the book may irritate, but there can be no denying that at his best J. P. Donleavy is a very brilliant performer indeed. Here and there among these Beastly Beatitudes there's just enough evidence to prove it all over again.

WILLIAM TREVOR

The d'Oliveira decision

M C C have never made a sadder, more dramatic, or potentially more damaging decision than in omitting d'Oliveira from their team to tour South Africa. Fifteen players have been named. The sixteenth will be a bowler. Jeff Jones of Glamorgan, if he is demonstrably fit after an operation on an elbow. If he is not, Higgs will probably be offered the place.

There is no case for leaving out d'Oliveira on cricketing grounds. Since the last M C C tour in South Africa, Test pitches have become grassy, ideal for seam bowlers, of whom South Africa deploy five. So England's tactical need is for a Test class batsman who is a reliable bowler at medium-pace, or above, to make the fourth seam bowler: only d'Oliveira, of our current players, meets that demand. He was top of the English batting averages in the series against Australia just completed, and second in the bowling. The latter may seem a statistical quibble, but when he bowled Jarman on Tuesday he made the break-through which brought England their close win in the fifth Test.

He is a useful, if not great, fieldsman at slip or in the deep. Decisively, to the objective observer, he has the temperament to rise to the challenge of an occasion, as he proved against the West Indian fast bowlers, and in both his matches against Australia this summer. His behaviour in what might have been difficult situations has always been impeccably dignified and courteous.

If politics, in their fullest sense, now transcend cricket in importance, it might have been wiser to take d'Oliveira to South Africa though he were not good enough, than to leave him at home when he is not merely good enough but eminently suited for the tactical situation the side will face.

In the first place, no one of open mind will believe that he was left out for valid cricket reasons: there are figures and performances less than a week old— including a century yesterday— to refute such an argument. This may prove, perhaps to the surprise of M C C, far more than a sporting matter. It could have such repercussions on British relations with the coloured races of the world that the cancellation of a cricket tour would seem a trifling matter compared with an apparent British acceptance of apartheid. This was a case where justice had to be seen to be done.

Secondly, within a few years, the British-born children of West Indian, Indian, Pakistani and African immigrants will be worth places in English county and national teams. It seems hard to discourage them now, for, however the M C C's case may be argued, the club's ultimate decision must be a complete deterrent to any young coloured cricketer in this country.

The final thought on it, however, must be one of sadness and that in the selection the M C C have stirred forces—for both good and evil—whose powers they do not truly comprehend.

JOHN ARLOTT

Cricket still needs Colin Milburn

That Colin Milburn should lose an eye is as savagely ironic as his immediate assertion that he will bat again is characteristic. To take his eye is akin to robbing a sculptor of a hand for he has always been predominantly a batsman of the eye, picking up the line of the ball so early that he can formulate an attacking stroke while others are still preoccupied with identification.

This capacity, physical and mental, for quick decision established him, from the day he went from school in Durham to score 100 against the Indian touring side of 1959, as potentially the most exciting batsman in English cricket these many years. He has realised that promise in full. He has the strength of a vast trunk and forearms, yet many of his most vivid strokes stem unforced from his intuitive sense of timing.

The incidence of the accident is almost as tragic as the result. Left out of the M C C team for last winter's tour by the selectors' endemic tendency to pick match-savers instead of match-winners, he went to play for Western Australia. His batting, which made him as popular there as he is in Northants, and his dramatically splendid late entry on to the unhappy scene in Pakistan with a century in the Karachi Test had, surely, established his footing in the England team beyond argument.

Earlier disappointed at being dropped from the Test side and concerned for his financial future, he had considered emigrating to Australia—'where they don't think it is a crime to weigh 18 stone.'

Last Thursday night, over dinner, he was emphatic that he wanted to remain in England. When I left him on Friday he knew he would be made secure to do so. Five hours later he crashed.

Cricket needs Colin Milburn as much as he needs it. In a day when spectators conspicuously stay away from cricket, they will travel and pay to watch him. A batsman of simple might, when he asserted command against Australia or West Indies, the finest out-cricket in the world could not check him, and he played the fastest bowling with huge relish.

Then, as he took a match in his hands and by vivid power reshaped it according to his own unique designs, he lifted the heart as perhaps no other batsman has ever done. Add to this his sense of fun, his modesty, his courage, and the steady depth of his friendship, and you have not simply a cricketer to admire but a man to enjoy.

He has said he will bat again, and there is no doubt that he will be in a net as soon as he can reach one. His problems of adjustment will be profound.

The focusing and assessment of a moving object is a two-eyed process: anyone whose left, or normal leading eye, has been lost has to alter his stance and his whole reaction pattern to sight the ball. 'Buster' Nupen, of South Africa, had only one eye but, although he was no great batsman, he judged the ball well in the field; and the Nawab of Pataudi has played outstanding innings at Test level since he lost virtually the entire sight of his right eye, also in a car accident.

If courage and possession of all the necessary supporting gifts can overcome the greatest handicap that can be imposed on a batsman, Colin Milburn will bat again; and everyone who has ever watched him play will hope that it may be so.

JOHN ARLOTT

The smell of an Englishman

Not long ago a group of Americans met to discuss a forthcoming Anglo-American project in which they were to take part. One of the more unusual bits of information they got was that although they could expect to find their British associates academically their equal, they should be prepared to find a high proportion of them careless in their personal hygiene.

As a British immigrant to the United States long before the brain drain, I must have been considered Americanised enough to be brought into the broader discussion which followed. The Americans themselves could be placed in three categories: those with little or no previous contact with the British who were shocked; those who had, and wryly agreed with the accusation; and one or two confirmed anglophobes.

This last class I had encountered before, and on the same subject. One of them related a story about British technicians on exchange in America who, on their first day, had been issued with company overalls. They had continued to wear these every day, ignoring the fact that their co-workers dumped theirs in the laundry-bin at the end of the shift, and drew fresh ones the following morning. Only when the grimy garments were quietly disposed of one evening after their owners' departure, did the message get through. The survival and repetition of stories grotesque as this—or mildly amusing as the one about the Englishman who was told that good soup could be made with his neck-tie—is a measure of American astonishment at the faintest hint of what is an undeniable truth to anyone familiar with both societies, that the British are indeed far less fastidious in their personal hygiene.

The American, white-collar or blue, regards as his birthright a daily bath or shower and clean underwear every morning. Another shower before even the most humble evening activity is the rule rather than the exception. On a more basic note, when away from home he can be seen to move from the urinal to the washbasin as instinctively as the Englishman moves to the exit.

If the British regarded American toilet practices enviously, denied to them only through lack of adequately heated homes and unlimited hot water, it should follow that new arrivals to America would be quick to indulge themselves in these commonplace luxuries. There's little to show that they do, and far from rare is the man who contends that there's something psychologically unhealthy about the American 'obsession' with cleanliness. True, the abrupt rise in the standard of living soon permits a clean shirt daily, but so often it will be with a suit worn far too long. (The number of times an American sends a suit to the cleaners in the space of a year is astonishing.)

But the greatest affront, in a society grown super-sensitive through sheer unfamiliarity with it, is a level of body odour which must pass unnoticed in Britain. Unnoticed, that is, until you've been away and returned. The joy of being in London again aside, I found travelling by the Underground last summer a much nastier experience than using American public transport when the temperature is in the nineties. The persistence of this particular problem is baffling, unless there's something to the theory that the offender is so permanently engulfed in his own under-arm aura that he is unaware of being different. It's a pity for there's a New World just an arm's length away.

PETER RUSSELL

Sir,—'The smell of an English*man*.' I was delighted with the title, and more so to find that the writer meant just that.

I am a female manager of men and have been totally amazed to find how big a problem this is. The majority of females are aware of the possibility of body odour and take the necessary precautions but in my experience most men would not know what you meant even if you mentioned it.

Recently, a medical examination was arranged for male members of the staff and on the appointed day a great commotion arose because one chap thought it was the following day and refused to see the doctor. When I asked him what difference it made, he replied: 'I would have had a bath and changed my underwear if I'd known.'

Female Manager

Lancashire.

Sir,—A Wigan teacher is reported to have sent a boy home because of his smell. The boy's mother sent her this note. 'Dear Miss, our Johnny smells the same as his dad, and his dad smells lovely. I should know. I've slept with him for 25 years. The trouble with you, Miss, is that you're an old maid and don't know what a proper man smells like.'—Yours sincerely,

Mary McLean

7 Lilac Grove,
Billinge, Wigan.

M. et Mme Clochard

It was one evening about halfway through last month that I first noticed the old man and the old woman encamped in the doorway of the Uniprix Store, in the Rue de Rennes.

On the pavement in front of them was a disintegrating cap, into which nobody had put less than a franc. One got the idea that the old man had himself put in the first franc by way of a pot egg, and that, faced by his flashing eye and majestic Assyrian beard, no passer-by had dared to fall below the expected standard. Apart from that, there was nothing remarkable about them, except, perhaps, that they were slightly off the usual beat for their kind.

Tramps, or 'clochards,' are a familiar enough sight in Paris, though they do not often go about in couples. One school of thought looks upon them as part of the local folklore. Another regards them simply as vermin, reproaching the police for not clearing them off the streets, but neither knowing nor caring where they would be cleared to. It is not unknown, if one of them, a bit more sodden than usual, falls, and damages himself, to hear voices saying: 'There's no point in ringing for an ambulance to take him to hospital. He's brought it on himself, and he'll only go and do the same thing again.'

The police handle the problem with a good deal of practical sense. They make a daily round-up of tramps, whom they take to the Departmental Institution at Nanterre for a kind of sorting operation. At the end of it, some appear before the magistrates for begging or vagrancy, some are persuaded to enter the institution permanently, and some are sent to hospital.

When the cold nights set in, the police run a salvage service, collecting the clochards, who are sleeping rough in conditions that might be fatal, and putting them into Nanterre temporarily. Last winter, mild as it was, they rescued 528 men and 152 women that way. For the rest, the average agent has a blind eye for the

clochard who has settled over a warm grating and is giving no
trouble to anybody.

The old man and the old woman had at their disposal one of
the biggest and hottest gratings in that part of Paris. The next
evening they were there again, and the one after that. Occasionally, during the day, I would see them about the Quartier, usually
separately, she with a shopping bag, he marching somewhere unknown with a more purposeful stride than the normal clochard's
shuffle.

Early evening, without fail, saw them back at base, in an atmosphere for which it was difficult to find the exact word. Established?
Settled? Dug in? Sometimes now, he wrote in a small notebook.
They chatted a good deal, between sallies, to the passers-by, and
clearly the old woman had a sharp tongue and the old man, imperious as he looked, bent before it. The right word did not come
until, returning home late one night, I saw them fast asleep in the
doorway, huddled together with a spare coat thrown over both of
them. It was domestic.

At the age of more than seventy, in the doorway of a popular
store, with gusts of the warm south coming up through the bars
of the grating in front and, behind, a Christmas glitter of blue
chains and pink baubles, they had set up a home.

NESTA ROBERTS

Back to school 1: the unhappiest days of my life

Down at elegant Eastbourne, salubrious and sunny by the silver
sea, I pace the prom and count the geraniums and lobelias slung
in baskets from dazzling white woodwork. Also, compulsively, I
play the game of 'Beaver,' so popular in the 1920s when beards
were out and rare. Now I count white-haired old dames in pink
cardigans. Already I counted 87—unless I am a little mad. But I
am never myself in Eastbourne. I am rather my little self of eight
years old, a doppelgänger by my side, tearful, bullied, neck chafed

by Eton collar, cap lost (beating in store), on the school walk back to prunes and suet in that hideous red brick mansion in The Meads.

My heart pumps as we foot it up the brick road. In a second—I am taller than I was at eight—I can look over the creosoted fence and see the very same cinder path behind the gym where Smith minor twisted my arm till I shrieked as I hope never to shriek again.

No permissive society, that. You were bullied and beaten and even at night lay awake home-sick listening to the 'acorns' tapping the panes in the salty breeze (all the windows to be open, always). Presently the under-matron came to shake the bed wetters awake and turned up the gas for a minute so that you could see if the dormitory bully were really asleep, in which case it might be safe to sleep oneself. But not always. You might be caught and chained with a bike padlock to a brimming chamber pot and spend the night on your knees beside it. Relenting in the dawn M, who later died splendidly in Normandy, asked why I was 'blubbing.' I am proud to remember I had the guts to lie 'One of my aunts has died.' *That* line worked.

The bed wetters had it bad. A favourite game was to line them up for execution by kicked footballs against the gym wall. Many of the staff were vulnerable, shell-shock cases too. We got on to that quick: as the master turned to the blackboard to write, twenty desk-lids would crash down in unison and he was back on the Somme, gasping and clutching his heart. Dear little things, prep school boys.

I liked the swimming, some of the games (at least I was an accurate score keeper, which meant the twelfth bottle of ginger ale at the end) and of course then cheerfulness as now did keep breaking in. We didn't smoke, had no more than romantic sex but on one Good Friday we crucified a Jew whose super-rich parents were rumoured to stay at The Grand for £1 a day, a fortune in 1920.

I lived then more intensely than ever before or since, every pore open, on the *qui vive* all the time. All character-forming decisions and battles took place in those halls smelling of Mansion polish, confectionery and chalk. Here I bargained with God, begged intercession in vain, learned to love the Bible, chess, John Buchan, and Latin gender-jingles, learned courage too, or at least resignation, when each new recruit to the staff thought of calling me 'hopeless Wallace'—and the turn over, what with buggery and nervous breakdowns, was pretty smart.

Did I learn courage? All I've known. And resource too. I sat out a siege in front of a plate of marmalade pudding for four hours, then packed it in my house shoes and was excused. Shoes later found in cistern, identified by Cash's name tapes. Beating. Chapel was best. Twice a day. 'A noble army, men and boys,' we bawled, 'the matron and the maid,' turning to stare at a florid nursing sister in a green hat which she hoped made her look paler and at Doris the maid, who coloured up rewardingly. Lovely moments, when the harmonium surged under the efforts of Mr Cavanagh (who wheezed in sympathy having been gassed in 1915) when it came to 'For those in peril on the sea.' And there was always 'Lord dismiss us' bliss at term ending, though I often wondered if I'd recognise my parents again after 13 weeks, a long time when you're not yet nine. I guess it is all subjective. Some boys dreaded the 'hols.' But to me they were release from purgatory. I can say, with Hugh Walpole, that nothing ever can be so bad again. Swing on, geraniums, lobelias and white-haired widows. But don't ask me to feel rational in Eastbourne.

PHILIP HOPE-WALLACE

Title: Back to school 2: I am, I can, I ought, I will

I was taught at home by a governess until I was thirteen. Her name was Ethelwyn Flower, which makes her sound mythical, but it was her real name. And although people think of governesses as Victorian, or at least Edwardian, Miss Flower was resolutely up to date until the day she died, last year. She was also decidedly different from the traditional idea of a governess. She was trained at Charlotte Mason's House of Education at Ambleside, where

Parents National Educational Union (PNEU) methods aimed 'to kindle the enthusiasm of childhood—not so much to teach children subjects, as to train in them the seeing eye.'

A PNEU governess was expensive, but I shared Miss Flower with another child who lived near by. Miss Flower came by train each day from the village of Maiden Newton, 13 miles from us on the way to Dorchester—in the Hardy country, as she liked to say. But Thomas Hardy was not in our curriculum. Sir Walter Scott, yes: history as well as landscape, pure romance, and chivalry. Scott was read aloud to us every day after tea, while we did our needlework.

A parcel of books from PNEU headquarters arrived at the beginning of each term. Opening it was as exciting as opening birthday parcels . . . a Shakespeare play, a new Waverley novel, poetry, biography, the intoxicating smell of new books. For 'Picture Study' there was a set of six sepia prints of pictures by the artist of the term. We studied the pictures, 'narrated' them, and then copied them in our drawing books. Finally, we framed the prints with glass and passe-partout.

Every morning we did half an hour's work before Miss Flower arrived—brisk and bracing, middle-aged, tailored costume, cloche hat with a feather pom-pom at one side, big fur tie of strong-smelling skunk. Miss Flower said you could always tell genuine skunk by its smell. In this half-hour before lessons began we learned poetry by heart and every term we acted a whole scene from Shakespeare to our parents. At 11 o'clock there was milk, Petit Beurre biscuits, and the *Daily Mirror*—for current events. The *Daily Mirror* was then 'a newspaper for ladies, by ladies'; it also had Pip, Squeak and Wilfred. Then we went into the garden for skipping, dumb-bells, or Indian clubs.

After lunch, handicrafts: framing the prints, making raffia mats, and toys for our Dr Barnado Christmas parcel, painting flowers in our nature notebooks, drawing ancient Britons' weapons and Roman domestic objects in our century books with Indian ink. On golden afternoons Ethelwyn (as we were allowed to call her after about four years) would proclaim a nature walk, and we would go off carrying a vasculum for specimens and a gravy strainer on a long stick for inspecting pond and stream life.

We always kept a flower list and a bird list each year, but of course we did not take birds' eggs, nor catch butterflies. Also we kept a common-place book, a habit I have never lost. I still possess the notebook started at 8 years old, written in careful handwriting acquired through Mrs Bridges's manual. My first entry was:

> *So still we glide down to the sea*
> *Of fathomless eternity.*

Then—'Knowledge comes by eyes always open and working hands. There is no knowledge that is not power.' Emerson. 'Self-control is strength, right thought mastery, calmness is power.' James Allan. 'Lucius Quintius Flamininus was so dissolutely and licentiously given over to his pleasure that he forgot all comeliness and honesty.' Plutarch.

Ethelwyn was a Christian Scientist, so was a looker on the bright side—'The blue of heaven is larger than the cloud' (Mrs Browning). The PNEU motto was: *I am, I can, I ought, I will*, and the greatest of all sins was to lay an open book down on its face, or mark it in any way. Ethelwyn had other maxims. Excuses are not to be allowed. Never play cards until the curtains are drawn. Waste not want not. This last was exemplified at a picnic by making us take home in a wisp of paper the salt that was left over from the hard-boiled eggs. I do not know if Ethelwyn approved of punishment, because we were never disobedient. We were virtuous and prudish little prigs, but we were tremendously happy.

My godmother, who lived in Switzerland (and so was in no position to judge my scholastic abilities), had known the Misses Lawrence who founded Roedean School, and she suggested that I should try for a scholarship. Only three awards were given each year: £120, £90, and £60. The full fees were £180, much too much for my parents. It was a drawback that I had done no Latin, geometry, nor algebra—but *I am, I can, I ought, I will*. It was arranged for me to be coached for two terms by a Girton graduate. My mother herself tried to teach me a little botany, which was not a PNEU subject. Nature study, yes; and flowers might be picked to paint, or to identify in the Rev. C. A. Johns's flower book. But to pull them to pieces to look at their stamens was utterly non-PNEU.

Scholarship candidates had to stay at Roedean for a week of examinations and interviews, and off I went in that summer term when I was 13, with my nature notebook and my century book, and my head full of Angela Brazil school stories, and my long hair down my back—everyone at Roedean then was Eton-cropped. I was an intensely shy child, but I cannot remember this plunge into a strange school in the middle of a term as being an ordeal—the girls must have been very friendly. Nor can I remember feeling worried about the written exams although—or possibly because—I had never taken any examinations before. But I do remember that all the other scholarship candidates wore enviably orthodox school uniforms, whereas I wore a jersey and kilt. And I remember the matron making me plait my hair in two pigtails.

Some weeks later a long letter arrived at my home from Roedean saying that Alison knew nothing. They were surprised that I should have attempted the mathematics and Latin papers at all, since these subjects were clearly quite new to me. My botany was negligible, geography sketchy, and so on, and so on. English literature was the only bright spot (Shakespeare and Sir Walter had stood me in good stead), but that didn't prevent my total marks being below all the other entrants. In the last sentence of the letter they said they had decided to award me the £60 scholarship.

In my first term I was put into the bottom form, whereas the other two scholarship girls were placed two forms higher. Somehow I got out of the Upper IV after the first fortnight ... *I am, I can, I ought, I will* ... but I was still a form below the others. I was definitely not scholarship material. Then why was I awarded one? Perhaps they sensed that my governess had achieved the PNEU aim of 'kindling the enthusiasm of childhood,' an eagerness to learn.

It may seem an unfair award from the point of view of the disappointed candidates whose papers had been so much better. But thinking it over now, I am satisfied that my need was greater than theirs. They, star pupils of excellent high schools, could not fail to do well and get university places. But I, with no good day school near my home, would have been sent to an inexpensive boarding school with indifferent teaching where the tennis coaching was good. One of the most valuable contributions of the great girls' public schools is—or was—to give *average* children wide opportunities. In my day, even pretty dim girls got their school certificate eventually and were not allowed to leave without some training lined up for a worthwhile career.

Whatever lies in the future for the girls' public schools, there will be no State takeover of private governesses. The Department of Education say they have no records of how many children are educated at home, and as far as the Ministry is concerned, private governesses do not exist. Gabbitas-Thring say that in this country governesses are a dying species, although they still get requests to fill posts abroad. I count myself supremely fortunate to have had Ethelwyn Flower before the species became extinct.

ALISON ADBURGHAM

The Peter Pan world of William

So in the end they all died within a year, the three writers whose books for children sold by the million and went on selling in an age when many thought them venerable anachronisms.

I don't come to bury Miss Blyton or Captain Johns, still less to praise them. They knew how to get the easy response, and got it. Richmal Crompton wasn't quite the same. True, she was with the other two in the best-sellers' league; she was with them in the children's book departments of those stores which found only Blytons, 'Biggles,' and 'William' books worth a display. But Noddy, the Famous Five, and Biggles were characters one was sorry to see a child engrossed with—characters to be recalled in adult life with mild distaste or, preferably, forgotten. William is a character to be remembered with affection.

He started in 1922. He was not initially meant for children, and is still alleged to be a secret addiction of many adults. In most ways he is a strictly adult conception of unregenerate boyhood—

perennially 11 years old, dirty-faced, stone-throwing, window-breaking, amusing at a safe distance. He's seen, typically, in progress along the ditch (in preference to the footpath), 'dragging his toes in the mud, his hands in his pockets, his head poking forward, his freckled face stern and determined, his mouth puckered up to make his devastating whistle.'

He's not at first sight a likely hero for small boys; you can see that Biggles, the intrepid airman, has certain natural advantages. Yet boys did admire and identify themselves with William. I am one of thousands who could no doubt testify to having called themselves Outlaws, to having fought 'mostly in vain' for William-like adventures, and even to having made and drunk liquorice water.

His appeal to youngsters is, I think, a dual one. On the one hand he is a small boy blown up a little larger than life: a born leader, a daredevil who gets recklessly into trouble and ingeniously out of it again, a boy who scores off the grown ups, especially the nasty ones. And on the other hand he is a figure to be patronised; naïvely credulous, believing any tale a rogue or beery tramp may tell him, forever misunderstanding the simplest things and blundering into disaster.

William is three dimensional but not exactly realistic; besides the daredevilry and naïve silliness, he has a wild imagination, and a magnificent line in sulky rhetoric. He is capable—and probably this is the essence of William—of page-long eloquence in defence against a grown up charge of unwashed hands or a proposal that he should visit his aunt.

William's character shows no sign of development in the 46 years of his life. This perhaps was not to be expected. The stories themselves, and the social background, changed a little. Their middle-classness has been remarked on by everyone who has felt impelled to write about them. Like that of the BBC's Dales, it changed a little outwardly while staying fundamentally the same. In the earlier books, William's parents, Mr and Mrs Brown, have a cook, a parlour maid and a gardener; since the war, Mrs Brown has made do with a daily help; but she is still the employing class —and the help is still the servant class.

Mrs Bott at the Hall—the vulgar little wife of Mr Bott, inventor of Bott's sauce—is unchanged to the end: 'An' 'oo's *this* meant to be, may I harsk?' she says in a late story, looking at a painting of herself. 'Not me, I 'ope. Hope.'

But then, Mrs Bott was never to be taken seriously. All the minor characters in fact are either caricatures or just foils for William. Mr Brown, his father, sardonic and disenchanted, emerges from time to time from behind the financial pages of his newspaper. Mrs Brown hopes unendingly for reform and tidiness. Elder brother Robert has just met the most beautiful girl in the world and hopes to take her to the tennis club dance. Elder sister Ethel holds suitor after suitor at a safe and virtuous distance. William maintains a romantic affection for the little girl next door, while being pursued by fluffy, deceptively angelic looking Violet Elizabeth Bott.

The stories themselves progress a little. In the earlier books they are simple, episodic and mildly seditious. Later stories understandably show signs of strain, rely more on concocted plot than spontaneous invention, and on the creation of ever more unlikely and eccentric adult characters. Yet complaints of middle-classness are probably unfounded, and efforts at updating misguided. The world of William, like that of P. G. Wodehouse, is not so much out of date as out of time altogether. For 46 years William has been out-Panning Peter. He was born in 1922, aged 11; he is still 11 in 1969 (he should by rights be 58); and he will go on being alive and 11 for quite a long time yet.

JOHN ROWE TOWNSEND

The writing lark, or a dog's labour

At this costly time of year I perceive sadly that for me on this earth it will never be *la dolce vita*, the fur-lined Bentley, a Duccio in the loo and six months in Nassau. Forty years on and I live like I did in the hungry thirties bed-sitter, wise in essence among shoes, piles of gramophone records, stooks of clothes not shabby enough to offer the WVS yet, a piano which is so loaded with sheets of music it can hardly open, a retreat where the lightest cough might start quite a serious avalanche of paperbacks.

This writing lark, short of acquiring some film rights, doesn't pay. As for criticism which nobody likes and everyone resents—unless it is praise which is not criticism, of course—that seems to be least paying of all. Certainly you are not going to be propped up in your declining years by the millionaire of whose daughter, after four years at the RADA and two thousand spent on private voice-coaching, you can find nothing better to say than that in the 'small but not unimportant rôle of the housemaid she achieved a certain wry charm.'

The only French Academicien I ever met, the late Faute de Mieux, once patted me on the head (though I seem to remember that even at that age I was the taller of the two, so perhaps I was sitting at a desk) and said: 'Young man—carry always a little note-book with you. At your age you do not know how to write, but one day when you are my age . . . hêlas' . . . and he shook his frosty pow and one was left to imagine the lack of ideas sadly voiding that distinguished head. 'Donc, toujours un carnet!'

I wish I had kept that notebook, though between you and me it would probably have been thick with sententious rubbish. It wasn't really until the war that I began to distinguish a beautiful aphorism from a real think-nugget (mentoid' was one dreadful word coined in the late twenties). But it would have been interesting. I find if I turn up old yellowing cuttings of my first efforts (which one preserved in those days, a sort of evidence that one *was* a writer, and some editors would demand to look at a cuttings book when you applied for a job and failed to return it when you didn't get it) I find that I can't recognise myself at all.

All writing seems to me a dog's labour beside which manual work of many (but not all) kinds often seem child's play. After a stint at the keyboard of an old battered typewriter gazing at the still far too wide swathe of uncovered paper, who has not gladly gone to do a turn at the sink? Tolstoy's boot-mending must have been one of the very least mischievous activities of the great artist humbug we revere. But I suppose with a steady grind you do gain a little competence (unlike skating and swimming and bicycling, which you never forget, but like the piano where you lose virtue if you stop for ten days) writing always seems to demand the same fresh insane expense of nervous tension.

Or do different people react differently about this? I remember on another paper when I was a very nervous tyro—watching the clock coming up to deadline, writing a word and then scratching it out—how I used to gaze at the awesome Charles Morgan, then critic *en chef*, who would spend most his precious minutes sitting, musing fingers to brow, like a statue of a romantic poet in his birthplace. Then with unruffled calm at the very last moment he would take push-pen and paper and write unhurrying a thousand words with never a pause or a slip.

I can write pretty fast myself now, if never so well, and I was the other night visited by the awful thought, have I now reached the predicted state of the late Monsieur Faute de Mieux who had come to the last of the thoughts in his *petit carnet*? Perish the thought. My belief is on the principle which Proust laid down about photographs of loved-ones which, far from reminding us of them, create creatures we *don't* remember—that a card index of 'ideas' is a coffin of the soul. Or do I hear a distant voice cry: 'How's that for a sententious non-mentoid! *Tempus est abire*: where you get off, fella.'

PHILIP HOPE-WALLACE

Something to celebrate

P. H. Newby says that nine tenths of his energy is devoted to the BBC, where he is Controller of the Third Programme. With what is left over he has written 17 novels, a book of criticism, and a biography of Maria Edgeworth, and has edited a selection of stories from *The Thousand and One Nights*. The seventeenth novel, *Something to Answer For*, published by Faber and Faber, has just won for him the first Booker Prize for Fiction, worth £5,000, which was presented in London last night.

He regards himself as a very old-fashioned novelist who does nothing that Conrad would not have thought old-hat; he has a story to tell and likes to make his meaning clear. But this is deceptive. He is a subtle and demanding writer, full of close meanings. He thinks of modern novelists as either historians (like C. P. Snow who, he says, regards himself as a latter-day Trollope) or poets (like Malamud or Iris Murdoch). Mr Newby, then, must be classified as a good deal more poet than historian.

He lives in Buckinghamshire in a house which his older daughter, aged 21, considers too much like a stockbroker's. There the other day, while his younger daughter, aged six, was being bathed upstairs, Mr Newby talked about the novel today, his own novels, and himself. Two cats listened or slept. The large black cat is called Hamlet and the little silver tabby Ophelia; Mr Newby, who did not name them, says he has always been a bit ashamed of the names.

He was born in 1918 in Sussex at Sir Arthur Conan Doyle's house which was then being used as a nursing home, and went to grammar school at Worcester and teacher training college at Cheltenham, qualifying in time to be called up in 1939 and sent to France with the British Expeditionary Force. He went to Africa, and was a corporal stretcherbearer with the Eighth Army until just before Alamein, when he was seconded as a lecturer in English literature to the Fouad I University in Cairo.

In 1964 he came home, published his first novels, and wrote reviews and short stories for *Encounter*, *Lilliput*, and *Mademoiselle*, a glossy American teenage magazine which regarded literature as an object of fashion and had the distinction of first publishing *Under Milk Wood*. He reviewed for *The Listener*, receiving 15 guineas for 1,500 words but making much more than that by immediately selling at half price the 50 or so novels sent to him each week.

In 1949 he joined the BBC as a sound talks producer, working mostly on historical and literary programmes with names like 'First Reading'. He once produced Robert Oppenheimer when he was giving the Reith Lectures under the title 'Science and the Common Understanding,' but could not see the talks until four days before they were broadcast, had no time to adapt them for reading aloud, and now thinks little can have been commonly understood.

For a while he did Light Programme talks. When I asked him what he thought of the present-day pop Radio 1 he replied, carefully, that it was not something that could have been foreseen. He has been Controller of the Third for 11 years now but prefers not to talk about that either. He likes to keep his broadcasting and his writing well apart.

He began writing early. Two novels written when he was 18 and 20 were unpublished, but after the war he was quickly successful. His first novel in 1946 won a Rockefeller Foundation award and his second the Somerset Maugham prize; later he was given a fellowship to travel all over the United States, and last year the novel which has now won him £5,000 was chosen as the *Yorkshire Post* book of the year.

'You have had a lot of prizes?'

'I have been writing rather a long time.'

Something to Answer For, which is perhaps really about the way a man's spirit changes under stress and how he comes eventually to believe that no one but himself is responsible for his own conscience, is set, like many of Mr Newby's books, in the Middle East. Did his stay there make that much of an impression on him?

'A determinate impression,' he says. Oriental life was so much more explicit and extravagant that it was like living in a human laboratory. People talked about the mysterious East, but London was much more mysterious than Cairo, where there were no inhibitions. A stranger would ask who your parents were, why you were there, and how much you earned. His students demanded to know why he was not married and whether he was a homosexual. He said he was not homosexual, and was engaged to a girl in England. He knew members of the Egyptian royal family and people from the slums. Everything was extreme.

Then there was the Arabic love of language which was used with relish now unknown here. He well remembers a man who used to go about the streets of Cairo, his voice raised in measured ecstasy, selling bits of wire to clean Primus stoves. 'You meet people,' he says, 'who get into a sentence which will not allow them to escape before they have offered you their house.' He was once at a party when he was unwise enough to tell his host he had a magnificent house. 'My dear Newby,' he replied, 'It is yours, I insist.' For a moment the man meant it, Mr Newby thanked him and accepted, and neither mentioned the matter again.

Mr Newby believes the novel nowadays is in a bad way. The Victorian novelist was an entertainer, a man to whom all people, prime ministers and kitchen girls, looked to have their imaginations fed. He had an awareness of being read by statesmen and scientists. But now the novelist was only one of many entertainers, and was swamped by films and television. If a man was single-mindedly to devote himself to novels—and to write a novel meant being alone for two years putting down words on paper—then he had to be sure that what he was doing was important, that someone might read his books when he was dead. This confidence could be attained only by a consciousness of addressing a whole range of people throughout society. Mr Newby is a successful novelist, who sells 8,000 to 9,000 copies of each book, a lot more than most writers, but his private nightmare is that his only readers are old ladies.

He says the novel has been changed by other media. Why should a man now write a detailed description of a scene, when a film camera could do better at a glance? Just as the still camera had displaced the portraitist and the painter had therefore looked to colour and abstraction, so the novelist was now looking to inner feeling and becoming more and more a poet.

'So we shall never have another Theodore Dreiser?'—'Out of the question.'

Back in 1950 Mr Newby wrote that the English mind was fast becoming self-conscious about money. He still thinks that a novel which made explicit people's greed for money might be shocking to some. He himself is a little reticent about money. When I asked what he would do with the £5,000 he said perhaps build a new study, but when he was first told he had hardly dared to think about it because any day the Publishers Association might have telephoned and said they were terribly sorry but the letters had got mixed up and the winner was someone else. 'And I should have said, "That's quite all right." '

TERRY COLEMAN

Invisible eye

The camera, of course, is a lying jade. Alfred Hitchcock made the point in *North by North West* when a member of the UN is stabbed in front of Cary Grant. Grant plucks the dagger from the victim's back just as a flash bulb goes off. Cut to front page of daily paper and picture of Grant, clutching dagger aloft, startled in the act of murder.

So the photographer has to find his own truth. Paradoxically, when painting since impressionism has so often sought the here and now, Henry Cartier-Bresson has used camera shutter speeds of fractions of a second to organise the informal into the hieratic image. Any still from a film of Godard—a careful selection, that is, from a filmed fiction—looks more natural than a picture of an actual event by Cartier-Bresson.

This is because Godard has a feeling for contemporaneity, but a 1932 photograph by Cartier-Bresson looks a lot like a 1968 photograph by Cartier-Bresson. It is not that the scene has remained the same but that Cartier-Bresson always looks for the human drama behind the trappings. His sympathy for ordinary suffering humanity is enormous: compare his portraits with Cecil Beaton's, lately on show at the National Portrait Gallery. Beaton is the Van Dyck, Cartier-Bresson the Rembrandt of photographers.

Cartier-Bresson has infinite cunning. He built his fame on the invisibility of the Leica that enabled him to take photographs without his subjects knowing. There is one marvellous picture of this sort taken in 1945 at Dessau: one released prisoner vengefully accuses another of being a Gestapo informer. At moments like this, Bresson takes his camera right into the group of people involved and photographs frontally; at other moments he approaches the truth obliquely: he photographs the Parisians watching the Algerian demonstration instead of the demo itself; he takes a back view of three Berliners peering over the Wall, instead of showing what is on the other side.

Cartier-Bresson is sympathetic when he photographs the peasantry or the proletariat; deadpan before the forces of authority; ironic before wealth and privilege. He takes the working class in close up, showing children playing or adults sitting by the Marne stately as Seurat's riverside picnickers. At Eton, he photographs from a height, placing the uniformed boys in their setting, masking their individuality and deploying them instead as ciphers for their class.

Paris, Valencia, Casablanca, Tokio, Peking, New York, Dublin, Moscow, Ahmedabad, Popocatepetl: it makes no difference. We are all brothers beneath the skin, exploiters or exploited. This is not to deny Cartier-Bresson's ability to record the peculiar grace of particular regions but in this he is one among many. In photographing people he is scarcely unique either; just the best.

MICHAEL MCNAY

A passionate curiosity

Fame obscures. Perhaps this has to be so: we cope with greatness by shrinking it into simpler, handleable forms. We compensate with adulation and go our way, not a little pleased at having doffed our caps so neatly. We own the great and thus admire ourselves.

It is essential to break the habit and the mould from time to time. The Leonardo da Vinci exhibition at the Queen's Gallery is an ideal occasion for this. We admire him so much and know him so platitudinously. The Royal Collection includes a great number of Leonardo drawings, many of them well known but many others unfamiliar. The exhibition consists of 160 drawings plus the three volumes of anatomical studies. These are in showcases, open now and to be opened at other points from time to time, and there are full-size photographs of many of them near by, accompanied by explanatory (and enthusiastic) notes by Dr K. D. Keele. The combined effect of all this material is shattering.

Leonardo's skill as draughtsman we take for granted—too readily of course. The moment we try to characterise his way of drawing we find that he had not one way but many. His drawings seem to belong to several ages. To his own, with its fine and brittle way of abstracting things into lines, and also its first attempts to map the surfaces of things by means of elaborate hatching. Other drawings suggest the seventeenth, eighteenth, and even nineteenth centuries—some that revel in the softness of flesh, and others that offer a glimpse, an impression, of Nature as though he had sat beside Corot.

The second obvious truth about him is the passionate curiosity that his drawings served. But here the important thing is not that he didn't divide scientific interests from artistic—why should he have?—but that he was impelled by a hunger for knowledge that is almost frightening. He almost invented drawing: drawing as the means of knowing, examining, remembering, reconstructing, explaining. He was not just a recorder of what he saw. His drawings can be diagrams, clarifying the complex mechanics of some part of the body; they can function as transparencies, revealing successive layers; they can be a workbench on which he constructs a model to demonstrate some process that he has never been able to observe. They can also be the subtlest, most melodic of paeans in praise of some beautiful person or object, seen or imagined.

It is the emotional charge in all this that is so surprising. This homosexual bastard, lonely and restless, needed to connect everything with everything else, to examine events, collect instances, illegally dissect corpses, not just to understand each thing but in order to reassure himself of the underlying unity of the world.

'Death sooner than weariness,' he scribbles to himself in his left-handed mirror-writing. 'I am never weary of being useful. No labour can tire me.' And again: 'I am never weary of being useful. Nature has so disposed me.' The majority of his drawings come late in his life, in middle age and after. On and on he goes, and then, among those he did before his hand became paralysed, come the apocalyptic deluge drawings. The forces he had studied with such passion, whose working he had traced under so many guises, erupt and destroy the world. About the same moment, north of the Alps, Dürer awoke from a nightmare and noted down, in word and image, a similar intimation of catastrophe.

NORBERT LYNTON

Florence's great restorer

He is a great man, not just a man of eminence, and when you see him with his students in Florence, you can measure his greatness far better than in the Hayward Gallery. Without Ugo Procacci we should never have enjoyed that marvellous exhibition of Florentine frescoes on the South Bank. These students—the three American girls whose Italian is rudimentary because they suspect Italian boys and therefore don't get much social life, the one whose Italian is excellent because a couple of weeks ago she became Signora Alberghini, and the Italian girl who is even more articulate than a Roman driver crossed at the traffic lights—these students know that as well as anyone and better than most.

Professor Procacci is not the first man to have taken frescoes off their walls so that they could be manhandled across Europe. Someone shipped a wall painting across town here in 1566. But Procacci is the man who studied the trick seriously for the first time in several hundred years, who perfected its technique and who began to create a whole new school of fresco restoration in the 1930s. He is the superintendent of all the endless art in Florence. He is the man responsible for saving so much and losing so little after those floods three years ago. All this is his eminence.

He has a lot of crow's feet around the corners of his eyes, and they have been caused by grinning and laughing. He has the patience to slow his rate of teaching to the capacities of his classes without any apparent concern. When one of those reclusive American girls stumbles over a question he has put, he gives her a small hug of encouragement. And when an itinerant journalist who has gate-crashed his lecture without one word of the professor's language to his name has been provided with two hours of translation, Procacci apologises with a grin for not having been able to discourse in English. These things are part of his greatness.

He stands in the courtyard of San Salvi, which was once a church but which is now a restoration centre, like a guide on the threshold of a conducted tour. And he is. With him he has Dino Dini, who actually peeled some of those South Bank frescoes from their walls. He follows his professor like an acolyte, a man dressed as carefully as a bank manager, but years of working in powdered plaster have left white rimes around the circumference of his finger-nails.

Years of working with all kinds of restorative chemicals have left Procacci's own hands and wrists bald of any hair. The professor's life has been absorbed with technique. He laughs a little at art historians who enthuse about this or that painter's background of red to a crucifixion (the artist's manifestation of divine wrath, so they say); they do not know, as he has painstakingly discovered, that the sky was originally blue but the pigment flaked off long ago because of some chemical change.

It may be naïve, but after seeing the immaculate presentation of those frescoes on the South Bank, a visit to San Salvi is a shock to the system. Inside it looks like, and is, a workshop. If there is anything more staggering than the frescoes of Florence themselves (and, of course, there isn't) it is the way they have been taken down. There are two methods and neither is substantially different from the practice of the Middle Ages. If the plaster beneath the pigment is rotten the restorers glue canvas to the surface and then peel it off the wall; when a restored surface has been prepared they glue the pigment back on and then remove the canvas; this is called the strappo method. If the plaster is still sound they still glue canvas on the surface and then they cut round the edges and ease canvas, pigment, plaster and all away from the wall with huge knives whose blades are sometimes as wide as an arm-span; this is known as the stacco method.

But do they never ruin a fresco by tearing off a strip of pigment and leaving the rest behind, or by having half the staccoed plaster and its paint fall in a disaster at their feet? Ask Procacci this and he shrugs, and the sides of his mouth curve down. 'It's impossible,' he says. He means that after 30 years of research into glues and pigments and plaster he has made it impossible. 'Just wait,' says one of the students, 'just you wait and see how they throw these things around in here.'

Inside the former church of San Salvi there is one fresco still in situ; the whole east wall is covered by Andrea del Sarto's 'Last Supper' and there is a nasty looking white gash running the whole length of the dado under the Lord's table; that was deliberately cut during the floods to stop damp rising into the main body of the work by capillary action. One day it will be fixed.

The frescoes that are being fixed right now occupy the whole of two storeys. They stand propped against the walls in frames, like the ones we saw in the London exhibition. They rest upon easels, so that someone can retouch small hair-lines where time long ago neutralised the colour. And, occupying half the floor space in front of the del Sarto is a vast painting on canvas. It is a fourteenth century 'Inferno' from S. Maria Novella, ten square metres and the second largest fresco ever to be removed in one piece; it is so big that one end of it curls up the wall. It is very difficult to imagine it in its proper place. Lying there floppy and a bit dusty it looks like some faintly shabby thing that might have come out of an extravagant Indian bazaar.

Procacci picks his way among these things which are at once priceless works of art and pieces of flotsam, and leads his students through their tutorial. He shows them a sinopia, which was the artist's first sketch on a wall. He tells them how it was used as an aide memoire, how the artist then plastered over as much of it as he could paint properly in one day, how he always worked from top to bottom of the composition, to avoid splashing what was beneath, how the pigment of true fresco—which was always painted when the plaster was wet—penetrated may be two or three millimetres at most.

He runs his finger around the faint lines which distinguish one day's work from the next. He goes into a detailed explanation of chemical reactions—how salts can rise to the surface and destroy a fresco, how the egg which was sometimes used as a binding agent would turn blues into greens—and only Signora Alberghini from Syracuse (NY) and the articulate Italian miss can follow his baffling distinctions between carbohydrates and carbo-sulphates clearly. So Procacci grins a bit and repeats himself a lot and gently rephrases his more obscure passages.

And then—perhaps because he is after all an Italian and there-fore a showman—he does something absolutely daft. He ap-proaches an enormous canvas on the floor, which may be the third biggest fresco ever to have been taken from its wall, a Christ hanging from the Cross in colours which are muted and lambent. He motions to Dino Dini and together they start to roll it up. Then they let it unroll itself, which it does with an acceler-ating whoosh and a flurry of floor-dust. If anyone dared to put a price on that Florentine fresco from the Middle Ages it would probably be worth half a million or more, and they have treated it like a length of linoleum. Professor Procacci catches my eye and grins again. 'It makes quite an effect,' he says, 'to throw frescoes around.' He should know.

GEOFFREY MOORHOUSE

Sitting on the future of Venice

The preservation of Venice can wait. The Government's inter-ministerial committee, created nearly three years ago, for the defence of Venice against sinking, flooding, and industrial speculation, held a plenary meeting yesterday in the lagoon city and decided to 'soprasedere' (sit on) a recommendation to Parliament for one rhetorical remedy which would cost nothing —that of declaring the city's entire 58,000 hectares to be an historical and artistic zone to be protected from the ravages of man.

A Christian Democrat committee member, Signor Dorigo, who speaks for the industrialists, objected that another pressure group was being led 'by a person with the same surname as a man who made his fortune from the creation of the first industrial zone at Marghera and who now opposes enlarging that zone.'

He could only be referring to the Countess Anna Maria Cicogna Volpi, the militant leader of the Venice chapter of Italia Nostra, the group which is opposed to the filling-in of more marshland at Marghera as a site for industries. Her father, Count Volpi, who also was Mussolini's Finance Minister, was responsible for the first Marghera filling in.

Italia Nostra experts, who are not all countesses, but include leading hydraulic engineers and geologists, contend that the marshes serve as a sponge which has saved Venice from many floods in the past. In the last decade Venice has been flooded 30 times, in the preceding 90 years only 28 times.

Though Unesco has established its interest in saving Venice from the sea, and the Government gave a small sum recently to the National Research Centre to open a special laboratory in Venice, the problem is too urgent for more committees to sit. In another generation they may be swimming.

The inter-ministerial super-committee was given £586,000 for its studies and has spent, with no notable results, all but £6,000. Now it is asking Parliament for some more—£150 millions—this time for some actual works such as a sewer system, restoration of public palaces, loans to private property owners for restoration, etc., and, of course, more 'studies.'

That the new industrial zone at Marghera is going to be built can be supposed from the fact, reported in the press and not denied, that a new 18-kilometre-long canal for tankers and freighters, begun in 1965, is again being dug after work was suspended some months ago, when the busybodies, who think Venice may be as worth saving as the temples at Abu Simbel, protested that the new canal should be stopped.

By the time it is finished, it will be outdated, as new tankers are tripling in tonnage. Then, to 'save' the industrial zone, the canal will be enlarged and deepened. From the top of the new Marghera factory chimney, some day one may be able to view the top of the Doge's Palace as it bobs above the water.

The national president of Italia Nostra, Signor Giorgio Bassani, the novelist, says of the petrol canal: 'I'm not accusing anyone, but I have a presentiment that the most formidable land speculation which has ever been attempted in Italy is under way.'

He is only a writer of fiction. Signora Cicogna Volpi is only a countess. But they, and others in league with them, know how things come to pass in their country, as, indeed, even some foreigners have learned. How can Signor Bassani be sure that the experts hired by the industrialists are wrong, and that his fears are right? 'I know by intuition,' he explains. 'Poets are good for something, you know.'

GEORGE ARMSTRONG

Echoing round

What Queen Victoria would have said I shudder to think, but the great dome of the Royal Albert Hall is now hung about with flying saucer-shapes made of glass fibre. I have long wondered what exactly the royal comments were when, on the opening of the new hall in honour of Prince Albert in 1871, it was discovered that Victorian technology had fallen badly short. A musician herself, Queen Victoria might well have approved of any scheme to eliminate the famous echo, and that is what is now promised—or at least half-promised—in the latest modifications to be unveiled next week.

I had assumed that the echo was an inevitable result of the circular design, but apparently not. The management of the hall decided recently to call in a firm of acoustic consultants. The experts of Acoustical Investigation and Research Ltd., (AIRO for short) found by careful analysis that the building's fault was not the whole of the dome but the smooth external circle. That smooth area produced an unpleasant high-pitched echo, while the corrugated middle area reflected only a low-pitched reverberation that was far less troublesome.

The first idea was to put a ceiling over the whole hall, cutting out the dome entirely, but then it was discovered that that would reduce the volume of sound by a third, and so the scheme was devised of glass-fibre flying saucers, between six and twelve feet in diameter. These have a plastic coating so that the right top and bottom frequencies are reflected and the right middle frequencies are absorbed. Extra damping has been put inside them so that the dome area does not acquire an echo of its own and go on reverberating when the rest of the hall is quiet.

It is chastening to realise that, according to the AIRO experts, in the worst seats (round about letter K, or six o'clock from the stage) the echo has until now been louder than the direct sound, and at yesterday's press conference a tape-recording of gunfire and a bassoon playing the *Teddy Bear's Picnic* was put on to prove it. Now with any luck it should be very different, and the BBC has kindly arranged a special concert by Colin Davis and the BBC Symphony Orchestra next Wednesday (invited guests only) when the new arrangement will be tried out in Berlioz and Bruckner. The reverberation period is going to be three seconds (still rather high for a concert-hall) but until now the middle frequencies have been providing a much longer reverberation-time than that, and they have been the trouble-makers. We can now only wait and listen, though Mr Frank Mundy, general manager of the hall, yesterday sounded a note of caution. The arrangement, he pointed out, was still experimental. He felt that if this first try at removing the echo provided the definitive answer, it would be 'a miracle.'

What is in fact little short of a miracle already is that the whole scheme is costing only £8,000, a mere nothing when you remember that the acoustic modifications to Philharmonic Hall in the Lincoln Center, New York, have already cost several millions. And in case anyone is worried about flying saucers landing on them in the middle of a concert, the biggest weigh only 83lb. and are held by chains capable of bearing over four times as much as that. They have even thought of the possibility of the roof leaking and filling the saucers with rain-water; tiny holes in the middle of each saucer will if necessary let the drips through.

EDWARD GREENFIELD

Karajan's Berliners

Last night, in a crowded and ravingly vociferous Royal Festival Hall, Herbert von Karajan conducted the superb Berlin Philharmonic Orchestra in and through the Seventh symphony of Bruckner, prefaced by the first Brandenbrug concerto of Bach. Not so long ago, within living memory, Karajan conducted the Vienna Philharmonic Orchestra and the Seventh symphony of Bruckner was his main occupation in this same Royal Festival Hall.

These continental conductors forget nothing. It would be a refreshing change if, for once in a while, one or two of them turned attention to, say, an Elgar symphony; after all, Sir John Barbirolli is bold enough, and persuasive enough, to conduct Mahler in, of all un-Mahlerish places, Rome. Perhaps Karajan doesn't know the two Elgar symphonies—Bruno Walter didn't when I asked him to perform some Elgar in the mid-1930s. Elgar might suit Karajan; at any rate, he has conducted a wonderfully vital performance of Holst's *The Planets*.

Karajan doesn't change his view of the Bruckner Seventh symphony. He emphasises the not generally well-known fact that Bruckner really could score richly, even sensuously, for the orchestra. The Berliners' strings revelled in the gorgeously written part-writing in the adagio.

Karajan remains for me something of an enigma. He is an orchestral master, comprehensive and sure of himself. He has the score in his head, and can send waves or pulsations of his personality into the instrumental ranks, generated from his inner dynamo, enforced by drastic commanding shoulder action, and arms thrust down from on high, then, at a transition, the hands suavely shape a phrase, almost kissing it good-bye on its way. He is obviously dedicated—whether to music in general, or his own aesthetic reactions in particular, I couldn't say. The Berlin Philharmonic respond as one man to his promptings with full and gutty yet incisive violins, velvet violas, rich brown 'cellos, and basses of vintage in the cellarage. Maybe the brass gets out of focus at times; and no horns or wood-wind can surpass our native own. But Karajan worries me as an interpreter; he tends to endow all composers with the same sound.

This performance of the Bruckner Seventh, for all its delights to the orchestral ear, made Bruckner (of all composers) appear rather self-conscious of the effects he was making on the audience. There is hardly a hundred bars in all Bruckner's output which postulate an audience, least of all an audience which is considerably a byproduct of records and television. Here and there, for all Karajan's fine artistry—and he is an artist—the symphony didn't quite get off the ground, a phrase which, I think, will come home rather meaningfully to Karajan. Yet the performance had its memorable periods: the spacious opening-out of the first movement, broad and far-reaching, and the truly valedictory coda of the Adagio, lamenting the passing of Wagner, echoing Valhalla.

Maybe the Scherzo needed more of geniality; I have never suspected Karajan of having an inexhaustible vein of humour. It is superfluous to report that the Berliners gloried in the Bruckner unisons; and in the angelic rise and fall of melody during the slow movement Karajan again levitated the phrases beautifully, sensitively timing the wood-wind responses, and getting the exquisite catch of breath at the entrance of the three-four violin seraphic song, at the beginning of the Adagio.

'Exquisite' may be an odd word to apply to Bruckner, or to Karajan. In the context of this performance it falls, as a description, trippingly from the pen. Moreover, I have heard Karajan conduct Debussy's *Pelléas et Mélisande* with a touch of quite exquisite fancy unequalled in our time. He is our most enigmatic and compelling conductor—almost *capable de tout*—capable even of making Bruckner sound, at times, aggressive, noisy, almost a Berliner himself. Karajan, by the way, used the 'cymbal crash' edition of the symphony, thus exposing himself to censure by the musicologists, under a solemnly laid-down penal sanction.

NEVILLE CARDUS

Pasmore takes a stroll

Victor Pasmore's recent work, at the Marlborough New London Gallery, is friendly and varied. Too much so? Now in his early sixties, Pasmore has earned the right to take his art for a stroll instead of marching it down some new-found path with bayonets fixed.

A stroll, you could say, around the territory he conquered and none of it far from home. In the late 1940s he stood out as a rebel, renouncing the delights of landscape and still-life for the rigours and logic of abstract geometry and construction. Yet we look back now and we see so much in the post-1948 work that already existed before 1948, and so little of the essential Pasmore has been lost, obscured or even amended, that it feels platitudinous to mention it.

To pick on one aspect: his feeling for locations in space. He has always gone for clear organisation. Horizontals and verticals are firmly established even in the sauvest landscape to contain any swirls of form he may permit himself. This clarity he counters with a mystery: the actual position of forms in space—in the illusionistic space of the picture, in the real and illusionistic space of the relief construction.

If he has a flat surface that announces its exact location too plainly, he will paint two rectangles of one colour on it, one larger than the other and thus apparently nearer the spectator. His low relief constructions of the 1950s, strict as they seem in their Neo-plasticist idiom, actually shift about ceaselessly because of their contradictory levels of projection and the occasional patch of soft, unlocatable colour.

This duality appears all through the present exhibition, in many different guises. It is accompanied by other, less fundamental but equally familiar ones: geometrical shapes versus free-hand (almost off-hand sometimes) execution; forms and textures given by the boards he works on and into, versus specific imposed marks and surfaces; a vocabulary of hard against soft, defining against diffusing.

There emerges a duality behind all the others. The sense of a lack of direction, troubling in a younger man's work, is the product here of a confident centre. The works are eccentric, peripatetic; the centre is Pasmore himself, not needing to assert intentions or advertise his presence, the same lyrical spirit as always.

NORBERT LYNTON

The youngest of the greatest

Sviatoslav Richter is the greatest pianist in the world, and so are Horowitz, Rubenstein, and one or two others. It depends on which one you heard last. Perhaps it is true to say that Richter is the youngest of the greatest pianists: he is also Russian and elusive, and any concert organisation which can include a recital by him in its series is not only rich but also lucky, like the Harrogate Concert Society which presented a Richter recital in the Lounge Hall last night after only one cancellation.

It is difficult to know where to begin with the praise, unless it is to say that his attitude to music—his programme design, choice of encore even, and his approach to the interpretation of each work —would be the ideal model for any performer, not only pianists. The piano is actually not of the first importance. His recitals are not a matter of filtering Bach, Beethoven, and Mussorgsky through one man's relationship with the piano. Last night there might have been three pianos. The instrument he used for Bach's French Suite No. 2 in C Minor sounded like one specially designed for the purpose. It was small, but bright in tone and precisely articulated, with all the properties of the harpsichord, together with the piano's sustaining power and range of colour. Perhaps he hit the Courante rather harder than a contemporary of Bach would have done, but the clarity and continuity of the several voices in the Allemande and the Sarabande were quite extraordinary.

Much of the secret of Richter's playing rests, in fact, in his use of the pedals. He can vary the tone of a note long after it has been struck, sustain some and not others with never a suspicion of jangle or fuzz, and employ effects which composers like Stockhausen have just discovered as sensations, and which Richter dedicates always with the utmost subtlety to phrasing, coloration, and clarification.

The instrument he used for Beethoven's Variations, Opus 35, although it was the very same Steinway, was bigger and stronger than the Bach one, and it seemed to grow with the stature of the variations and with the accumulated strength of the interpretation. The word for this is economy, and yet he never seemed to hold back, and was never afraid of the grotesque and eccentric Beethoven whom so many pianists attempt to ennoble. For Mussorgsky's *Pictures at an Exhibition*, it was an even bigger piano, of course, with an enormous range of sound in the instrument itself, and a superb technique on the pianist's part. But this was not the most impressive aspect of the performance, for there was an uncanny power of characterisation, confirming Richter's greatest quality of all, which is the obvious compulsion he has to work out his own personal relationship with every work he plays and every bar in it.

GERALD LARNER

Interrupted pilgrimage

The opening Concert of the Aldeburgh Festival has become a sort of pilgrimage. One returned to The Maltings on Saturday afternoon as though to some favourite cathedral, a sanctuary even more beautiful in sound and sight than one had remembered. Within hours of that first concert the place was gutted, a desecration almost too harsh to believe, something which now leaves one with a dreamlike memory of an occasion that showed Benjamin Britten's qualities as an interpreter with almost ironic exaggeration.

Playing the piano in Schubert's 'Trout' quintet, he welcomed his first visitors to the festival, the Amadeus Quartet, with what you might describe as a musical bear-hug. We all know that the Amadeus players are the best-mannered in the world. They are not given to violent eruptions. Their style is smooth and it sounded smoother than ever in The Maltings for the first half of the concert, Purcell's Chacony in G minor (the first work ever heard at the festival back in 1948) and Mozart's great G minor Quintet.

Then with the Schubert something—or rather someone—hit them. Unashamedly Britten gave them an exhilarating bumpy ride. He even had the temerity to grin impishly at the ends of movements. As we know from 'Winterreise' with Pears and the F minor Fantasy with Richter, Britten's way with Schubert is almost improvisatory. He recreates the argument, lets the inspiration of the moment take the music heavenwards—very different from the refined, scholarly manners of the Amadeus. To give them credit they seemed finally to get used to the idea, and enjoy their Suffolk outing.

On the day following the disaster one had little heart for music bravely as Benjamin Britten and his helpers were trying to provide it as usual. But if music there was to be, Bach at Blythburgh was more consoling than anything you could think of—two of the violin and cembelow sonatas played raptly by Norbert Brainin from the Amadeus Quartet and George Malcolm, plus a partita for each of them solo. As I went in I had a word with Benjamin Britten. He had spent the morning at the rehearsals, but there was no time for more meditation. He was off to The Maltings, already consulting with the engineers and architects, already determined that his great concert hall will be restored long before next year's festival.

EDWARD GREENFIELD

The agony of the first hole at St Andrews

The ultimate challenge of golf is the ability to produce one's best when it matters most and, except on rare team occasions, the mattering is entirely a personal affair. Long ago it was written: 'Golf is not a wrestle with bogey; it is not a struggle with your mortal foe; it is a physiological, psychological, and moral fight with yourself.'

This applies to every golfer, from the great man striving to win an Open championship to the humblest performer with his heart set on breaking 90. Whatever the degree of aptitude, technique, and experience, performance eventually depends on nerve; anyone can produce his shots on the practice ground, but the simplest stroke in a competition often strikes fear to the heart.

In all golf there can be no more revealing instance of this than the first hole on the Old Course at St Andrews. Few golfers are not familiar from personal experience, pictures, or hearsay with the hole's classic simplicity. The drive down the vast spread of greensward, unbroken by hazard of any kind, must be the most straightforward in the world, although this in itself can sometimes be a snare; but, except for a slice or hook of prodigious wildness, the ball is always in play. Then comes the problem.

Ahead lies the Swilcan Burn, from a distance just a faint dark line curving over the turf but, in fact, eight feet wide. It must be crossed if the round is to continue. The green, a generous, inviting expanse, lies immediately beyond the burn; the flag flutters enticingly; and apprehension mounts in the heart of the golfer— particularly those unaccustomed to precise keeping of their scores.

The approach can vary enormously, according to the wind and length of drive. Occasionally, it is prudent to play short and pitch over with the third, but even this is fraught with peril. The shot is delicate. One tries to nurse the ball close to the flag, perhaps 15 yards across the burn; it is early in the round and nerves are taut. How easy it is to quit on the shot so that the ball, feebly struck, plops gently into the clear waters or, jabbed with convulsive anxiety, races across the green and three putts invariably follow.

The awful psychology of the thing is that if the second shot goes into the burn, and the distance to the flag always looks shorter than it is, one is now playing four and trying desperately to avoid a six. There should be little difficulty; a simple pitch and run of 20 yards, no more; but there is the accursed burn at one's feet. Last year I faced this stroke. Deep in my heart I knew I was not going to make it.

The mind said: 'Get the club back, swing smoothly through the ball, and don't look up'; but the club stopped with the sickening abruptness so familiar to the fluffer, and the ball just had sufficient impetus to roll over the edge from a range of six feet.

Months before playing in the Spring Medal last week, I resolved that, come what may, I would take enough club to carry the burn with plenty to spare. True contact with a 3 iron would have sufficed easily, but contact was minimal; the result, a perfect lay-up position for a short pitch, and what should have been at worst a five. Then the sabotaging forces, 'the unconscious cerebrations,' did their evil work; the ball rose in a feeble parabola and vanished.

I fashioned the traditional seven, as did one of my partners, a golfer long experienced at St Andrews, who hit a 5 iron plumb into the burn. He said later that he knew he should have taken a four but, as millions of golfers do, he made the deadly, false assumption that he would hit the shot perfectly, and from damp grass early in the morning.

All this may sound faintly ridiculous to those who have never played a Medal in agony at St Andrews, but I can assure them that it is not. The very next day, two eminent golfers of comparatively recent international vintage also opened with sevens. One chipped into the burn twice and tore up his card before he even crossed it, which must be some sort of a record.

Although the burn is the obvious villain of the piece, the essence of the plot is the fear from within. If one played a Medal round every week over the Old Course, fear would diminish, even vanish, and the burn would seem to be the pleasant stream that it is—and not as one Australian golfer described it years ago, as the '—— drine.'

It all boils down to competitive practice; there is no conceivable substitute for anyone, Casper, Nicklaus, you or me.

PAT WARD-THOMAS

Raymond Postgate's Roman dinner

GUSTATIO
Murenae burdigalenses Mulsum (lus in murena elixa: piper, ligusticum, anethum, porrum, coriandrum, mel, vinum, liquamen. caleficies et amulo obligas).

PRIMAE MENSAE
Perna cum caricis Vinum Aquitaniae (Perna, ubi eam cum caricis plurimis elixaveris et tribus lauri foliis, detracta cute tessellatim incides et melle complebis. Deinde farinam oleo subactam contexes et ei corium reddis; et cum farina cocta fuerit, eximas furno et ut est inferes).

Cauliculi
(Cauliculos elixatos mediabis; summa foliorum teres cum coriandro, cepa, cumino, pipere, passo vel caroeno et olio modico).

SECUNDAE MENSAE
Uvae atque dactyli Vinum Mosellae.

We were entertaining to dinner our friends Margaret and William, and I had determined to cook the dinner. As one of our guests is a famous cook and the other a chef of the first rank, this was a reckless and arrogant decision. But during a recent illness I had thought seriously, as one should, of things that I had left un-

done and of knowledge that I had not tested. In particular I had not gone thoroughly into ancient Roman cooking and ancient Roman wines; I would, therefore, do so now. The food might turn out to be terrible, but at least it would be new even to these alarming judges.

Roman food was not like Trimalchio's banquet, or the grossnesses satirised in Horace and Juvenal—a sequence of grotesquely combined dishes like thrushes in wild boar's bellies, consumed by guests lying around on sofas, a sure method of getting indigestion. These were recorded or imagined, for the reader's contempt; Roman food was on the whole rather frugal, but it did call for a large number of flavours, some of them very odd.

The two most favoured are, unfortunately, the two most mysterious. One is called *laser* and also silphium; it is thought to be asafoetida and the encyclopedias tell me that in Persia it is called Devil's Dung. (What useless information one is offered. There is not a single Persian shop in Kent.) Its smell is so revolting and its taste so disgusting—it is added—that more than a drop will ruin any dish. I decided not to use *laser*.

The second is called *garum* or *liquamen*. Sometimes *liquamen* is said merely to mean 'stock,' but this cannot be correct; it was a very strong sauce made basically by leaving the entrails of fish out in the sun. A jar of it, the ancient equivalent of HP sauce, has survived; it says

Liquamen
optimum
saccatum
ex officina Umbrici Agathopi

('Best strained liquamen from the factory of Umbricus Agathopus.') Anchovy sauce seemed to me the nearest I could come to it without distressing the neighbours. I would be sparing of that, too.

The chief authorities for Roman food are Varro, Columella, Martial, Pliny, and above all, Apicius. The last is a real cookery book whose original author lived under Tiberius, but what we have now bears as much relation to what he wrote as the later 'Mrs Beeton' does to the original. Incomparably the best edition is by the Misses Flower and Rosenbaum, who have not only translated it but themselves cooked a number of the dishes. This is the more necessary as Apicius's recipes are the briefest of notes —mere reminders to an experienced chef—no times, no quantities, nor even always a sequence, as you can see from the menu printed herewith.

226

The first course presented the first problem. It was usually called *gustatio* (there are various names for the course, but never mind) which is usually translated 'hors d'œuvres' and, indeed, what the poet Martial (reign of Domitian) expected was very like what I got when I first adventured into Soho—sliced eggs with tunny, prawns, crab, lettuce, olives, sliced beetroot, and leeks, all in oil and vinegar and perhaps *garum*, but no devil's dung for once.

I could not get Varro's favourite—dormouse with chestnuts— so I decided on a wholly authentic substitute, the most luxurious *gustatio* of all, lampreys. You observe the instructions say 'boiled lamprey in gravy, pepper, borage, leek, dill, coriander, honey, wine, and *liquamen*; heat through and bind with corn flower.' This was extremely good, in a rather rich manner, and the judges were kind. Halfway through, my wife (as wives do) blew my gaff. 'John Arlott got us the lampreys, tinned from St Emilion,' she said. Well, as tinned, the lampreys had the wine and leeks already with them; but at least I did the flavours.

I fell down on the wine; with a *gustatio*, *mulsum* was compulsory. *Mulsum* should be a mixture of dry white wine and honey. I had tried this with Soave, which is Virgil's favourite wine—Rhaetian, and it was insufferable. (I have since found the fault was probably mine, for the ingredients ought to be kept together for a month— Columella says more—and then run off into a fresh *amphora* and hung in the chimney smoke.) So I did my best with a dry white French wine and some of our own syrup of blackberries. This is like what today is called a Kir, from a canon who lived about 90 years, mostly as the immovable mayor of Dijon, and popularised it. It's all right; you can't say more.

The real success I would claim is for the *primae mensae* which consisted of ham and cabbage. Apicius for once is almost lo- quacious. 'After boiling the ham with many dried figs and three bay leaves, peel off the skin, make criss-cross cuts and fill them with honey. Then cover it with a paste of flour and oil to replace the skin' (or, 'put the skin back on'—unlikely). 'When the pastry is cooked, take it from the oven and serve it as it is.' I did just that, using the cheapest most withered figs and a pressure cooker for the first part, and puff pastry for the casing. I think perhaps hot-water pastry would have been better, as it would make better eating when cold. I also kept some of the juice left in the pressure cooker as gravy. This dish I shall do again. I like it very much.

The only interesting thing about the cabbage ('when the cabbage is boiled, cut it in half, slice all the leaves'—or, 'the top of the leaves'—'with coriander, onion, cummin, pepper, sweet wine or reduced wine') is that you cook it whole, which kept the taste fresher. I made too little of the elaborate flavouring to go with it. No other fault. I used a white cabbage.

The wine should, theoretically, have been the famous *Falernian*. But after 2,000 years that has become one of the dreariest of Italian wines. So I chose wine from Aquitania where the vines were first planted by Messalla Corvinus about the time of Augustus—one from St Emilion, one from Cissac, and one from Margaux, in all of which places winegrowing dates authentically from Roman days. The temptation to buy Château Ausone which takes its name from the late Latin poet Decimus Magnus Ausonius was resisted (1) because it is so confoundedly dear; (2) because though I won't deny Ausonius may have owned that vineyard, his favourite one was across the river at Lugaignac, which means it is now an Entre-deux-mers. That would have been a dull white wine.

The last course, *secundae mensae*, was fresh grapes and dates, and a wine from the Moselle. Ausonius wrote a whole poem about the Moselle and its vines, which except for one epigram, is the best thing he ever did.

I have nothing more to report except my hope that, if anyone is moved to follow my example, he will choose the recipe for boiling an ostrich (Apicius VI, i, page 141 in Flower and Rosenbaum).

RAYMOND POSTGATE

Milady

I met her by sheer chance. In the summer of 1929 I was writing some 8,000 words weekly in this paper about cricket and music, stationed in Manchester, but nearly every week I went to London to cover a concert, or a game at the Oval or at Lord's. One day I described a Lord's Test to the length of 1,500 words, then on the evening of the same day I rattled off 1,200 words about Covent Garden Opera.

During the Canterbury Festival of that year, when I was coping with Lancashire and Yorkshire at Old Trafford, a letter came to me, my first from her. It was written in pencil, on a page torn out of a notebook. It informed me that she had strained an ankle, was lying 'prone' in bed, and unable to go to Canterbury to see Woolley batting. 'You,' she wrote, 'will surely understand the deprivation I am undergoing.' I couldn't ignore the tone, the charm, of the letter, so I replied, suggesting that one day we might meet.

A month or two later, I had to go to London for a Kreisler recital. We arranged, by post, to meet at the bookstall in Charing Cross Station. We described roughly our individual appearances. On October 8, 1929, I positioned myself at the bookstall in Charing Cross Station. For ten minutes I waited; no sign of anybody who answered to her self-identification. Then, as I was about impatiently to depart, she emerged from the ladies' waiting room, where she had been, as she put it, 'carefully inspecting me.' Frankly, I was disappointed by her appearance and dress; she looked pale and might have been the next suburban office girl.

We walked from the station across Trafalgar Square; and while we were dodging the traffic she asked me if I would lend her ten shillings. She had laddered her stocking, and had come out without her purse. I gave her a ten shilling note while we were having coffee in a café in the Haymarket. After an hour's more or less conventional talk I told her that I had to leave for an appointment, which wasn't true. I could have taken her to lunch, spent the whole day with her, with dinner and a theatre in the evening.

I got rid of her on the pavement opposite His Majesty's Theatre, where I called for a taxi. I asked her if I could give her a 'lift' anywhere. She said, 'No, thank you, goodbye.' Before the afternoon was over no stronger notion of her remained with me than of a pleasant young woman with beautiful eyes and a large generous mouth.

Next day, or the day after, she sent me a ten shilling note, and a letter of one sentence: 'I really did leave my purse at home.' A month afterwards I met her again; I hadn't the heart to let her think that one look at her had been enough for me. I arranged to take her to dinner one Saturday in the Howard Hotel, near the Embankment. I waited for her in the lounge. She came through the swing-door on the minute. In my dying hour I shall remember the radiance which now emanated from her. Her eyes were more lustrous (and alluring) than any I had ever before seen. Her high cheekbones were vivid, her natural colour. Her lips were rose red, also by the dowry of nature. She walked with a suggestion of a swaying side-way motion. Later, when Richard Strauss came to know her, he said, 'She walks to the music of the *Dorimene* movement of my *Le Bourgeois Gentilhomme* suite.'

This time she was simply but charmingly dressed; a small grey hat, which followed the shape of the back of her head, her hair coiled in wheels about the ears. When she uncoiled her hair for me—but not yet!—it fell to her knees. She was thin, or rather, slender; and not too tall. Her head fitted perfectly into my shoulder. When I took her arm to lead her into the restaurant I felt the life in her trembling. I had known this sensation only once before, when I held a bird in my hand. At dinner she talked as if she had known me for years. I asked her why at our first meeting she had looked—er—looked 'so different.' 'Engine trouble,' she replied.

She burned a flame of sex and being. She had found my wave-length, and it was a flame blown about fitfully now and then. Between her eyes a line would sometimes appear, a straight thin wrinkle. I guessed that she had gone through some troubles, not to say endangering experiences, one time or other. She sensed what was passing at this moment through my mind, and in a low voice with her chin resting on her hands, said: 'Yes, I have been naughty, but I was educated in a convent in France, and always help with the harvest festival at our church.'

I do her no wrong, this wonderful girl, if I write that whenever I introduced her to anybody redolent of English middle-class flavours, I would stand aside to note their reactions to her. I could almost hear them asking themselves: 'Who—what is she, *really*?' But abroad, in Germany and Austria, men such as Huberman, Schnabel, Stefan Zweig, Arnold Rose, and Weingartner, at once fell under her spell. She could, as she would put it, 'produce' herself, given the occasion. In London she was admired by Sir Thomas Beecham; and C. B. Fry invariably addressed her as 'Milady.'

We were together in Salzburg during the festival of 1932. Deep in conversation we crossed the road, near the Stein Hotel, failing to take note of a prohibited sign to pedestrians. A policeman charged after us, crying out officiously, 'Durchfährt verboten!' With a regal toss of her head she said to him, 'Durchfährt yourself,' and we proceeded on our way.

At Salzburg, this same year, if I remember well, Anton Weiss of the Vienna Philharmonic Orchestra insisted that we should go on to Vienna, at the end of the festival, to hear Weingartner conducting *The Ring*. Weiss assured us that he would give instructions at the secretary's office of the Staatsoper that tickets would be waiting for us, reserved seats for the performance of *Das Rheingold*.

So, on to Vienna we journeyed; and on a golden September afternoon I entered the secretary's office, to pick up the promised tickets, leaving my beauteous one waiting on the pavement outside. But there were no tickets for us, no seats reserved, the performance was ausverkauft—sold out. I protested—'But Herr Weiss promised.' No avail; there had been a mistake. I departed from the office and, outside, told her about it all. 'It doesn't matter,' I said, 'I don't particularly want to hear "Rheingold." I'd much rather we went to Hartman's for dinner.' But she expostulated. (And how she *could* expostulate, eyes and mouth.) 'I'd like very much to hear *Das Rheingold* in Vienna. Besides, we were promised. *I'll* go and see to it.' Through the imposing doors she walked, in spite of my protestations that it would be useless for her to argue.

For nearly an hour I stood in the street; opposite was a jeweller's shop bearing the name of 'Hugo Wolf.' I paced up and down. I furtively peeped into the corridor leading to the secretary's office. No sign of her. Then she reappeared, holding in her hand a card of admission that evening to the Director's box—du lieber Himmel, to the private box of Weingartner! 'Good God,' I exclaimed, 'but how—how did you get this?' 'I persuaded them to take me to Dr Weingartner,' she said. 'And,' said I, 'what then?' 'I was NICE to him,' she replied. And I find it necessary, for the purposes of true and living communication, to have the word 'nice' printed in capital letters.

We proceeded that evening to the Director's box, armed with our imperative card of admission. When we arrived at the Director's box it was crowded—crowded with civil servants, hangers-on of the Staatsoper staff. They were all cleared out, every one of them, and we sat there alone throughout the performance, opera glasses in plenty digressed from the stage to look at her. Next day the Vienna press printed inquisitive paragraphs about 'die schöne Engländerin.'

After this *Rheingold* performance, we went to Hartman's restaurant, and soon Weingartner himself entered, accompanied by one or two famous artists, himself straight from the conductor's desk. He was wearing a long cape, and before divesting himself of it and seating himself with his guests, came to our table. He took her hand and kissed it and, with accent and intonation of an aristocrat, hoped she had enjoyed the performance. Then he kissed her hand again, clicked his heels, bowed to her, and departed to his own table, taking not the slightest notice of me.

There was no artificiality about her. When she projected herself it wasn't to impress others, but to get the best out of herself in a given situation or scene. I would watch her when she wasn't aware that I was watching. Like a young girl she would review herself in front of a wardrobe mirror, swirling around, showing herself to herself.

She pretended to no wide culture: and whenever she was with those who knew their subject, she was discretion itself. But she was a good and careful reader, with so sure an instinct for the best music, poetry, and literature, that often, while formally educated people were talking nonsense, I could feel that, as she quietly listened, she was thinking devastating sense.

She never ceased to surprise me by her contrasts of extrovert enjoyment followed by abrupt transitions to a quiet self-indulgent seriousness. She could achieve a crisis which would ruin a day out with her. If she caught a chill she at once wanted her temperature to be taken. A tight shoe would put an end to a walk in the country almost before we had gone a hundred yards.

The irony of these imagined maladies is that she was victim of the most cruel asthma, which at nights would overwhelm her until she terrified me by her gaspings for breath. She never suffered this way in my presence; she would go into another room, assuring me that the affliction wasn't dangerous, just something she had to go through, like 'the curse' every month. In the adjoining room she would burn some medicinal paper, inhale the fumes, and wait patiently for the paroxysm to pass. Next morning she was as fresh with the bloom of life as ever.

At the height of a riot of an enjoyment of herself, with a laughter which, in an English restaurant, invariably provoked pained glances towards our table, she would make a decrescendo worthy of Furtwängler and ask: 'Do you think that *Hamlet* really is two plays patched together?' If I affected to exhibit on any subject a more expert knowledge than truly I possessed—and to tease her I frequently did so pretend—she would say, 'That'll do, my dear: save it for Sir Thomas.' Always she told me to 'save' my blarney for Sir Thomas Beecham.

As I say, she wasn't a systematic reader, but had the gift to get to the core of a book as though intuitively. Her sense of words was gorgeous. She savoured them on her tongue, licked them with her red lips. She had no time for primness in writing, and she went so far as to cast Ernest Newman out of her court, much as she admired him as critic, because he persistently used the word 'commence.' One day I wrote a cricket article in which I referred to a batsman's 'vivid hook.' She was at the other end of England, but next morning, as soon as she had seen the *Guardian*, she sent me a telegram—'I like vivid but isn't it a bit highfalutin'?'

She knew much of Shakespeare by heart, revelled in Dickens, delighted to read from Montaigne to me, and chortled at the Sitwells—'all dutifully writing every morning in their different apartments, like a sort of writing-sewing guild.'

She was certainly born for the theatre. James Agate repeatedly, and with irritation, said to her, 'Why the hell didn't you go on the stage?' Her wit was a constant joy. One autumn day we went to Windsor for an outing. We were walking along a narrow street, and I stopped to look into the window of a bookshop, while she went a few paces ahead. Then, suddenly, I saw her objectively; I was often trying to look at her with detachment. Now, on this autumn morning of ripe sunshine, I saw her as though anew; she was wearing a scarf loosely tied.

I looked at her like a painter inspecting a canvas brush in hand. And I flew to her, embraced her, kissed her. She received the kiss with the whole of her indulgent mouth. And, at this crucial moment, a line of small Eton schoolboys came round the corner and saw us. 'My God!' I exclaimed, 'what an example we have given to them. So young and innocent.' And she said, 'Let them begin with the classics . . .'

At a theatre or a concert she was a perfect companion, never saying the wrong thing. During a performance of *Tristan and Isolde* she would have tears in her eyes when Kurvenal died. In the intervals of the same opera she would be saying, 'Oh, these bloody shoulder-straps!' When she was present at Noel Coward's *Bitter Sweet* (or whatever it was) and the hero was suddenly and fatally shot or stabbed, she cried out, from her seat in the stalls, so that the entire audience around her could hear, 'Crikey!'

She was Eliza Doolittle before and after Professor Higgins had taken her in hand. But I never grew accustomed to her face; it constantly changed, responsive to her volatile mind and temperament. Even in her sleep her face didn't have repose; she was alive in her dreams, 'producing' them, herself the principal and endearing character. She came out of the same stable as Mrs Pat Campbell; but was gentler. She had the voice of Mrs Pat. In my last moments of this life I shall hope to hear her reading, *not* reciting

> *Go not, happy day,*
> *From the shining fields,*
> *Go not, happy day,*
> *Till the maiden yields.*
> *Rosy is the West,*
> *Rosy is the South,*
> *Roses are her cheeks,*
> *And a rose her mouth.*

All in a tone as soft and low, and as beautifully modulated as the viola of Lionel Tertis. Life in her was too abundant and self-consuming. It couldn't last. She died, suddenly, still young, a rare gift to the gods, rare and premature.

NEVILLE CARDUS

Index of Authors

237

238